What people are s

Travelling the

Morgan Daimler's *Travelling the Fairy Path* is a wealth of knowledge, not only on the rich history and folklore of fairy but how we can practise this path in a modern world. Daimler offers the reader an invaluable roadmap to walking this spiritual path born from years of personal practice and experience. Where this book shines is in the practical real world tools it offers to those interacting with the Otherworlds and its inhabitants. Much of what is in these pages can be applied to all aspects of magical practice. Having had the honour of sharing ritual space and adventures in Ireland with Morgan I can tell you there is no one better to be your guide on your journey.
Stephanie Woodfield, author of *Celtic Lore and Spellcraft of the Dark Goddess* and *Dark Goddess Craft*

What Morgan Daimler doesn't know about the world of fairy isn't worth knowing. In my humble opinion she is 'the' fairy spokesperson. This book does not disappoint. With a combination of personal experience (which is vast), myths and cold hard facts and very sensible advice, Morgan has put together what is quite possibly the best fairy handbook ever written. Get a copy now, or even two.
Rachel Patterson, author of several books on Witchcraft including *Pagan Portals: The Cailleach* and *Witchcraft into the Wilds*

If you really want to know the truth about fairies, Morgan Daimler's books are the ones to turn to. She is renowned for her impeccable research as well as having years of genuine experience travelling the fairy path, which is exactly the subject of her latest book. While *Fairies: A Guide to the Celtic Fair Folk* demonstrated her historic and folkloric knowledge and *Fairycraft: Following the Path of Fairy Witchcraft* offered a practical way of combining traditional fairy lore with modern witchcraft, *Traveling the Fairy Path* offers the insights from a life of interacting with the Good Neighbours, including personal breakthroughs, mistakes and gnosis. Having had some encounters with the Fair Folk myself, this book absolutely resonated with me. Read it – and heed Morgan's advice – if you yourself feel drawn to the fairy road.

Lucya Starza, author of *Pagan Portals – Candle Magic* and *Pagan Portals – Poppets and Magical Dolls* and writes A Bad Witch's Blog

Morgan's book is a bit of a departure from others in her series dealing with Fairy Witchcraft, in that this work is more personal, and written in a slightly different style, presenting the material in a more conversational manner. It's hugely informative, as are all of her books, and touches upon issues that are rarely mentioned in other books in the Neopagan world. Discussing the difference between spirits and fairies, how to work with verified or unverified personal gnosis, looking at the lore from the perspective of poetry and music as well as practical information on glamour, shape shifting and more, this book is a great addition and complement to her other works. There is even an entire compendium of ogham knowledge in the appendices, which is extremely useful. I always look forward to more works from this author, and highly recommend her to everyone in the Pagan community, as well as those interested in all things Celtic.

Joanna van der Hoeven, author of the best-selling *The Awen Alone: Walking the Path of the Solitary Druid* and *The Hedge Druid's Craft*

Travelling the
Fairy Path

Travelling the Fairy Path

Morgan Daimler

MOON
BOOKS

Winchester, UK
Washington, USA

First published by Moon Books, 2018
Moon Books is an imprint of John Hunt Publishing Ltd., No. 3 East Street, Alresford
Hampshire SO24 9EE, UK
office1@jhpbooks.net
www.johnhuntpublishing.com
www.moon-books.net

For distributor details and how to order please visit the 'Ordering' section on our website.

Text copyright: Morgan Daimler 2017

ISBN: 978 1 78535 752 7
978 1 78535 753 4 (ebook)
Library of Congress Control Number: 2017956154

A CIP catalogue record for this book is available from the British Library.

Design: Stuart Davies

Printed and bound by CPI Group (UK) Ltd, Croydon, CR0 4YY, UK

We operate a distinctive and ethical publishing philosophy in
all areas of our business, from our global network of authors to
production and worldwide distribution.

Contents

This book is dedicated to Jaime. You were one of the most amazingly cheerful and thoughtful people I have ever known. I will always miss you. Until we meet again my friend.

Introduction

Walking into the Wilds

Still I sing bonny boys, bonny mad boys
Bedlam boys are bonny
For they all go bare and they live by the air
And they want no drink nor money.

I've written several books now on Fairy Witchcraft and one on the Fey Folk themselves, and I like to think those books have real value to some people. I also write regularly online, with some of that material finding its way into print in a modified form, shared in my books for those who don't read my online writing and because I think some things deserve a more permanent preservation. These efforts are meant to serve a specific purpose, to help people find their way onto a spiritual path that is often obscured by mist and hidden among an array of other more straightforward options. The path of what I choose to call Fairy Witchcraft is definitely not an easy one, although it has its rewards, and the first challenge is often simply to find it. That said though, I realize that just offering a signpost pointing at the entrance to the path isn't necessarily enough; people may want further guidance in walking on that path. However, this is not the sort of spirituality that lends itself to step-by-step instruction. Nor is it the sort of thing that I think is ever meant to be a cookie cutter religion, where everyone has the same experiences in the same ways.

Walking the road to Fairy is and will always be a deeply personal thing. There can be shared moments along the way, communal glimpses beyond this world, times when we together experience the Otherworld, and there is a large corpus of shared folklore and folk knowledge. But most often we will walk this path alone.

With that in mind what I want to do here is take a more personal approach, I don't want to point your way down the path, but I'd like for you to walk with me for a bit along my own way. And maybe those seeking to further their own journey will find value in seeing some of what I do and how I do it, by sharing my experiences, mistakes, and breakthroughs. *'Giorraíonn beirt bóthar'* (two people shorten a road) as the saying goes. This is my invitation to you, to walk down the path a ways with me, only remember that I can tell you and talk to you about this as much as I want but like any other path it's for you to walk yourself; this isn't something to passively study but to actively do if you really want to experience and understand it.

I'm going to write about my own journey, but also the things I've learned that might be useful for other people. This book then isn't meant to be a beginner's introductory book or step-by-step instruction manual so much as it's a guidebook. For those who have learned the religious side of Fairycraft and want to delve into the magical practices, and for those who simply want to know what it is to actively practise this spirituality two and a half decades on.

One of my favourite songs, in all its many variations, is the traditional 'Bedlam Boys' a song about madness. Madness and fairies go hand in hand, and it has long been a saying in Ireland that those who are mad or those who are connected to the fairies are called 'touched'. Doing this work and practising this kind of witchcraft means being open to a reality, to another World, that doesn't exist for most people and it means experiencing and accepting, for good and ill, a much wider range of possibility than other people accept. Some people call that madness, although it isn't in the diagnostic sense. Every chapter of this book begins with a verse from the song, and each verse, to me, has a profound meaning that ties into what it is to walk this path.

Chapter 1

Stepping onto the Path, or How I Got Here

To see mad Tom of Bedlam
10,000 miles I'd travel
Mad Maudlin goes on dirty toes
To save her shoes from gravel.

We all have a different story about how we found our way to the Fairy path, some of them straightforward, others long and winding. Just as the path itself is something that is unique to each person walking it, so too our stories about how we got here and our lives within this spirituality will be different from one person to the next. To begin this book I want to talk a little bit about my own background and how I got to the point I'm at today, which is certainly not a place I ever anticipated being. If a bit of autobiographical material bores you, feel free to skip to Chapter 2; if on the other hand you're curious about why I'm writing this book or what my qualifications are to write this – if you want to know whether I'm a worthy guide for you on your own journey – then this may interest you.

I have seen and interacted with spirits and Otherworldly beings for as long as I can remember and have been pagan since I was around 11 years old. Unlike most of my peers I wasn't raised Christian. I tend to say I was raised a secular agnostic because that sums it up fairly well. We celebrated all the main American holidays but without any religious overtones – Christmas was when Santa came in his reindeer-pulled sleigh to magically bring us presents and Easter was when a bunny brought us baskets of candy. I include the agnostic part because there was no firm disbelief, but neither was there any clear structure within any particular faith. We grew up hearing stories about our family's history and culture mostly Irish-American and New England with all the folklore and belief that came with that. I spent a lot of time outdoors in nature, connecting to the wild world. I also had the added personal quirk of seeing spirits, something that (luckily for me) my family humoured for the most part. I built little houses for the fairies and left them notes on my windowsill for as long as I could remember. But actual formal religion, there wasn't any.

I was always a spiritual seeker, maybe because I saw things other people didn't. At various points I was curious about different religions, attending church services with my friends, reading about Judaism, I even read up on Mennonites and the Amish. Nothing ever quite fit though. And then when I was in middle school (the early 1990s) one of my best friends introduced me to a book by Scott Cunningham called *Wicca: a Guide for the Solitary Practitioner*. For the first time I was reading about a religion – witchcraft and paganism – that made perfect sense to me. Gods and Goddesses, spirits, magic, these all resonated with me and fit into the world, spirits inclusive, that I already knew existed. I was mad for Irish culture at that point so it wasn't much effort to add in Irish mythology to everything else and begin reading about the Irish Gods.

I went to the library and found a few other books, and used my babysitting money to buy a couple more and I read what I could get my hands on at the time: Buckland's *Complete Book of Witchcraft*, Sybil Leek's *Diary of a Witch*, Laurie Cabot's *Power of the Witch*. Although my friend quickly lost interest and went back to Catholicism, I was enamoured with pagan witchcraft. At the advanced age of 12 I decided to perform a self-dedication ritual, out in the cold on Imbolc. Because at 12, I was certain that this was the most amazing religion ever.

Of course, within a few years, by the mid 90s, I'd started to focus more on what I'd later learn was called Celtic Reconstructionism and by 1997 I'd joined a CR Druid group called the Order of the

White Oak. In 2001 I joined another Druid group, Ar nDraoicht Fein, and in 2006 I joined Our Troth after I began studying Heathenry/Asatru. I had long since stopped considering myself Wiccan but I never stopped practising witchcraft and throughout it all the Good People – by any name – were the bedrock of my belief system and practice. The Fairy Faith – the belief in the Hidden People and the practices that went with those beliefs – had always been a core of my life and became the thread that bound my religious interests together. From one perspective it might be called an Creideamh Sí, from a Norse perspective I might label it Álfatrú, but by any name it was essentially the same, a spirituality that hinged on respecting and offering to the Hidden People.

I remained a dual-trad person, both an American reconstructionist Irish polytheist and a Heathen but I also began to see that over the years I had developed my own type of witchcraft, my own flavour if you will, based on and built from my fairy beliefs. So, in 2013 I wrote a book *Pagan Portals Fairy Witchcraft* which would be published the following year that described my witchcraft and my belief system, formed from a lifetime of experience and woven from the Fairy Faith and a reconstructionist approach to working with the Other Crowd. That of course led to another book, *Fairycraft*, and another, *Fairies: A Guide to the Celtic Fair Folk*. I felt compelled to write these things to share what I was doing, but also because I feel like Themselves have something to say.

I was content with my spirituality as it was. My spirituality was complex, woven from multiple cultural threads, but it was cohesive because of the Fairy Faith and witchcraft practices. I saw myself and my place in the grand scheme of things laid out pretty much in that context. I had taught my first public class at a Pagan Pride event in 2000, a workshop about fairies (aptly enough) and now I do what I can to write about the older folk beliefs and practices and to show people one way that those beliefs and practices can be preserved and blended into modern paganism. But for all that I still saw myself firmly as a polytheist focused primarily on the Gods and on doing their work in this world. Like many people I don't like change very much. If you'd asked me a year ago where I expected to be at this point I'd have said probably in about the same place, spiritually speaking. The spirits, of course, often have other plans for us.

Although as I've just discussed, the Good People (fairies) where always a main aspect of my spirituality; I considered myself devoted to the Gods I honoured and was formally dedicated to two in particular who I served as a priestess. I was a Celtic Reconstructionist, a Druid (although I have since stopped using that term), a witch, and these were more than enough to keep me occupied as I tried to balance my Irish paganism and Norse Heathenry, my dedication to Odin and my dedication to Macha. The daoine sí – and the huldufolk – were always a factor, and an important one, but I still saw them as only one portion of a complex spirituality.

And then I went to Ireland.[1]

This was a first for me, the culmination of a lifelong dream to travel across the sea. I left for Ireland on October 25th, 2016 to help co-facilitate a Morrigan sacred sites tour. I was very excited, and had high expectations of connecting more deeply with the Morrigan, Badb, and Macha on their own sacred ground at places where their stories had taken place. The tour had been arranged by Land Sea Sky Travel and hit, in my opinion, all the major sites I'd want to have gone to from the well-known like Teamhair (Tara) to the more obscure like Boa Island. It was a wonderful opportunity to connect to the Morrigans and I hope, very sincerely, that it served that purpose for the people who went on the trip.

My own journey went sideways, as they say, almost immediately, and that's the story I'd like to tell here. Because its mine to tell and because parts of it I'm compelled to share publicly.

On a trip like this I honestly expected that the main focus would be on the Gods – the Morrigan, Badb, and Macha – and on connecting to the land itself in a broader sense; that the Good People, while obviously always a factor, would be a background consideration. It became clear almost immediately that this was not to be the case, and then increasingly obvious that everything altogether was shifting in ways I had not anticipated. But now I'm getting ahead of myself.

After a bit more than 24 hours of travel time we landed in Dublin, a day before the tour was to start. Me and my friend Melody, who was travelling with me, met up with my co-facilitator Stephanie Woodfield and her companion, and then Vyviane Armstrong of Land Sea Sky Travel. Since we had come in early, a group decision was reached to take the day and go down to Kildare; I was excited to see Brighid's Well (or wells as it turns out). The drive was lovely and I was struck the entire time by how much everything felt like home to me – not in a deep metaphysical sense exactly but in a literal, visceral way. It was actually disorienting; I don't travel much and I'm used to, when I do travel, feeling very much like I am somewhere foreign whether I'm in Florida or California or western New York. But that wasn't so in eastern Ireland, it all felt like I could easily still be home, and it was an odd feeling to be sure.

So we went to Kildare, to what I am told is Brighid's Well 'the old one' – of course there are many Brighid's Wells – but this one did feel powerful and special and I quite liked it. I won't say exactly what happened there, but I had a moving experience that was both odd and beautiful praying for my younger daughter who has several health issues. Then we went to the other well, the more well-known one with the big statue and nice shrine, and the sideways-ness began. Because as soon as we got near it, well it wasn't Brighid at all that I was aware of there but Themselves entirely. And that wasn't what I'd expected. It wasn't bad exactly, but it was strong, and obvious that I had their attention. All things being equal I dismissed it since things like that can happen – have happened to me – and I assumed it was the location and being in Ireland.

The second day we joined up with the people going on the tour, and a more excellent group no one could hope for. I could write paragraphs just about how wonderful they were, but just take it as a given from here out that they were the most amazing 15 people because their stories are their own though and I don't feel it's my place to speak of them, except where they touch on my tale here.

We got everyone together and we went to Knowth and Sid in Broga (Newgrange). I will confess that Sid in Broga itself underwhelmed me although I quite liked Knowth. That aside though for the second time in as many days I found that while I was aware of the presence of the Gods it was the aos sí that dominated my attention. We had had lunch at the centre's cafe and I had kept several of the wrapped pats of butter, stored in a plastic bag in my bag[2] and as we roamed the grounds at Sid in Broga, while the others felt obligated to pour out offerings to the Gods, I found a tree near the boundary which was Theirs and made my own offering there, to the Other Crowd.

At the end of the day we went to the lovely cabins we were staying at for the first part of the trip. I found a post on the fence line, right in front of a small stream, across from our cabin and set about making offerings there; it would become a sort of impromptu altar for the time we were there and I would make butter and cream offerings there every morning. That night I ended up giving a spontaneous workshop on the Other Crowd, Good Manners, and How Not to Get Taken by the Fairies after one of our tour people went out walking and heard voices in the darkness calling him to join them (not human voices). Being he is a skilled musician I was fairly concerned by this and it became a running joke – of the seriously-thought variety – to make sure that person stayed among the mortal people.

When I went out the next morning to make an offering of cream there was a fairy ring in the grass in front of the post I was making the offerings at.

Have you ever had to go into a cabin full of people you either just met or possibly don't know well in person (my travelling companion excluded) and try to explain why the spot you've already mentioned as a place to make offerings to the Good Neighbours now has to be approached with care due to a fairy ring? It makes for interesting breakfast conversation.

The next day we went to Heapstown Cairn and then Cheathrú Chaol (Carrowkeel). Heapstown Cairn is associated with the well of Slaine and is a place with strong ties to the Tuatha Dé Danann, especially Airmed. We did our opening ritual there and it was a good solid ritual to the Morrigan. But if you're guessing that, just like before, I felt the presence of the Gods but was far more keenly aware of the Good People you are starting to see the same pattern I was catching on to, although at this point I was ignoring it. I was here to honour and connect to the Morrigans as a priestess of Macha and that was what I wanted to do. I was seeing this as a once in a lifetime opportunity for that connection, and while I did appreciate the feeling of intense association, I suppose you could say, with the aos sí that wasn't what I had intended the focus to be.

You know what they say about the best laid plans ...

Heapstown Cairn had a strong presence of the Other Crowd, both within it and in the little groves around it. I felt it and so did a few others in the group. It was an old feeling but quiet, contemplative. Cheathrú Chaol though – oh that place! I loved it from before I saw it. I loved it as we approached it and I saw the rising wall of hills. I loved it as soon as I set foot on the ground. We drove in and the mist came down like a wall, so that we hiked up to the cairns in a shroud of white. We arrived at the first cairn, cairn G, and I went no further – if I were to say I had arrived home anywhere in Ireland it was that place. It is sacred, deeply so I think, and it is very full of the Otherworld. I went in to the cairn and refused to come out again until I was genuinely afraid that Vyviane might have to come get me, and I wouldn't let that happen. I won't share my actual experience there, but I feel like I left a piece of myself behind, and I walked away with two Irish pennies and shell in exchange. It was a fair trade. When I die I am reasonably certain that a person looking for me would be wise to go to that place and seek my spirit out among the stones and heather.

The next day we went to Boa Island for a ritual to Badb in the cemetery where the two Janus stones are. That place is quite amazing all on its own, and the feeling of walking on the ancient dead is strange, but the energy overall is very peaceful. We chose to do the ritual under the cemetery's only tree, towards the back and I stood with my own back to it, just in front of a large white quartz stone thrusting up from the ground. The tree was being overtaken by ivy and honestly that was all I noticed before we started. This, dear readers, was a serious error on my part.[3] So, we began and as we got to the part where there is a ritual meditation, and Stephanie began reading it while people relaxed and tranced out, I became keenly aware of a door opening behind me in the trunk of the tree. My eyes focused on the small branch hanging over my head and down in front of my face and it occurred to me, suddenly and simultaneously with the door appearing, that the tree was a hawthorn.

Sitting inside our warded space with a group of people mostly in open trance.

Oops.

Suffice to say I handled the situation and everything was fine, because we had a motto going on this tour of *'no crow left behind'* (crow meaning tour participant) and I have a strong sense of duty to people I feel responsible for. I will not make that mistake again though and afterwards I was sitting on our coach eating salt from a packet out of my bag to help ground myself. Salt and butter, by the way are great things to carry around for emergency situations.

Rathcroghan was next on our itinerary, on the dark moon the day before Samhain. We started at Ogulla, a triple holy well, then went to the Rathcroghan mound. Walking up the mound I could feel that it was a sí but at this point I was kind of accepting that all the old cairns and burial mounds in Ireland are. We were being led that day by Lora O'Brien, who is an amazing guide that knows Rathcroghan and Medb and the Morrigan better than anyone else I can think of. When we reached the top, up the eastern entrance, Lora had us all take 16 big steps out to demonstrate the size of the mound; I found myself walking straight towards the western entrance/walkway and had an almost overwhelming urge to keep walking. I knew in the moment that I had to go down that way, just as I'd come up the east. Had to, like a compulsion. This was almost immediately problematic, however, as Lora began talking about the mound and its history and mentioned the two paths, east and west, and shared that in her own opinion the western walk was not for the living and we were all to go down the east, the way we'd come. And the hell of it was that what she was saying resonated as true with me but still I knew I had to go down that way. She had us focus on connecting to the ancestors and Medb, and probably to no one's surprise at this point I ended up connecting to the Fair Folk in the mound instead. Then when we were done and it was time to leave, I discovered I had a problem – I could not go down the eastern path. Could not. Physically could not. I wandered the top trying to figure out what to do because this was most certainly a case of 'do as I say, not as I do' since I knew no one else should follow me down the western path and I was afraid to just go down and have anyone else follow me. In the end I found Lora and talked to her, and then when everyone else had gone down the eastern path I went the way I had to go.

Maybe you're wondering why?

At the time I didn't know, only that I had been told I had to go that way and then found that the east was physically barred from me. Later in the cave, though, it came clear.

There's more than one kind of initiation.

We left Rathcroghan and we headed to the field where Uaimh na gCat is located. I saw a rainbow – the first and only one I saw while in Ireland – as we went and then as we walked to the field. When we arrived there was a kitten[4] playing nearby who darted in and out of the cave; later he would escort me the final few yards out of the cave tunnel. All of these seemed like good omens to me and I was eager to get into the cave and finally connect in that profound way I had been expecting with the Morrigan. In the cave I ended at the very back, perched precariously on a slip of muddy ledge just above Lora and another person with the tour. There is a piece of time in the cave which I do not remember and I hope if nothing else that I did act as Her priestess for others while we were in there; sometimes when I go into a deeper trance I don't remember it. I do remember towards the end yelling at people as they left not to set foot outside the cave without thanking Herself first, so there's that.

Most clear in my memory though is the vision of the back of the cave opening up into a great golden hall, the sí of Cruachan. And as to that, I'm not sure anything I can say could ever do the experience justice. I think I would almost certainly have broken my neck trying to get to that doorway, though, if I wasn't in the position I was in right next to another person who I would certainly have injured if I'd tried to climb higher, and that thought alone, of hurting someone else, held me in place but barely. To this day part of me regrets not trying.

That night after the cave I dreamt of the sorts of things you'd imagine after something like that and I woke early in the darkness full of inspiration. You see our group was going to Tlachtga, the Hill of Ward in Athboy, that night to celebrate Samhain at the big

Samhain Fire Festival. I, along with Stephanie and Vyviane, had been asked by Gemma, the amazing priestess co-ordinating the ceremony, to take a role in the ritual itself, helping, by holding banners at the quarters and reciting some of the sacred space casting and such in unison with the other priestesses present. In addition I had been asked to say something in the ritual to honour the aos sí, and up until that morning I had nothing prepared. Not for lack of trying but because no matter how I'd tried nothing had come to me that didn't seem trite or foolish. When I woke up that morning in the darkness of the early hours, while everyone else still slept, I had to immediately go and write down what had come to me in the night and it felt good and right.

We arrived on the Hill and the rest of the group went off to Trim to shop and explore. At this point I didn't even blink to feel the presence and know it was a sí. Of course it was. The energy in the air was amazing and the people who put on the ritual were even more so; it was an honour to meet them and stand side by side with them later on. Everyone who was involved with that Samhain ritual was wonderful and I wish I'd had more time to talk with them – as it was it seemed like the night went too quickly. The crowd was epic, estimated at around 2000 and it was filmed by a Japanese television crew who seemed to be ubiquitous throughout the night. There were fireworks. There were bonfires. It was cold. It was windy. It was utter madness in its way. It was gorgeous.

I don't want to detract from the beauty of the ritual itself or the hard work of the group who put it on; but for my own small personal experience I will say that there was a point where I was introduced to say my blessing for the aos sí and was given the title of priestess of the aos sí, something that resonated and presented me with a choice to accept or reject it. I accepted it, and the geis that I could sense came with it,[5] and I said the blessing I'd written as well as one additional line, added spontaneously.

Daoine Uaisle
Daoine Maithe
Daoine Sith
Noble People
Good People
People of Peace
You who are due part of the harvest
You who are due a portion of the milk and bread
You to whom the wild harvest belongs after Samhain
You who can give luck or take it
You who can give health or take it
You who can give fortunes or take them
We remember and honour your presence
May there be peace between us
May there be friendship between us
May the old ways never be forgotten
Beannachtaí na Daoine Sí daoibh

The next morning, still Samhain by my reckoning, we went to Emhain Macha. We went to the Iron Age re-enactors village where they were celebrating Samhain and also acting out the funeral of a village member, and – you guessed it – much of the event revolved around the Other Crowd. Because it was Samhain there was a lot of talk about the Good People and protection against them, even to the point of the re-enactors handing out sticks of rowan to several people for protection from unseen powers. And lest anyone reading this get the wrong idea about me or think I am a better person than I am, I'll be clear that I had to fight the entire time to behave myself; it took a monumental effort when asked where we were from as part of the 'funeral' not to say we'd come from the sí of Tlachtga. I still wonder how the re-enactors would have reacted to that.

The site itself was beautiful and there's something that's hard to put into words about walking the same ground that my

14

favourite myth takes place in. As a group we went to the mound of Emhain Macha and then over to a smaller mound adjacent to it and held a small ritual there. It was really moving to stand where the stories took place and retell them as part of that ritual. The main mound, where the old temple stood and was burned, had a good feel to it where I could have happily stayed all day. But the place that drew me the strongest was the smaller mound to the side of it, which – you guessed it – is a sí. We did ritual there with me as always offering butter, in the ritual and before and after. It can safely be said, I think, that I buttered my way across Ireland.

After that we went to Cloch na Fhir Mhóir (Clochafarmore) the stone where legend says Cu Chulainn tied himself as he was dying. It was dusk and I stood out in the field and told the story of the stone. I have never considered myself much of a storyteller but there was something about being there and standing where we were standing that was inspiring and I found the words flowing in a way they hadn't seemed to before.

The final day of ritual occurred for us at Teamhair (Tara) and Sliabh na Caillí (Loughcrew). Teamhair, like Sid in Broga, did very little for me personally although I think the ritual there went very well. Sliabh na Caillí was another thing altogether. The hike was pure determination and I wouldn't have made it without my friend Angela encouraging me, but once up there it was worthwhile. The view alone was worth the effort – imagine standing so that you can look down on the backs of crows flying below you – but the cairn was amazing too. I did see the Hag's Chair and touched it, but felt that it was not right for me to sit on it, so I did not. I was drawn into one of the smaller open cairns, cairn S, to the side of cairn T, and as usual Themselves were there strongly. At one point I had lost my sense of orientation and wasn't sure where the way out was, and said out loud that I needed to find the gate to leave – and immediately looked over and saw it. If you guessed a butter offering was made then you'd be correct. On the way down, as I was walking with another member of our tour, I jokingly said out loud that I hoped I didn't fall on my backside, but the Fey would probably think that was funny, and of course I promptly felt as if a hand had grabbed my ankle and fell on my butt. I wasn't hurt at all and I laughed it off, but it was a valuable reminder not to speak foolishly, especially when I knew they were around.

I could tell you more, about the hawthorns and the hawthorn twigs showing up everywhere, about the shells, about the magpies. But I think this is enough. You'll notice I haven't mentioned the Morrigan much so far. She and They were present but I found that while I served them by serving as a priestess to others on the tour for myself there was nothing on that end, excluding a feeling of Macha's presence at Emhain Macha. No, this entire trip for me became a different sort of thing entirely and it was life-changing in a way I never would have anticipated. I am still not sure what it all means or what will happen now, but I am contemplating it all, still. After returning home I found myself being released from my dedication to Odin after a decade and I found a Fairy Queen reaching out to me. One dedication ended and a new service began.

On the trip I was given a title I didn't expect or look for: priestess of the aos sí. Usually I don't worry too much about labels, I do what needs doing and people can call me what they please for it, as most labels are transient and shifting. On the other hand, some labels are titles with weight and obligations that only a fool would ever take lightly, and priestess of Themselves is such as that. I was named Their priestess and it was spoken in sacred space, in ritual, on Samhain, on the hill of Tlachtga in front of thousands of people – it was spoken aloud and I did not reject it when it was said.

Priestess of the aos sí is something I will spend a lifetime living up to, and it is more work, in truth, than any one person can do. But I will try my best to do my best.

Sometimes the path is unclear and hard to find, the footing unsure.

Other times though, the path before us is plain and only the walking is left for us to do.

Endnotes

1. The following has been expanded from a blog post I wrote after returning from Ireland in 2016.
2. Yes, this is basically the sort of person I am – 'look butter, this will come in handy later for offerings. Into the bag it goes'. As you may imagine I am rather interesting to travel with.
3. I make mistakes. Some of them more serious than others.
4. By an odd coincidence it turned out later the kitten belonged to the man who lived next door to the cave, who was the nephew of a friend of mine. He was an absolutely adorable little kitten, and delighted our whole group while we were there.
5. Everything has a cost. Anyone who tells you different is lying. In this case, accepting a role specifically as a priestess of the aos sí meant accepting that they had a prohibition for me, something that I was not to do again from that point on.

Chapter 2

Trucking with Spirits

I went down to Satan's kitchen
For to break my fast one morning
There I found souls piping hot
That on the spit were turning.

This path hinges on two main things: knowing the beliefs and practices relating to fairies and actively dealing with them. Knowing the beliefs and practices is essential groundwork and really can't be downplayed at all; you have to know who the Fey Folk are and how to deal with them before you begin trying to deal with them, if you want to do so safely. There's really no shortcut to that except to become as familiar as possible with as much folklore as possible, and to try to get a feel for what the traditional beliefs about fairies were and are. Modern culture has its fairy beliefs as well, of course, but modern or pop culture fairylore is a minefield to traverse because it is, as often as not, created from an author's imagination rather than based on actual experiences or stories passed down. In other words there's a big difference between traditional folklore which comes from people who truly believe that fairies exist and modern fairy fiction created by people who just want to sell a product or write an interesting story. I'm not saying throw out all modern fairy stories, movies or books, just that there's a lot of straight fiction seeping into modern belief that one needs to be cautious of. If you truly believe that these beings exist as real, tangible presences that can and do affect our world – which is the entire crux of Fairycraft – then you must understand the important difference between a tried and true traditional belief and a modern fanciful invention. Seek out the tried and true to guide you, and enjoy

18

the fiction for what it is.

In a later chapter we'll take a closer look at the Fair Folk themselves and the Otherworld, but to begin I wanted to discuss how best to approach the nitty gritty of actually dealing with spirits. It may seem counterintuitive to do things in this order, but I think that it's important to start with an understanding of the differences between dealing with fairies and other types of spirit and how to handle approaching fairies correctly before we jump into more complex dealings with them and deeper discussions of who and what fairies are.

Dealing with spirits in any way beyond the most superficial level is something that needs to be done carefully and with an understanding of some basic esoteric concepts. These include the power of the names we use for ourselves as well as for the beings we are dealing with, the importance of cleansing and purification, and basic etiquette with both spirits and fairies.

The Power of Names

There is a lot of power in names and naming, something that we see coming into play in mythology and folklore and something that directly impacts deeper magical work. This is an important subject to understand, in particular for witches, because there can be confusion around the idea of True Names and magical names within modern paganism, and it's vital to know the differences. So, we're going to look at what True Names and magical names are, and the difference between them, with some examples from mythology and folklore as well as practical advice for how to work with these concepts yourself.

A True Name is the name that resonates with a being's soul or otherwise identifies that being on the deepest level. This is not necessarily the name you are given by your parents at birth, although we'll look at the power that your birth name can have later. Your True Name is a deeper metaphysical thing, something that you may or may not ever find if you are human, and something that you guard as more precious than your life. Every being has a True Name, and that includes nature spirits, humans, fairies, and Gods. Knowing a being's True Name gives you power over that being and allows you a level of control over them. In the Cath Maige Tuired we see this when the Dagda encounters a Fomorian princess who demands he carry her on his back; he refuses until she has asked him his name three times[1] and he is forced to reveal his True Name; knowing it she repeats the request using it and he must comply with her request. In the familiar story of Rumpelstiltskin we see knowledge of a True Name as the only way for a woman to get out of a contract she has made with a dwarf. This motif and variations of it are found throughout Europe, with either the firstborn child or the woman herself as the agreed upon pay for the Otherworldly being unless the Name can be discovered. Knowing a True Name means knowing the true nature of a being which allows that being to be commanded against their will, and this is exactly why knowledge of a True Name was hidden.

As I mentioned, your birth name also has power over you. Perhaps anyone who has ever experienced an angry parent yelling their full name at them is already aware of this. Seriously though, even though your birth name is something given to you by others it has the power of blood and kinship bound up in it, and it is tied to your soul all the same, although not as strongly as your True Name. In most folklore it was understood as unwise to give your name to Otherworldly beings, because knowledge of your birth name gave them knowledge of you to some degree. We see examples of this in stories such as 'Maggy Moulach' where a fairy (in that case a Brownie) futilely loves a mortal who does not feel the same way for him; when he asked her name, she concealed her true identity and told him it was Mé féin (Myself). The young woman eventually is forced to throw boiling water on the amorous fairy, mortally wounding him, and when he was later asked who had harmed him he answered

'Myself' preventing his mother from seeking revenge against the girl.[2] Names have power, even the ones our parents have given us, and we should remember that power and also the importance of guarding our birth name from potentially unfriendly beings.

Beyond the names we are given at birth we can choose our own names as we get older. We can assume nicknames, or we can even (in most countries as far as I know) legally change our names when we are adults. There is a long and deep-seated tradition of adults changing names to shed the name they were given at birth and assume a new name symbolizing in many ways their adulthood, usually to better reflect who the person had become. We see this in mythology with Setanta becoming Cu Chulainn; Gwion Bach becoming Taleisin; Deimne becoming Fionn Mac Cumhaill. There is power in naming ourselves, but we should choose wisely as well, because just like birth names, the names we give ourselves hold power over us and create connections. Cu Chulainn taking his name also meant taking a geis against eating dog meat, and his ultimate fate was bound up in that taboo. To choose a new name as an adult is to make a statement about who we perceive ourselves to be and who we want others to see us as. From a magical perspective it still is a name that is tied to us, perhaps more so because it is a name that we have chosen ourselves to better reflect our true selves – although I would strongly advise against ever using what you believe is your True Name as your legal name or the name you go by in any public way.

It is from the power that your name has, I believe, that we see magical names coming in, particularly in ceremonial magic. A magical name was originally meant as a pseudonym, a way to keep your identity hidden from spirits and likely to act as a layer of magical defence from unfriendly people, witches and non-witches. Or perhaps we might say more aptly it was used to create a specific alternate identity for dealing with them. Magical names, like any good persona, were about creating an ideal image for the self, rather than a true reflection of the self. So, for example someone's True Name might be Echaire (horse-keeper) but they may take a magical name that is much grander and more impressive sounding like 'Storm Raven' or 'Ocean Rider'. People often use the names of deities, mythic heroes, past famous magicians and powerful animals for their magical names. Magical names do build power with use, but could also be shed and remade as needed. Think of them a bit like clothes or armour. A magical name in a way is like a nickname in the sense that it can change or evolve with a person as the person grows and the person can use it with others – in this case both humans and spirits – without the idea that the person is being deceptive. It is after all still one of your names, just a more flexible and transient one than your birth name or True Name. Even with this though, there was historically usually a layer of secrecy between a person's magical name and real name, an attempt to keep the two separate and distinct, so that in ritual or with fellow practitioners no other name would be used except the magical, and outside of those contexts no name except the birth name would be used.

At some point in the modern era I think the ideas of True Names and magical names were confused somehow, so that people began to think that a magical name was supposed to be a true reflection of self rather than a projection of power and confidence. From this we start to see two things happening, firstly magical names that are intended to reflect as much of a person's soul as possible, and secondly, the public use of magical names in non-magical contexts. Or basically the entire concept of magical names became less about esoteric spirit work naming and more of a tribal assuming-a-new-name-with-a-new-community process. One is not better or worse than the other, but they need to be understood as distinctly different things. A public name that you use because you feel it fits you better than the one your parents gave you isn't a magical name. And it isn't your true name either, or I hope it isn't if you're sharing it around so publicly.

One who is dealing with fairies would also be wise to remember that it is dangerous to allow them to give you a name. The act of naming, itself, has power of its own because giving a name is a type of gift-giving and gifts always create a debt if they are not repaid. Henderson and Cowan discuss this in their book *Scottish Fairy Belief*, specifically in relation to Tam Lin who they suggest was given his name by the fairies as a means to keep him bound to their world. They quote one of the multitude of versions of the ballad in which Tam Lin says that first his name was Jack and then it was John then says *'but since I lived in the fairy court; Tomlin has always been my name'* (Henderson & Cowan, 2007). This implies that as a mortal boy and young man his name was John, probably given the nickname Jack by his family, but after he was taken by the Fairy Queen he was renamed. We will discuss the meaning of the name Tam Lin and its ties to Fairy in Chapter 5, but at this point what matters is that his renaming was likely significant and may have been part of what tied him to Fairy and kept him from leaving. Katherine Briggs also discusses the power of giving a name or nickname to a fairy as a means of driving one out of a place, reinforcing the power of naming. I would highly recommend you keep control of your own name and choose what you are called and don't let others name you, no matter how flattering it may seem in the moment.

Names have power. We can take control of that power by choosing what we want people to call us, by naming ourselves. Even assuming a nickname is an act of power. We can use magical names, and in Fairy Witchcraft we *should* use magical names. In fact I strongly encourage anyone on this path to have a magical name that they use in spirit work, particularly when journeying or dealing with spirits or fairies. We can also seek, and sometimes find, our True Name which can be one way to better know ourselves and claim our own power. But we shouldn't forget the lessons that mythology and fairy tales have taught us about the value of the power of the names and the need to guard the names that mean the most to us. Not all names are meant to be shared.

Cleansing and Purification

Another very important aspect to this practice is purification and cleansing. Really any witchcraft practised should be sure to include a strong basis in purification, but in my experience many don't emphasize them. For Fairycraft, however, proper purification and cleansing are essential. Before we engage in any magical working we want to be sure that we have cleared anything from our own energy that might interfere with what we are going to do. Pre-ritual and pre-magic purifications are essential to this. We are also intentionally putting ourselves into situations where we may be exposed to dangerous or harmful spirits and energy, as well as things that may not be blatantly harmful but could cause harm unintentionally, and it's important to be certain that we aren't bringing any of that home, so to speak, or allowing anything harmful to stay with us in ways that can and will affect us. Cleansing and purification then are just good magical hygiene, like washing our hands before and after cooking meat.

When we look at pre-Christian forms of paganism and traditional witchcraft we mostly find the idea of what harms people embodied as spirits, and so we see means to fight or drive off these spirits, but we do also see in some cases the idea of magic or energetic illnesses that affect people in negative ways, such as Cu Chulainn's wasting sickness or Aengus's love sickness. Practising magic then opens people up to risk on two levels: the chance of a spiritual entity attaching itself to a person on some level and physically, emotionally, or spiritually affecting them, or the chance of being afflicted with an illness that is based in an energetic injury or connection. Making sure to cleanse helps avoid or minimize these risks and can help deal with these issues if they arise.

We also find the idea that people through their actions can place themselves into or out of society, with people outside of society having a distinct and dangerous energy to them that must be purified before they return to civilization. We, as witches who deal with uncanny beings, would qualify as people stepping intentionally outside society and for that reason alone it would be important to make sure we ritually cleanse and purify after doing magic.

There are a variety of ways to approach cleansing of course from simple to more complex. The main ones that I tend to use involve direction of movement, use of specific herbs, baths, and ritual purification with a specially prepared ointment or liquid. Which one you would want to use at any point would depend on the circumstances, how much time you have, and what situation you are dealing with. Generally it's good to have a routine of basic cleansing that you do regularly, whether that's burning purifying herbs or taking a cleansing bath on a weekly or monthly basis.

Probably the simplest method which is useful to draw in blessing energy is to walk or turn sunwise (clockwise). Just as moving counterclockwise or against the sun has its uses including opening pathways to Fairy and hexing, when we move with the sun we are drawing positive energy to ourselves. So a very easy way to cleanse and bless is to turn sunwise. You can do this with objects or yourself and you can walk around spaces sunwise to bless them or cleanse negative energy from them.

Another method involves the use of herbs,[3] especially burning different herbs to cleanse away baneful energy. The most well known in Irish and also Scottish culture may be juniper. Juniper is mentioned by various authors, including Danaher, Evans, and MacNeil, for its protective qualities in folk belief and for the widespread practice of burning juniper in the home and stables on the Quarter (Scottish cross-Quarter) days to be rid of dangerous energy and to bless the space and people. Another herb that is less well known for this in modern times is mugwort, which can be burned for protection against evil spirits and baneful magic and was also kept around the home, tied onto livestock, and worn on a person's clothing for purification and to ward off fairies and witches (MacCoitir, 2006). Rosemary is one of my personal favourites, historically used especially as a fumigant in sick rooms, carrying the idea of cleansing away lingering illness or baneful energy in the atmosphere. An enterprising person could gather and dry the three together or make a blend of the three herbs to burn; even hanging them in a bunch together would have protective effects around the home.

Bathing with oils or herbs is a method I recommend using on a regular basis, even if you also burn or hang herbs. For this purpose I like to use a rose oil blend for lighter cleansing and birch essential oil for heavier duty purifications. I don't know that rose has any long history for this purpose but I have found it personally very effective at both gently cleansing and blessing. Birch was historically used to drive out spirits and purify, so birch oil is excellent for heavier duty cleansings. When I use these in a bath I generally add between three and five drops depending on how strong I'd like it – sometimes more if I feel it's needed – and also a small amount of sea salt. Salt of course also drives out negative spirits, is protective and cleansing, and has some blessing properties.

In mythology and historic ritual practices we find hints that indicate that people who intentionally stepped outside of society needed to be ritually cleansed before re-entering it. Specifically, there are indications that a person who had left society to live in a wild state and who wished to re-enter society needed to be ritually cleansed using a process that featured a ritual meal, usually a broth (McCone, 1990). This process may have involved the broth being consumed as well as asperged over the person, or symbolically bathed in. This broth would have been made from food that was being ritually offered to the Gods and so was sacred by association as it were. The Fianna, who lived a portion of their time outside society, seem to have had cleansing rituals in order to re-enter society later and these rituals may have involved ritual anointing with milk or butter (PSLV, 2011). In this way we see that the food used for ritual feasting could play a role in purification, particularly the more significant or serious purifications including redeeming people who had been living wild or as outlaws. For our purposes this kind of heavy purification might be considered after doing any magic that would be seen as out of societal bounds, perhaps cursing for example, to bring the person back into alignment with society. A very simple modified ritual might involve offering some butter to the Gods and Good People and using a small amount to anoint the forehead while praying for cleansing. Another method might be used on one of the Fire Festivals (Samhain, Imbolc, Bealtaine, Lughnasa) by making a small food dish involving a traditional meat like pork and offering a portion of it to the gods and spirits while again using a small amount of the juices to anoint the forehead and pray for purification.

For those seeking to work the magic of Fairy Witchcraft or follow such a spirituality, maintaining a good habit of purification and cleansing is essential. A good habit of cleansing is important for any witch, really, but perhaps especially so for those who seek to walk a liminal way or who intentionally step outside society's bounds on a regular basis. The more baneful or harmful energy you may be around the more important it is to make sure you purify and cleanse often, but even if you live within society and keep on the straight and narrow (as it were) it's a good idea to at least purify and cleanse on the major holidays. I recommend a combination of the above mentioned methods, although I favour incorporating moving sunwise (or depending on circumstances against the sun) into everything you do, with intention.

Fairy Etiquette

Now that we've discussed the importance of names and of regular cleansing, the next step for dealing with fairies directly is to have a really firm grasp of what they consider good manners. The Good People operate on their own system of honour in many ways but they nonetheless expect us to adhere to it and they don't grade on a curve. If you want to be successful in dealing with fairies then your best bet is to know what their expectations are for behaviour – where this gets complicated is that there is no universal standard, so what is rude to a Celtic fairy may be acceptable for a Norse one. I highly recommend reading up on the fairies of whatever culture most interests you. Personally my main focus is the Celtic – specifically Irish – and Germanic fairies but since in my experience the Irish fairies are strictest in what behaviour they expect, I tend to follow that protocol. This is also the etiquette that I am going to relay here but keep in mind what I said about variations with different groups. I'm giving you what I use because it's the equivalent of 'high court' manners if you will and I feel your chances of staying safe are best by taking this approach. Don't look at this as written in stone, though, it's only meant as a guideline.

With that said consider this a bit of a crash course – or the cliff notes version – in fairy etiquette. Like anything else on this subject for every rule or guideline there's an exception but this offers the broad strokes. Before reading this it's important to keep in mind that the Fair Folk in general are not humans and are not like humans; as Yeats would have it they have few unmixed emotions and are beings of extremes, both good and bad. Often what they do seems perplexing to us, sometimes capricious and sometimes cruel. We should not think that we understand their motivations or project overly human feelings onto them if we want to be successful in our interactions with them. We cannot approach this subject expecting them to be or do what humans would in any circumstance but we must look at the system they operate in as a guideline to understand their etiquette which is distinct from our own. For example, the Good People have no compunction at all about stealing from humans or harming humans, although we see in folklore that they do have some strict rules about humans doing those same things to them and a set of rules about how members of Fairy are expected to treat each other; it is not an equal playing field but one on which they have different sets of rules for themselves and for mortals. This must be understood to understand anything else about them.

So then, this guide to etiquette is not so much about the etiquette of fairies among themselves, but of etiquette for humans dealing with fairies. Which is really the essential thing for a witch seeking to deal with Themselves anyway. Keep these points in mind, as much as possible, when you are interacting with the fairies in whatever context you interact with them, be that dreams, journeys or if you feel like they may be around you in this world. These are the basic rules I'd suggest for you:

Don't lie to the Good People – Fairies are always honest; in folklore and my own experience the Daoine Maithe don't lie but always speak the truth. I suspect this is why they can be tricked in ways we perceive as 'easy' sometimes, such as the story where the girl tells the Brownie in the mill her name is 'Mé Féin' (myself) and he believes her. Of course, as I have mentioned more than once before this does not in any way keep them from tricking us by telling us nothing but the truth in ways that get us to assume a conclusion that is not true. Semantics is an art form of which they are masters. But because they do not lie they don't expect dishonesty from humans either and as you may imagine they react badly to being lied to.

Keep your word – Building off that last one, should you ever be in the position to make a promise or take an oath to a member of the Othercrowd under no circumstances should you break your word. They don't make exceptions to this – a promise is a promise and an oath is an oath. Do what you say you will do. If circumstances arise that mean you can't keep a promise then understand that they will be angry and they will either expect some sort of recompense for the broken promise or they will exact a punishment. This is why I suggest never to promise anything you are not certain you can do or follow through with.

Lending, Borrowing, and Stealing – It happens that the Good Neighbours do sometimes ask the loan of things from us, and it's usually wise to give it. This can range from food to grain to items (usually household items or farm equipment). They always repay their debts, most often with interest but not always in kind; for example there is a well-known anecdote about a man who lent the fairies wheat and was repaid with more than he gave but in barley. There are also stories of fairy mothers who ask a nursing human mother to let a fairy baby nurse just once from them in trade for a blessing; again this is considered good to do. Humans may also borrow from the Gentry but slightly more caution is required as folklore tells us that a deadline for re-payment is always set and must not be missed. Just as with the above point about keeping your word you should always remember that if you borrow from the fairies you are basically entering into a contract with them and must keep to the letter of the agreement. A final note here on giving and taking: the fairies are well known to steal from humans and in some cases humans steal from the fairies. Not surprisingly this generally works out much better for the fairies than the humans. If an item you value disappears and you suspect fairy involvement they can sometimes be encouraged to return it if you simply ask, and other times if you offer a gift in exchange. Sometimes, though, you may have to accept that the item is simply gone. On the flip side of that I highly discourage anyone from trying to take anything from the Fair Folk without permission, and by that I mean explicit permission. If you have any uncertainty, don't take it.

The Issue of Wash Water –This one is a bit complex, but generally speaking, one should not throw dirty water on the ground without an audible warning first, to alert the fairies, and one should not pour such water out over a large rock, lest it be the abode of fairies. Fairies abhor filth and seem to have an especial hatred of dirty water and urine (both of which can be used as protection against them). There is also the matter of having dirty water standing in the home, something that was more common in the past when people would come in and wash their feet; this 'foot water', depending on the area of belief, would either drive fairies away or conversely allow them entry into an otherwise protected home. It may seem strange that I'm including this here but it's something that should be kept in mind by witches seeking to deal with fairies. I find that people who weren't raised with these cultural prohibitions often don't even give a thought to dumping out a bucket of water in their yard or leaving water standing in their sink overnight or similar things. In this case, however, these are things that do need to be thought about and treated with deliberate care.

Gifts – If offered a gift it is wise to accept it and to offer something in return; however, fairy gifts are rarely what they seem. That which seems valuable initially often turns out to be worthless and that which seems like nothing at first is often revealed to be quite valuable. Fairy gifts are also, as often as not, traps, and so great caution should be used with them. In many stories we see something given as a gift that does indeed bring luck or happiness to the person who receives it, but in others, the item – particularly if it is food or drink – may act to trap the person or bind them to Fairy. Gifts are never straightforward. You really have to use your head here, because accepting them can be a good idea and refusing them can anger the fairies, but sometimes refusing them is the best choice. A general rule of thumb is to consider who is giving it: food and drink offered by the higher echelon fairies, especially the Queens and Kings is usually safe to take and eat and would be dangerously rude to refuse; food and drink offered by anyone else though could bind a person to Fairy forever. While there may be some romantic appeal to that idea for some people the reality is far less pleasant and it must be kept in mind that you really don't want to be taken on anyone else's terms. If you eat or drink and are thereby trapped you will be bound there against your will, without your freedom, and almost certainly in the capacity of a servant of some type. So if you are offered food that you feel isn't safe to eat but you are worried about refusing you have a couple options: you can divert to something else, such as playing a game; you can take the food but not consume it; you can refuse as politely as possible. Whenever possible it is wise to give a gift in exchange for a gift. You don't want to put yourself into debt to any being of Fairy if it can be helped.

Nothing is Free – Related to the subjects of lending/borrowing and gifts, try to keep in mind that nothing is free. Even gifts that are given as true gifts without hidden traps still come with obligations. Fairy is a very feudal system in that respect; everything is tied together through debts and obligations and what's owed to whom. If you give to them then they owe you in return, even if that owing is paid back simply by not causing you mischief. If they give you gifts then gifts are expected in return. Reciprocity and obligatory return are the foundations of their society, at least in much of folklore and my own experience. Some caution is required in this area as tangible gifts aren't the only thing to take into account but intangible things can also accrue debts including aid in situations, advice given, and displays of loyalty. One of the main ways that you build relationships in Fairy is by slowly creating alliances with those who are willing to work with you by exchanging these things with them over time.

Never Say Thank You – It is a widespread belief, although not ubiquitous, that one shouldn't say thank you to the fairies. I have heard one theory behind this, that it implies a debt to them, a blank cheque if you will, that would allow them to decide how you repay them. This is somewhat supported by the etymology of the phrase 'thank you' which is rooted in the concepts of gratitude and obligation (Harper, D., 2017). Another theory suggests it is dismissive and implies you feel superior to them. Whatever is the case you should try to avoid saying it. Offering a gift in exchange for something you feel you've received can be a good idea, or saying something else along the lines of expressing gratitude for what happened without saying thank you directly, such as 'I am so happy with … ' or 'I really appreciate … '.

Silence – it is possible for a person to have the favour of the Other Crowd and to gain by it. However, the fairies have a strict rule about a person not speaking of experiences or blessings they get from the Good People. I think this is why we have more negative stories than positive and why we have more stories of single encounters than multiple ones. A person can sometimes get permission to speak or to reveal things, but the general rule is that to keep their favour you must stay silent about their activity in your life. Those who brag about fairy blessings or gifts almost always lose them and the future possibility of them. Keep this in mind and remember that most of your own experiences and interactions should be treated as private. My general personal rule is that if other people witnessed or experienced it with me then it is alright to share or if I have been told to share. Otherwise I try to keep it to myself or only speak of it if I feel strongly that I need to or am explicitly told to.

Privacy – Fairies really, really do not like being spied on or having their privacy invaded, a point that probably ties directly into our last one. Many stories in folklore involve a person who stumbles across the Good People doing their normal thing, is seen watching, and punished severely – in only a few cases does the person manage to talk their way out of any repercussions. For the most part if one happens upon the Good People, particularly if they are in the midst of some activity, it is best not to acknowledge seeing them. It is also generally better to not make a big point of calling attention to anything you do think might be unusual or fairy-related while you are experiencing it, although I will say that if you are being pixy-led saying that you are aware of it, aloud, can break the enchantment, in my experience. You need to use your best judgement on this one, whether it's better to pretend you don't see what's going on or to call attention to it. In some stories a person who admitted they could see the Fey folk was blinded for it; in others they were rewarded.

On a related note, it's a good idea to respect their places and to trust your instincts when you feel like you should or shouldn't go somewhere. If you do happen upon fairies it is probably best to stay quiet and hidden, and wait for them to move on, unless they make it clear from the start that they know you are there. Take your lead from them and try to be aware of what their mood is, although, also, always be aware that their mood can turn on a dime as it were. In an anecdote from Ireland preserved by Dublin City University a man was passing by one night and saw a group of fairies playing with a ball; when they saw him they began calling out his name and kicked him the ball but when he kicked it back to them they attacked him and beat him senseless (Dúchas.ie, 2017).

Moving on from a basic etiquette guide, I'd like to add seven tips for dealing with fairies. These are things I've picked up along the way that I feel can be helpful to anyone seeking to create ties to the Fey. If you already have ties to the Fey then maybe just keep this in mind if you decide to branch out into new or different groups of Themselves.

1. Start Small and Think Local – that isn't a pun; actually most

of the fairy folk aren't small anyway and some are literal giants. But in this case what I mean is that instead of aiming for the most important, powerful being you can think of or find right out of the gate, think more humbly. Nurture connections with the fairies which are closest to you on a daily basis, hearth and home spirits and those who live on or around the land you live on. It doesn't matter where you live, trust me, there are fairies around you. In the city or in the forest, in the suburbs or the wilds, they are there. And for as long as we've had folklore we've had stories of those beings who intentionally choose to live close to humans. These are the ones who are generally the most inclined to be nice to us and the most willing to interact with us – after all they prefer to live near us or even with us in our homes. These are exactly the beings who will be most receptive to you extending a hand in friendship, so that's the best place to start. The idea with all of this work is to create a web of alliances and friendships that will protect you and help you in your witchcraft, and that is something that takes time to build up. The best base for that though is a strong connection to home and local spirits – as those solidify, you'll find that the other connections will come along as well.

2. Remember the Value of Gifts – we already talked above about the importance of gifts and the way that fairies lend and borrow. When you are beginning to reach out to spirits think of it like showing up at a holiday dinner at new friends' or new families' homes: you don't want to show up empty handed. And it is always better to start off by offering gifts than it is to not give anything and find yourself in a debt you didn't expect because you didn't realize they were keeping track. Trust me, they always keep track. You never want to be in debt to any being of Fairy if you can avoid it and should you find yourself in that position, you want to get out of it as quickly as possible. Giving gifts up front can help avoid that situation and also put you in a stronger position overall. I recommend butter or cream, but

I'm a bit of a traditionalist. I'd avoid offering blood – your own anyway – or anything else with heavy metaphysical implications for you. Other options can include fresh pure water, jewellery (especially silver), food, and crystals. Be aware of how and where you give these gifts though, if they are tangible physical objects, because you don't want to do anything that could cause harm to the environment or animals. In the case of dreams and journeys, which we'll discuss in more depth in a later chapter, all I'll say here is to remember that (to paraphrase a popular movie) 'just because it's happening in your head doesn't mean it isn't real'. You can give gifts in dreams and journeys, and you can accept them, and the same general rules apply.

3. Negotiate – whatever happens, even when dealing with the most powerful beings in Fairy, never forget that you have the ability to negotiate. It is not unheard of or even uncommon for a person to find themselves in a situation where they desperately need something and are suddenly being offered it, in exchange for something else. What they ask for in exchange may be obviously valuable or it may not, but don't rush into anything. If they want it always, always assume it has more value than you are seeing. And if they are asking for it don't assume they are joking or mean it in any other way than literally; so if you find yourself in a situation where a fairy is asking for your child in exchange for their help please understand they mean they want to take your child, or your lover, or your soul. That's not hyperbole. Although speaking of hyperbole they won't lie but they can ask for things that represent other things without explaining the details to you. For example, asking for three tears may seem harmless, but what do those tears represent? What do they contain? What power will they give that fairy over you? A tear is never merely a tear, a simple drop of fluid from your eye, it is always something more. If they want it then it is not worthless, don't forget that. And don't think you can get one over on them because maybe deep down you want to go live in

Fairy anyway so it seems a small price to pay to give up your soul to them; *you don't know what they are going to do with it.* Don't ever be afraid to negotiate and don't ever be afraid to say no. You can make counteroffers of other things, and ultimately you can decide to just walk away from the deal all together. And if you do make a deal make absolutely sure you write it down because the exact wording always matters and trust me it will come up later.

4. Write Everything Down – like I just said above. Words have power and this is an important detail to remember with the fairies. Semantics is not just an art form for them it's kind of a passion and so it's really vital for you to be able to remember exactly what was said in any interactions you have, as best you can. Whether this means dreams, meditations, journeys, or any other type of encounter; you should write down every detail you can remember especially anything that is said. If it comes up later it may be important to know these details and having a clear reference matters. I have had it happen that something is brought up years later and if I hadn't written it down and didn't have that to go back and check I may have agreed to something – thinking I already had agreed to it – that wouldn't have been in my best interest. It can also be very useful on a purely mundane level to help you remember when a thing happened or how long something has been going on for or to notice patterns that you might not otherwise see.

5. Be Aware of What You Are Using – There have long been things that traditionally protect against fairies and you should, of course, know what these are and how and when to use them. However, in the context of working with the Good People you also need to develop a sharp awareness of when not to have these things around. Think of it like having a human friend with a severe allergy – you wouldn't invite them to your house and then deck your house out in the thing they are allergic to, would you? Well, the same thing applies here. You can't establish a

good relationship with the Good Neighbours if you iron plate your house and hang broom and Saint John's Wort over every threshold, at least not if you are planning to have them in your home. Obviously if your intention is to establish a separate space in a different location, like out in the woods, to meet with or honour them, then this applies less to you, but you still need to think of what you are wearing. In my experience hag stones, those stones that have a natural hole in them, will ward off any type of spirit or fairy around you which can be very useful sometimes, but obviously don't wear one if you are trying to reach out and connect to the Fey folk. The same for iron or steel, as much as possible, and rowan. If you are in a position where iron or steel are unavoidable due to health or mobility issues cover the metal with cloth as much as possible, preferably silk, but any covering is helpful; I'd also suggest saying out loud that you mean Them no harm and explaining why the metal is there.

6. Remember Your Place – If you want to be successful as a witch dealing with the Other Crowd then you have to have a strong sense of what you can and can't do and where you fit into the grand scheme of things outside a human framework. I find that many humans approach the Fey folk as if humans were the be all and end all of living things and that attitude, in my experience doesn't get a person very far. When it comes to the Otherworld there is a food chain and just like in our world we fit into that, and just like in our world we aren't at the top without external aids, but other things are. I mean let's face it if you are lost in the woods without a weapon and run into a hungry bear the bear is going to win. In the same way if you are wandering around the Otherworld without a means to defend yourself or the right allies and run into something bigger and meaner than you, you have problems. But just as you can survive unarmed in the woods if you stay alert and never forget your position relative to everything else, so too can you get along just fine in Fairy if you keep sight of where you fit in. Know exactly what

you can do and how far you can push it, and have a good idea of what is above you and what is below you in the grand scheme of things.

7. Always Have a Backup Plan – directly related to that last point, always have a backup plan. And then have three more for if that backup plan goes sideways too. Very rarely will things go as expected, and a key to being successful is to try to anticipate ways that things may go awry and how you could compensate. Know how to get out of any situation as quickly and safely as possible, whether we are talking about in a journey or in the real world. Have an idea of what to say or do if you find yourself facing something angry or hungry, and that includes knowing when to stand your ground and when to run. There's a quote from the movie the Last Unicorn: 'Never run from anything immortal; it attracts their attention.' That is something to keep in mind but you may occasionally find yourself in situations where running is your best option. I mentioned in the last chapter when I was talking about my experiences in Ireland about being with a group doing a ritual in an old cemetery, and realizing we were standing under a fairy tree only when a passage started to open out of it; these things do happen and you won't have a lot of time to react.

Hopefully these points and tips have given you a good basic grasp of what it's like to deal with fairies and how to approach doing so safely. The reality of course is that safe is a relative term and we learn as much from our mistakes as our successes.

A Final Thought on Dealing with Fairies:

Beware when you seek to trade
With those we call Good Neighbours
They'll never break a deal that's made
But words are ever their weapons
It's true they pay back barley for wheat
And they give more than they'll take

But they always choose what to keep
And we often, to our grief, mistake
What is worthless for what we need
We never value what we should
Until, seeing only gold and greed,
We barter away what we can't afford.

Basic Guide to Dealing with Non-Human Spirits

The point of this book is obviously dealing with fairies; however, fairies are not the only types of spirits out there and certainly not the only ones a witch will deal with. No discussion about trucking with spirits would be complete without a look at the differences between non-human spirit and fairies and the different approaches to dealing with each. These differences can be significant and the way one approaches and handles a fairy versus a ghost versus a non-fairy spirit can be profoundly different.

There are some basic ways to differentiate between fairies and other types of spirit, although I want to be clear that sometimes it is a blurry line dividing what is a fairy from what isn't. However, in general terms we can define fairies as those beings who are primarily from or connected to the Otherworld or who belong to it in some sense. We also tend to lump nature spirits into the category of fairies, although by the strictest definition they may not be, but they have been considered fairies in folklore for so long we might as well keep including them. Also as I've mentioned before my main focus is on Celtic and tangentially Norse fairies, although I apply the term fairy to beings from different cultures across the world as a generic term.

What then are we talking about here when I say a spirit that isn't a fairy and isn't a human ghost? There are many terms for them in the various paranormal and spiritual communities, all of course lumping different things into a generic category. Usually they focus on the dangerous ones and call them shadow people, or negative entities, or dangerous spirits. Some people even call them demons, although I would personally differentiate a true demon, which is an entity from a specific plane of existence which may or may not be particularly dangerous to us, from a strongly malignant entity that resides in our world or is attached to it. The main things that differentiates them from fairies are: while they may be from another plane of existence, such as the astral plane, they are not from any of the fairy Other Worlds; while fairies can have a tangible physical presence in our world these spirits generally do not; while fairies do not verbally lie these spirits can and do; and their interest in humans is usually different.

When it comes to how to tell if you are dealing with a fairy or a non-fairy spirit there are a few basic clues to look at. Fairies usually don't mess with electronics, while spirits do. You may see fairies as movement out of the corner of your eye, or even directly see them if they choose to be seen but often these other spirits appear as dark shadow shapes. In my experience dogs aren't particularly bothered by fairies but they are very alert to the presence of other spirits. While fairies can and often do physically touch people, and are known for specific things like tangling people's hair while they sleep (called elf-locks) as well as pinching and bruising people, other spirits are known for leaving scratches, particularly in groupings of three lines. Fairies will take things; spirits will move them.

If given a choice I much prefer to deal with fairies, they have a strict but understandable code of honour and behaviour. It takes a while to understand what that system is but once you do there is a certain reliability to it. Non-fairy spirits, however, are much less understandable, at least to me, and so I tend to approach them with more cynicism. It consistently baffles me that other people are so trusting of any and all non-human entities. There are many things about modern spirituality that perplex me but one in particular is the immediate trust that people give to spirits. The most savvy, smart people seem to throw all their critical thinking skills out the window when dealing with non-corporeal beings of any kind and often problems ensue. Because of that, let's look at some basics in dealing with spirits.

Spirits lie. Even the Fair Folk, who in my experience don't tell verbal lies will still deceive you into believing that day is night by speaking only the truth in ways that lead you to assume all the wrong things. And spirits who aren't the Gentry can and do flat out lie. There is no reason to immediately assume a spirit is telling you the truth, any more than you would assume a strange human you just bumped into was being totally honest with you. And the problem here isn't just that they can lie, it's that they will lie if it suits their purposes and you can really screw yourself over if you believe them. Let me tell you a story that happened about 15 years ago when my mother-in-law and several of her friends decided to play around with a Ouija board. They believed they had contacted the spirit of a child from the colonial period, and this spirit immediately began giving them a tragic backstory about being orphaned while it was alive, and dying terribly and wandering the spirit world looking for its mother for the last 300+ years. And asked them to invite it in to give it a place to stay because it was sad and lonely and they seemed so nice ... this was already a field of red flags to me when I was being told about it later but of course they believed every word and invited it in. And of course the next day when one person was alone in the house this had occurred in, the spirit began harassing her, telling her to kill herself, and trying to convince her that the other women were out to get her. And since they'd invited it in they found they couldn't get rid of it (which is where I came into the picture). And if you were wondering, no it wasn't a human ghost it was a negative entity that fed on human pain and misery; everything it had said to them was lies designed to worm its way in so it could influence them and feed on their suffering. The moral of the story – don't trust everything a spirit tells you without trying to verify what you've been told.

An important thing to remember with this kind of spiritual work is that just *because* it's a spirit doesn't mean it has your best interests in mind. I know some people believe that anything without a physical body must be some kind of enlightened being or guide that is here to help us evolve or something, but that is just not true in my experience (see my last story about the Ouija board). I'm going to be blunt here and I'm sorry if this offends anyone who believes differently, but humans are just not the centre of the spiritual universe around which all other manifest creations circle, eagerly looking for a chance to help us be the best we can be. Just like life with other people and animals, some are nice and helpful because they want to be, some will help if motivated to, some are just jerks, and some will actively try to harm us. Much like assuming spirits won't or can't lie, assuming that spirits are only ever trying to help us can cause real problems for us. It's also important to keep in mind that sometimes they are telling you the truth, and sometimes they are not trying to hurt you – they may even really be trying to help – but that doesn't mean that you won't get hurt. Spirits don't always understand what a person's physical limits are, or emotional limits, and their ideas of what's best for us are not always in line with what is actually healthy for us. You have to keep your own limits and safety in mind all the time and set boundaries that keep you safe.

Manners matter with spirits just like with fairies. I am often horrified by the books I see suggesting we treat all spirits rudely, with blunt orders and an assumption that they must obey us. I highly recommend not doing that around the Fair Folk if you like living and having your health, and when dealing with non-fairy spirits it often starts you off on the wrong foot right out of the gate. Unless you are working in a ceremonial magic tradition (or similar) that explicitly requires you to summon spirits with coercion, bind them, and force them to do your bidding using commanding language and you understand which spirits that's appropriate with, there is no reason in my opinion to go into spiritual interactions acting like you're reading from the Key of Solomon. There are certain times and reasons to command spirits, even Otherworldly ones, but if you are reading this and you don't already know what those times and reasons are, then for the love of all that's holy, please don't try randomly getting an attitude with spirits; they won't take kindly to it and you are probably going to make your own life much harder than it needs to be. Putting aside the fact that common courtesy is free and easy, looking at a range of any folk stories demonstrates pretty clearly that having good basic manners gets you much, much further with most spirits than acting like a spoiled, entitled child. But, for one example from fairylore, you might read the story of Lusmore. I will note that there is a slight exception in not saying thank you, but there are plenty of other ways to express gratitude, and also that prohibition isn't universal. When in doubt silence is usually a safe way to go, but general polite speech is always a good choice when you do speak. Unless and until you are in a situation where things have already become aggressive and you need to stand up for yourself, that is, and then, as they say, take no crap and enforce your boundaries.

We talked already about cleansing and purification, and this is another area where that's a big deal. When you are interacting with spirits, be they human ghosts or non-fey spirits, it's very important to make sure you are fully protected and that you cleanse well afterwards. You don't need to drape yourself in talismans but it's a good idea if you are into a spirituality like this one where you will be actively engaging in spirit work, that is intentionally interacting with spirits, to make sure you are cleansing yourself and your space, warding it, and also have some kind of protections. Actively dealing with spirits, whether it's doing divination work, making offerings to house or local spirits, or trying to connect to Otherworldly spirits will attract both things you want and things you don't want. Kind of like putting out a dish to feed local stray cats is going to get you both cats and visitors from the local wildlife. You can and should try to be selective in your advertising but no matter how careful and clear you are in what you are willing to allow in and deal with you're still going to occasionally get other things showing up. Maybe they're curious. Maybe they're bored. Maybe you just look tasty and they're hungry. So common sense: cleanse out the space regularly of stagnant energy (just like you'd physically clean it), ward it to keep out what you don't want (just like you'd close your doors and windows to keep out animals and weird people from your house), and have protections (just like you'd lock your doors). For example on the Fire Festivals it was a common tradition in Ireland and Scotland to burn juniper or a similar cleansing herb in the house and barn. This way at least every three months the space was blessed and cleansed; you can of course burn a blessing herb more often and you can also use other methods like ringing bells to cleanse a space. Space can be warded by walking the boundary with fire or sprinkling blessed water or salt along the border. An individual might bathe in salt water. Hag stones might be worn or hung up for protection, as can iron (although don't use this if you are actively trying to connect to the Fair Folk), and twigs of rowan. Many religious symbols are also worn for protection, which in the case of Fairy Witchcraft would mean the seven pointed fairy star.

This may sound cynical but it really is true that you can never be too careful. To quote Tolkien entirely out of context, 'all that glitters isn't gold'. Plenty of things look too good to be true precisely because they are, and the more beautiful and tempting a spirit seems, the more careful you should be. If it reminds you strongly of someone you have strong feelings for, or of yourself, or in any way hits on emotional triggers for you those should all be big red flags for you to stop and take stock before proceeding. The spirit world is full of tempting things that are, in effect, baited traps and this applies just as much to Fairy as it does to non-fairy spirits. Remember points #1 and #3 and understand that many spirits can change their appearance and that they can and will use this ability to manipulate you. It's also worth keeping in mind that just because something doesn't look attractive is not a reason to assume that it is bad or dangerous. Spirits are not a matter of the inside matching the outside, and I honestly don't know why people assume they will be. Also bear in mind that human beauty standards are not actually a universal measure, so what we happen to find attractive might mean nothing at all to certain spirits (I'm fairly sure Brownies, for example, don't see their lack of noses as a blemish). Just because you think it's ugly doesn't mean it's bad or evil – and just because it's gorgeous doesn't make it good. Most fairies in folklore that seduce and harm mortals show up in darn nice packaging to do so and by some accounts demons like succubi and incubi are very beautiful beings. If something is going out of its way to appear, well, appealing to you then at the least you need to ask yourself why. It might be harmless; a way to establish a connection with you, or it might be hiding a trap. This is not the sort of thing you want to figure out after you've already engaged with the spirit.

Always, always, *always*, trust your own instincts; this one should seem obvious but so often I see people not listening to their own gut, to their grief. By all means don't throw common sense out the window and look without leaping – think things through before acting because we can be influenced without realizing it. Some spirits specialize in getting us to do just that by manipulating our feelings or affecting us on levels we aren't consciously aware of, so learning to act slowly and deliberately is a good thing. But generally speaking if something feels bad or makes you uneasy, don't do it or deal with it. At the very least it means it's not something you're ready for and at worst it's something that is dangerous to you. If your gut is saying bad idea, your gut probably knows something you don't. Don't let your head talk you into doing something stupid, it doesn't matter if all the cool kids are doing it, or if you've done it before, or if someone told you that you have to do it to unlock the next level of spiritual awesomeness or win a gold star. If it feels wrong trust that it is wrong and try to figure out why. It's not like there's some video game time limit where you have to *Do the Thing* right now or start over at level 1 again. Take your time and be sure it's safe before you do it, agree to it, or go into it. This applies triple when oaths or promises are involved. Because if you do something wrong with a spirit the consequences can be profound and very, very real in the 'real' world. And some mistakes can't be fixed.

One way that fairies and other spirits are similar, that is worth mentioning, is that nothing is free – even free things aren't free. Most spirits work on some kind of barter system, although what they consider a trade may not be what we expect – for example, plenty will help us for an exchange of energy that we don't even notice, or for the entertainment value. Others may ask for actual payment in some form, be it a physical offering later, an action done, a task completed, or similar. Some will also help us out on the theory that we then owe them something, a debt that can be called in later (yes I do deal mostly with the Good Neighbours so I may be jaded). Even those who don't work on such an obvious system however, like our ancestors or spirit guides or mentors of different varieties, do assume a certain system of obligation or reciprocity is in effect – you can't expect your ancestors to show up and help you out if you consistently ignore them or actively refuse to acknowledge them. Now some people may say that angels and similar spirits operate on a different system, but I'd argue that working with them or calling on them still requires a level of engagement and belief which is, in itself, a kind of payment. Don't underestimate the value of attention as a method of payment and type of currency to spirits – there are theories after all that some types of spirit who require human attention and energy and are then lost to human consciousness literally cease to exist, which may be as close to death as previously immortal beings can get (depending again on what kind of spirits we're talking about – some can actually die and be reborn in a new form, others do not seem to die in a sense we understand). As part of this, never assume something – including help or guidance – is free. Ask what the cost is and remember that negotiation is always an option. If you don't ask and just blindly agree then you are accepting whatever terms the spirit wanted, and that's usually not a good idea.

To summarize: treat spirits the same way you would treat strange humans (or animals) with the same politeness and healthy mistrust, apply Wheaton's Law to everything, (i.e. don't be a dick), always read the fine print before signing the contract, and don't do anything that makes you feel uncomfortable. Do all that and you have a much better chance of successfully dealing with spirits.

May the odds be ever in your favour.

Dangerous Fairies and Knowing Your Limits

I want to end this chapter with a final thought that I think is vital for anyone who gets on this particular path to always remember. It's something that I hold in mind in any interaction I have with spirits or fairies and something you will probably see me emphasizing one way or another throughout this book. Knowing your limits.

When I was at Pantheacon in 2017, I taught a class about the Unseelie Court. It was a fun class to teach, late at night and with a good crowd. I may have been slightly delirious from jet lag and sleep deprivation. I may also at one point have uttered the now somewhat infamous line in response to what to offer them *'I wouldn't offer meat because then you're going to attract the sorts of things that eat meat. And you know, we're made of meat.'* So, it was that sort of class which is really the best sort of class in my opinion.

My purpose in teaching it was to address some of the misinformation that goes around about the Dark Court, painting them as more sympathetic and more kind than they generally are, but also to discuss ways that we can work with the more dangerous members of the Other Crowd safely. That may sound like a contradiction, but it isn't – like most things in life it isn't that all of the dangerous beings should be avoided completely but that they should be understood for what they are and respected. Part of dealing with dangerous Otherworldly beings safely, probably the most essential part, is knowing your own limits, because we have to know where and what our boundaries are in order to know how we can safely push those limits.

In the course of the class I mentioned how in the area I live in I am aware of the presence of an Each Uisge (water horse) in a local reservoir[4] that has drowned many people over the years. These types of fairy are definitely considered Unseelie Court and have a penchant for tricking people into riding them and then eating them. Someone asked what I had done about the Each Uisge being there and I told them I tried to spread the word that it was a dangerous place. But people wanted to know why I didn't try to go in there and actually get rid of the Water Horse or fight it, so I said, rather bluntly, that a Water Horse was beyond my ability to safely deal with. People were quite surprised to hear this and wanted to know how I could know it was there and dangerous and not try to do something about it. I had to try to explain that even in folklore that sort of being is notoriously hard to deal with and extremely dangerous. It's a thousand-plus pound animal with human intelligence. It's fierce. It's fast. And if you touch it you can't let go again.

Let's be realistic here, I may be fairly experienced with these sorts of things but I'm not Buffy the Vampire Slayer. And I'm not stupid. I know my limits and taking on a homicidal fairy horse on its own turf is not going to end well for me.

For those who seek to truck with uncanny things, to create allies among the Otherworldly folk, to work with the Good Neighbours, one of the most important things you must always keep in mind is your own limitations. Magically and physically know exactly what you are capable of doing. Especially when you're dealing with things that are known in folklore to consider humans a food source. Because this isn't a fun exercise in visualization, a game, or the plotline of a teen novel, and there can be some real and serious consequences when you mess up. You can be hurt physically, you can be hurt emotionally, and what I've seen most often is you can be deeply wounded in the soul or spirit. And sometimes those consequences are permanent and sometimes those consequences are fatal.

This is true with any kind of magic or working with spirits (angels scare me spitless, quite frankly with their Old Testament activities) but it should be common sense if you know you're intentionally going to be dealing with something dangerous to treat it as something dangerous. In the mundane world you wouldn't walk up to a wild bear or wolf and try to pet it, and in the same way in the non-mundane you should approach Other Folk with caution. But just like you can handle a wild animal safely if you know how and you know exactly what you personally can and can't do, what your physical limitations are, just so you can often handle spirits and Otherworldly beings as long as you know your capabilities. And even in unexpected situations you can bluff or manage your way out provided you know your own limitations – and a good grounding in folklore doesn't hurt.

There's a certain amount of risk that's required of anyone who seeks to connect to the Good People. But be wise in what you risk, and know exactly how far you can push.

Endnotes

1. There is also significance to the repetition of the number three, and of asking a question three times.

2. At least the girl is saved temporarily. As it happens later in the story she is at a party and brags to several people about the events with the Brownie and his mother, the eponymous Maggie Moulach, hears and immediately descends on the girl and punishes her for the murder of Maggie's son.

3. Anything involving herbs, including burning or bathing with them, you should consult a specialist or do some research and be certain they are safe for you personally to use. Herbs can interact with pharmaceutical medications and with other herbs, and those interactions can be dangerous. This includes breathing them in and absorbing them through the skin, so please be careful. I learned the hard way that woody nightshade can have euphoric and hallucinogenic properties when burned and inhaled and I'm very lucky I didn't kill myself in the process because I didn't stop and think before burning some. Don't be me. Be smart.

4. I call it an Each Uisge because that's the name that seems to describe it best. It's a large dark horse that lives in the water and drowns people. It doesn't physically consume them as far as I know, but it does feed on their emotions and spirit; if it isn't an actual Celtic water horse then I don't know of any local folklore that explains what it could be.

Chapter 3

Personal Gnosis, Omens and Intuition

There I picked up a cauldron
Where boiled 10,000 harlots
Though full of flame I drank the same
To the health of all such varlets.

I write a lot in my other books and various other places about a more academic view of my spirituality – facts, myths, translations. Hard, verifiable, provable things. Sometimes I think this may lead people to believe I don't get as much into the experiential side of things although I do try to write about that as well, it's just harder to talk about the more personal end. I'm also limited by the code of silence that the Gentry have in place when it comes to many interactions with them; quite simply I can't talk about many things that I may want to. Beyond that though personal gnosis is a huge factor in my spiritual life, but because it is so personal it doesn't lend itself to sharing much. It's hard to discuss a personal experience without reducing it to something that sounds silly or opening it to sceptical review which I have no interest in. I do try to share what I can of my personal experiences when I feel it will help other people, or if I am curious if other people are experiencing the same thing or getting the same messages, but generally I don't see much point in putting my personal gnosis out there knowing it largely won't be understood. That all said, however, mysticism and the gnosis that comes with it are inevitably key aspects of Fairy Witchcraft and anyone on this path should both be aware of the concepts and have some idea of how to approach it and make use of it.

Gnosis is of course a big and controversial topic in paganism, something that is both often misunderstood and misused. The word gnosis itself just means spiritual knowledge, usually with the understanding that it's knowledge obtained through direct experience or insight. What may perhaps otherwise be termed an epiphany, although in my experience it is also knowledge often gained directly from Gods and spirits. Gnosis is often shorthanded in the modern community to U.P.G. meaning unverified or unsubstantiated personal gnosis but ,honestly, I prefer to just call it personal gnosis, because how can we verify that Freya likes strawberries or the Morrigan likes whiskey? Certainly – and this is the usual view – we can rely on seeing if this gnosis is shared by other community members and how widely (becoming then shared personal gnosis or S.P.G.) but the flaw there is that – in my opinion – the vast majority of gnosis is never meant to be shared. Some of it is and should be (as the above examples are) but much of the 'knowing' we get in our spirituality is personal for a reason, in that it represents knowledge and messages which are tailored specifically for the individual.

I'm keenly aware that much of what I perceive as personal gnosis is just that – personal. It is something that applies to me in the specific context that it occurred in, but it may not be relatable at all to anyone else. And you know what? That's okay. Personal gnosis doesn't require validation on a public level. If I feel that something is true to me then I may not need anyone else to share that belief for it to be true to me. Just because I believe it, doesn't mean you have to believe it too. And this is where I believe that gnosis is misused in the community because I often see people taking what is, to me, clearly meant to be insight for themselves and then projecting that outwards as a general belief for everyone. Sometimes this works out okay, but sometimes it doesn't, because there may be a good reason that a deity or spirit tells someone to do something a certain way that is only meant to apply to that person, but not to others. Or why someone perceives a deity or spirit in a certain unusual way that is meant to be unique to them. Too often it becomes a matter of 'I believe this so everyone else must believe it too', and good rarely comes from that.

The other issue with gnosis is whether or not to accept it at all and this is also a sticky wicket. Some people reject all gnosis entirely but that's no better than throwing the baby out with the bathwater. On the other hand though there are people who accept absolutely every notion that goes through their head as if it were sacred writ and that isn't any better. Either extreme – total rejection or total acceptance – is ignoring the importance of discernment and I think discernment is absolutely vital in spiritual matters. Sometimes a dream is just our subconscious trying to work a problem out – or as Scrooge would have it *an undigested bit of beef'* – and it would be an error to take every dream as a deeply significant message. However, that doesn't mean that some dreams aren't messages or communications from spirits; land spirits and deities are well known in folklore and myth to talk to people in dreams and I don't think that should be discounted. In the same way, when we use methods like meditation and Journeywork there is always the possibility that we are interacting with our own mind, but there is also the possibility of genuine connection and gnosis. The key is to learn how to tell when we are talking to ourselves and when Something Else is talking to us.

My basic rules when it comes to personal gnosis:

1. Is it something I would tell myself? Basically does it sound like me talking to myself: is it in words I would use, is it something I have said to myself before, does it reinforce something I already believe?

2. Is it exactly what I want to hear? Is it a message I would expect to hear or want to hear? If I was daydreaming, is this how I would imagine this going? Not that the Gods and spirits can't give us messages that we want sometimes, but in my experience often we don't get exactly what we expect or would like. Much

like in dealing with other people, the experience shouldn't feel like it's in our control. To use a personal example that illustrates – I hope – my point: I had suspected a certain connection between myself and something else for a long time without any real reason for thinking that way, but I had always hoped I was wrong (personal reasons), but recently had my suspicion confirmed in a personal gnosis moment. Part of why I trusted it was that it wasn't really something I wanted to hear.

3. Can it be independently verified? Some gnosis is unable to be proved and as I mentioned that's fine when it's personal. I'm firmly convinced Nuada likes offerings of Gentlemen Jack, but there's no empirical proof of it. But I have had gnosis before that provided knowledge which was verifiable. I've had several dreams involving the herb yarrow, for example: once I was told a way to prepare it to use it as a treatment for wounds, and when I checked later I found out that yarrow does indeed have anti-bacterial properties;[1] I also had a dream relating to yarrow as a symbol of fidelity in love which was later verified in folk tradition as well. I recommend always checking what you get to see if it can be verified. Best case scenario – you will find out that what you received in your dream or journey can in fact be objectively verified, which is always a good feeling. Possibly you will be unable to confirm or deny it, and you'll have to decide whether to use it or not. Worst case scenario – the information you received will be directly contradicted and then you will need to reassess the source or decide how to proceed from there.

4. Does it contradict known folklore or mythology? I'm really cautious of anything I get that actively goes against existing folklore. This requires a lot of questioning and extra checking. It is possible that you may be told something that is meant to have a very particular meaning to you that contradicts existing folklore and mythology but in my experience, more often, this happens because either the message is actually the person's own mind talking to them or else has got muddled along the way.

Humans are, after all, all too often imperfect receivers of psychic information, and like playing the children's game of 'Telephone', things can get garbled along the way.

5. Is it dangerous or does it encourage dangerous behaviour? I'd also be really, really cautious of personal gnosis that is harmful to you or encourages harm to you or others. Spiritual insight should *not* be actively dangerous to life and limb. This isn't to say that this means the message may not be genuine, but as I pointed out in the last chapter not all spirits have our well-being in mind and not all spirits or fairies have a good understanding of human limitations and physiology. Ultimately you must be the one watching out for your own health and well-being and that means having a strong awareness of when you are being told something that you shouldn't do or that would put you in danger.

Beyond those basic guidelines I see personal gnosis as a set of personal beliefs and knowledge which may or may not be shared but that should, ultimately, shape the person's spirituality in positive ways. It is, you might say, the bones of our spirituality. Vitally important and deeply personal, and unique to each of us. The spiritual knowing that we get from our active practice is something that shapes us over time which we also learn to trust and to rely on as a guide.

My main sources for personal gnosis are dreams and journey work. I write everything down and use those notes later to keep track of what I have been getting and also to make further notes on any research I do pertaining to information I might get. For example, in one experience I was shown a four-petalled white flower by a Fairy Queen I am connected to, which she told me was called 'alasam' and said should be used for protection. I hadn't seen or heard of it before but later I drew a picture of what I'd seen and wrote down the experience; research showed that the plant was *Lobularia maratima* whose common name is Sweet Alison or Alyssum and whose name in Irish is Alasam.

Similarly, research showed that in folk magic the plant does have protective qualities, although in fairness as personal gnosis I probably would have used it for such even if it didn't have any known associations for that.

Omens

Personal gnosis is one valuable tool for anyone on this path but it is often one that is better for the long term than immediate answers. I find that what I get from personal gnosis experiences are often like puzzle pieces, where I have to work out exactly what the information means and how best to integrate it into my life. There are moments though where I need more immediate answers or information and in those cases I turn to divination. Of course traditional divination methods are an option, such as tarot, but more often than not I find these moments occur when I am driving in my car or out walking or otherwise not in a position to do formal divination. In these situations I look to omens and for this section I want to discuss two very different types of omen we can utilize.

Natural omens are always an option and one of the main forms I use (which I've written about in another book) is ornithomancy or bird omens. I like this method because it involves watching for signs in the natural world and is something that can almost always be done. It requires some practice and experience to learn when the actions or appearance of a bird are an omen and when they are purely natural behaviour, but once you get into the habit of paying attention I've found it to be a great method. Below I'm going to include a basic guide to some bird omens which I use based on folklore but please remember you would likely need to tailor this to your location.

Ravens – One of the most well-known birds of omen is the raven. Anytime ravens are in the area their activity, calls and direction of flight might be noted and interpreted, and in most folklore they are seen as a bad omen. If a raven arrives just as a new task is beginning, it is seen as an omen that the work will not end well; and a raven near a home signifies a death (O hOgain, 1995). A raven hovering over a herd of livestock was thought to indicate disease among the stock, and to steal a raven's egg would result in the death of a human child (Anderson, 2008). On the other hand, should a raven with white on its wings fly to the right-hand side of a person and call out, it was thought to be a sign of great luck for the person (Anderson, 2008).

Author Glynn Anderson suggests that most Irish lore about the raven is shared by the Norse and reflects Viking influence, which may be why the bird is seen simultaneously as a symbol of death and of wisdom, having been associated with Odin and used as symbols on the banners of different Vikings (Anderson, 2008). In Irish myth ravens are associated with several deities including the Morrigan, and Lugh (Anderson, 2008). Ravens are seen as psychopomps who are able to travel between the world of the living and the world of the dead, as well as the Otherworld. They have strong associations as messengers, which may be why they are seen as such powerful birds of omen.

Personally, I see ravens as omens to pay attention and listen. They are rare in my area so seeing on is significant. When I do see a raven I pay special attention to what it is doing and if it is making any noise, then I consider what that context means to me. For example, a raven perched by the roadside, calling out, might be warning therefore I may slow down or be especially aware as I drive. A raven flying towards me might be interpreted as a message to listen to what the Gods or spirits are trying to tell me.

Crows – Crows are seen as a similar mix of good and bad omens. It was believed that witches, fairies, Bean sí, and Baobhan Sithe appeared as hooded crows (Anderson, 2008). As with ravens, a crow landing on the roof of a house or flying over a home was an omen of death or disaster, but others believe that bad luck comes when crows leave an area (O hOgain, 1995;

Anderson, 2008).

I have always had a fondness for crows, so I tend to consider them to be lucky. They are not always what they appear and can act as messengers from the Otherworld, particularly from or for some of the darker beings. They are one of the special birds of the liminal goddess, the Queen of the Wind. When I see them I usually count them and think of the old nursery rhymes about counting crows, of which I know two versions:

One for sorrow
Two for mirth
Three for a funeral
And Four for a birth

And:

One for sorrow,
Two for joy,
Three for a girl,
Four for a boy,
Five for silver,
Six for gold,
Seven for a secret,
Never to be told.
Eight for a wish,
Nine for a kiss,
Ten for a bird,
You must not miss

Swan – It was believed that swans could actually be Otherworldly beings or transformed people, so killing them was prohibited and to do so, even by accident, was very bad luck (O hOgain, 1995; Anderson, 2008). While the feather of a swan was seen as a talisman of fidelity, it was believed that the bodies of dead swans should not be touched (Anderson, 2008). In mythology swans were associated with the children of Lir who were cursed into that shape by their step-mother; in several myths deities and people of the sí assume the shapes of swans including Angus mac Óg, Midhir, and Etain. Seeing a swan in flight was an omen of good luck, and one charm in the *Carmina Gadelica* invokes a swan to heal a child with the words *'Leech of gladness thou/ Sain my little child/ Shield him from death/ Hasten him to health'* (Carmichael, 1900).

Seeing a swan flying first thing in the morning is a great omen of good luck. I have always thought that seeing a swan in any context, swimming or flying, is a good sign, however, seeing one in distress or dead is a very bad omen. Swans are beautiful birds but they are also powerful and fiercely territorial, and I take this into account when I am thinking of what they represent.

Robin – Here in New England Robins are seen as signs of spring coming. In Ireland they represent a happy home, peace, and hope (Anderson, 2008). As such robins were never killed and if caught accidentally were always released; it was even believed, once, that cats would not kill robins (Anderson, 2008). It was said that anyone who killed a robin would be afflicted with tremors or swollen hands and his cows would give blood with their milk (Anderson, 2008). Some say that the Robin got his red breast by bringing fire to humanity (as did the swallow) while others attribute it to his aiding Jesus on the cross or bringing water into Hell to give to suffering souls (Anderson, 2008); when the first robin of spring was seen a wish could be made, and as long as it was completed before the robin took flight it would come true (Anderson, 2008).

Robins may be associated with the god Bel/Bile/Belenos. Because they are omens of spring they would be viewed, in Fairy witchcraft, as birds of the Summer (Seelie) Court.

Wren – In the old traditions the wren and the robin were said to be married, and Anderson suggests that this may reflect an older belief that the two birds shared the year, with the wren representing darkness and winter while the robin symbolized light and summer (Anderson, 2008). The wren was a sacred bird to the Druids who sought omens from its song and saw wrens as messengers of the gods; the goddess Clíona was said to take the form of a wren (Anderson, 2008). Possibly due to this, wrens were demonized by the church and hunted on Saint Stephen's Day, December 26th; although it may also relate to an older pagan practice of killing wrens at this time to symbolize the death of winter which they represented (Anderson, 2008). Since wrens were associated with winter and the gods of winter, I see them as related to the Cailleach Bhur, although that is purely my own opinion. Folk belief prohibits killing wrens or disturbing their nests at any other time of year, the only exception being December 26th (Anderson, 2008). The wren is said to be the king of the birds, after using cunning to win a contest among all the birds of Ireland; it was decided that whichever bird flew highest would be the king, so the wren hid on the back of the eagle and at the height of the eagle's flight leaped up to win the crown.

The wren is the special bird of the liminal goddess, the Lady of the Greenwood. I see wrens as omens of good luck, of magic, and of potential. As with any other bird omen I look at where they are when I see them and what they are doing for context, but generally for me they are symbols of good things coming and a turn from difficulties or troubles into better times.

Eagle – Eagles were seen as symbols of wisdom, magical power, long life, speed, and vision (Anderson, 2008). In folklore some types of faery, such as the Púca, are said to appear at times in the shape of an eagle. Personally I associate eagles (and hawks) with the Irish god Nuada and the closely related Osprey with Manannán mac Lir. Additionally, eagles appear often in Irish and more general Celtic mythology as symbols of knowledge.

For me the eagle is a symbol of strength and also a message

to pay attention to any messages that are already around me that I may be ignoring. Eagles are uncommon in my area but we do occasionally get bald eagles and for me they have additional symbolism of freedom and courage. When I see them I often look at what I was thinking about or doing immediately before they appeared.

Hawk – Generally hawks were seen as messengers of the Otherworld, were connected to the willow, and believed to symbolize memory and 'clear sightedness' (Anderson, 2008). The oldest of all animals, according to myth, was the Hawk of Achill. It was believed that if hawks suddenly abandoned an area it was because an evil spirit was present (Anderson, 2008).

The hawk is the special bird of the liminal god, the Hunter. I have always seen hawks as omens of a message coming through from the Otherworld and usually take unusual sightings of hawks as signs to meditate or perform divination. I have also found that they often appear as answers for me, as well, when I ask to receive an omen.

Owls – Owls have often been associated with death and bad luck. Hearing an owl hoot, seeing one during the day, or having one fly across your path was seen as very unlucky, although throwing salt in the fire or turning one's clothes inside out should deflect the bad luck (Anderson, 2008). The methods for deferring the ill-omen are strongly reminiscent of methods to defend against fairies, so one might surmise a connection between these birds and the Good Neighbours.

Owls are one of the birds connected to the Queen of the Wind and may act as her messengers and symbols. For me owls are a symbol of the winter (Unseelie) Court and can also be messengers of the dead. Different types of owl may have different associations for me personally and I urge individuals to trust their own instincts when looking at what owls might mean to you.

Dove – Doves have long been viewed as symbols of peace

and love. Irish folklore tells us that no ill-intentioned spirit can take the form of a dove (Anderson, 2008). To me doves are omens of peace and calm and may show up to represent a need for compromise.

Heron – Herons are strongly associated with magic, enchantment, hidden truths, divine messages, and mystery; they are especially associated with Manannán and the Cailleach (Anderson, 2008). When I see herons, or the closely associated cranes, I think of secrets and hidden knowledge and of magic. For me, they are omens that more is going on than I am aware of and that magic is afoot.

Blackbird – Blackbirds are associated with Druids and witches, and were believed to be able to pass freely between our world and the Otherworld (Anderson, 2008). Blackbirds could open the Otherworld to a person, or place a person in a trance by singing, as well as being said to carry messages between worlds (Anderson, 2008). When blackbirds appear I pay special attention to where they are going and what they are doing. I often see them in large groups and so I note the group as a whole rather than the individual bird.

That covers one method of omens, but certainly not the only one. There are many other types out there and it's always best to look at what you feel works for you and that you relate to the most. If you are trying to force yourself to use a system that just isn't connecting for you then you will never get clear answers and it will always feel like a struggle.

We've taken a look at one of my favourite methods, ornithomancy, which is a traditional one with a lot of folklore behind it but I also want to take some time to look at more modern options. I have found that for many witches we get so caught up in our idea of our spirituality being a certain way – read: primitive – that we can be a bit blind to some things. Like the way that modern life and technology intersect with ancient Gods and spirits, for example. In my experience we tend to focus so much on ideas of spirit communication that are based on older methods – dreams, oracles, card decks, natural omens like animals – that we may ignore other methods just because we are biased against anything more high tech. So, I thought I'd compile a list of things that are modern means of communicating with deities and spirits which I use or am familiar with that other people might consider or find useful. These are all things that I do pretty much daily and which I have found to be immensely helpful in my spiritual practices. All of these work on the basic principle of focusing on a question and then observing the next thing that happens in relation to the method being used for your answer.

Music – I've seen this happen through multiple means, including the radio and my MP3 player. The idea is that the songs and song lyrics which play seemingly at random actually provide insight or messages. For example, when I am asking Macha for an omen and Sara Bareilles's song 'Brave' comes on simultaneously I take this as an answer from her; this has happened so often I actually think of it as Macha's song now. For the Good Folk, there are a variety of options, but if I'm listening to Pandora, the radio, or my MP3 player on shuffle and something comes up that has strong connotations I would associate with them or whose lyrics resonate with my question, I take that as an answer.

The television as oracle – Basically the same idea as music except with the television. Since there's no shuffle setting on a television, as far as I know anyway, I use this by either flipping through the channels and stopping randomly or simply focusing on a question and then seeing what happens next. Both this method and the music one are simply higher tech versions of bibliomancy.

High tech bibliomancy – Speaking of bibliomancy, you can very easily adapt that method for modern technology. Instead of focusing on a question and flipping to a random page in a book, stopping randomly and pointing to text to get an answer or insight you would do the same thing on a kindle or other e-reader. It works the same way, but using modern technology instead of a physical book.

Omens and portents, oh my – Most pagans will tell you to keep your eye out for natural omens like animals or weather phenomena, but I have found that omens can come in a variety of forms, some of them quite unexpected. I'll never forget driving on the highway one day, worrying about how to handle a problem relating to a Norse spirituality issue, when a truck passed me with the words written large on the side 'Need a hand? Call Odin today!' (it was a moving service named Odin, I kid you not). This method involves keeping your eyes open but not limiting what you are paying attention to – anything around you can be an omen or carry a message.

Synchronicity – This is one of my personal big ones and I especially pay attention to it on social media. Repeated messages with the same theme, recurrences of the same animal, deity, or concepts, or seeing a message relating to something I had just been talking or thinking about can all be significant. I tend to watch for repetitions in quantities of three but sometimes it can be different iterations of the same thing like the word elves showing up in different ways in different places. For example, one day I found that no matter what I was doing the subject of the Good People and humans interacting kept coming up, from songs to episodes of television shows, to conversations started by other people.

Numbers – Numerology isn't my thing, but I have many friends who swear by the significance of seeing the same numbers repeated. For instance, if it's always a certain pattern of numbers when you look at the clock. If you keep seeing repeated numbers in different ways, perhaps, or noticing a certain number standing out. Even something like waking up at the same time over several nights. What exactly the number means will be very personal and you will have to figure it out yourself, but if it keeps recurring it will likely be important.

Tech glitches that aren't – This happens when our technology, be it phone, computer, or anything else seems to malfunction, but in such a way that it provides a repeated message. For example, a phone ringtone resetting itself to something that has a specific meaning to you or an image coming up on your computer that carries significance. I have even had this happen with broken text messages that suddenly appear days or even weeks after they were sent, but at a time when I needed to see a specific part of what they were saying. I have also experienced this when I am edging into writing something I shouldn't. I recently had this happen to me when I was going to share something on social media related to a personal experience with the Fair Folk; when I went to type it we lost power for several seconds, causing my computer to shut off and later, when I tried again, we lost power a second time for a longer period. I didn't make a third attempt as I had got the message not to share by then.

Intuition

The final thing I want to touch on here is related to these others, in many ways the key to them and that is intuition. We need to know how to listen to our intuition in order to know what is personal gnosis and what is just our own head talking and we need to understand our intuition to know the difference between an omen and a random event. It took me a long time to truly learn to trust my intuition because the rational mind always wants logic and rational reasons for actions. But when you work primarily with the Good People you find that life becomes less about rational choices and much more about following your gut, your instinct. It should be a given that when you step into a place and your brain says that it is a nice place but your gut is saying get out, always trust your gut. But this also applies to other areas as well. When you are practising magic you sometimes find that you feel drawn to do more or less of something than what is recommended in the book, so to speak. I struggled a lot with this when I was just starting out because I wanted the guidance that a book offered and I was afraid of making mistakes. Eventually I realized that mistakes are inevitable, no matter how closely we try to adhere to any guideline, and I slowly learned to rely on my own instinct instead of outside rule.

Like so many other things, of course, this is not ever a straightforward subject. We need to learn to trust our instincts but we should also not get so caught up in relying on instinct that we foolishly ignore outside advice and warnings.[2] Our intuition, no matter how keen, is not going to be right all the time and there are some cases where our intuition and feelings can be influenced by outside factors including different types of fairy. We should never blindly trust our feelings any more than we should blindly trust any other source. Just like I urge people to use discernment and to always fact-check things before using, when we are feeling an intuitive urge it is always good to double-check the same way we would check personal gnosis. Part of learning to trust our gut is knowing when and how to listen to it. Unfortunately the best way to do this is through trial and error, by listening to that inner voice and then seeing what happens. Sometimes it will be good, sometimes bad, and sometimes it will take you into unexpected things that can't fairly be described as either.

I mentioned in the opening chapter how when I was at Rathcroghan we did a meditation on top of the mound and our guide was very clear that people were to go down the way we'd come up, the eastern path. My intuition immediately told me that I needed to go down a different way even though I knew our guide was spot on with why everyone had to go down the way they'd come up. I could certainly have gone against my instinct – gone against that little inner voice – and it would have been much easier to do so quite frankly. But if I had done what I was told and not followed my intuition I would have missed out on the most profound initiatory experience of my life which began with that single choice to go down the mound the other way.

Only time and experience can teach you how and when to trust your intuition; it is never something that can be learned from any book or any in-person teacher. Yet for this particular type of witchcraft it is essential and so I offer these simple suggestions. Start paying attention to your own feelings about things and that quiet inner knowing that speaks to you. Make note of when you listen to it and when you don't and what subsequently happens. I have long been an advocate of keeping a variety of journals and you might think of having a small notebook where you can jot down thoughts about intuition and your experiences with it. I have found that I learn as much from when I don't listen as when I do, because either way the results and consequences are a lesson.

Endnotes

1. With anything related to herbs, do not play around with them please. Consult an herbalist. Herbs are not a simple thing to deal with and they can have complex and dangerous interactions with people and with other herbs and medications.

2. Much folklore exists to warn us about possible dangers we may come across in Fairy and with those who live in it or come from it. Although trusting our intuition is invaluable we should never totally discount what we know from folklore and tradition; there are beings who thrive by manipulating people into letting their guard down such as the Each Uisge who lure the unsuspecting into riding on their back only to tear them apart and eat them. As Fairy witches we must strive for a balance between trusting our inner knowing and trusting our wisdom and the wisdom of tradition.

Chapter 4

The Otherworld and Those within It

My staff has murdered giants,
my bag a long knife carries
For to cut mince pies from children's thighs,
with which to feed the fairies.

In Chapter 2 I talked about trucking with spirits and specifically about some basic guidelines of working with fairies and differentiating between fairies and other spirits. In this chapter I want to take a closer look at fairies and the Otherworld and some aspects of the very difficult subject of what exactly are fairies. As you advance into an actual working relationship or alliance with these beings its essential that you move beyond the usual 101 book understanding of them. Most books for a variety of different reasons tend to reduce fairies to the easiest possible discussion points in order to understand them, but to seriously engage with these beings you have to let go of any narrow view of them and embrace their ambiguity. Ultimately with Fairy there will always be more unanswered questions and uncertainty than firm truths.

Hierarchy

Fairy works under a hierarchy. At the highest level we have the most powerful spirits, beings which for simplicity's sake we call Gods.[1] Gods have the greatest and most pervasive degree of influence over the widest areas, and the fewest limits on their actions and influence. I have seen Gods take an active interest in individuals for both good and ill, and I think it is always unwise to forget the level of power a deity is operating with. There is a range, of course, from an upper end of extremely powerful to a lower end of still-a-god but not as powerful. Gods also, again in my opinion, have the greatest scope of knowledge both of current events and of things yet to come. Why do Gods have an interest in individual people? Well that's going to vary by each person, but ultimately the Gods have their own purpose and agenda, and sometimes they need us to forward that. They work on a scope and scale which is so vast it can be hard sometimes for us to understand the why – although sometimes it's pretty obvious. They need us, and we need them, on different levels. Why do I say there are Gods in Fairy? Because that's my experience and because that's what folklore and mythology tells us; in Irish mythology we find stories of the Tuatha Dé Danann going into the Fairy mounds and into the Otherworld where they became known as the aos sí, or people of the fairy hills (another name for the fairies as well). Many of these Gods, the Tuatha Dé Danann, later became known as queens and kings of Fairy in their respective areas.

Besides the Gods there is also a wide array of spirits, including those who are almost Gods themselves to those who are almost on the same level as humans, and those below us (influence-wise). Many of the Good Neighbours can be just below the Gods as far as influence and power goes, which is part, I think, of why they have always been so respected and feared. Others, however, are much closer to us and less dangerous to us. And if you take, for example, a spirit like most ancestors or human ghosts, they are very close to us indeed influence-wise and while they can and do help us and provide us with information they usually aren't a significant threat to us unless something unusual is going on (or unless it is an ancestral spirit that has been or is elevated to a higher level, which is possible – nothing is fixed, everything is fluid). The closer a spirit is to us the more logical it is for that spirit to want to help us or have an interest in connecting to us.

All of this is of course very loose and there are a lot of grey areas. What I might call a God someone else might call a fairy and neither of us would necessarily be wrong. And I do believe that there is the potential for movement both up and down in this system, so that an ancestor who is honoured and prayed to by enough people over enough time can become a deity and a deity who is forgotten and ignored for long enough can lose power. Much like so many other areas of life, nothing is set in stone; rather our relationship with the Gods and spirits is a symbiotic one where both sides benefit. I'd also argue that ultimately it really doesn't matter whether what you are connecting to is a god, per se, or a powerful spirit, or one of the Daoine Maithe, if it benefits you to have that connection.

It is vital, though, to know this when you are potentially journeying to Fairy or connecting to these beings. You may well be connecting to fairly low-level beings who are less powerful but still important – or you may be dealing with beings who are or have been Gods. You shouldn't underestimate anything you encounter and it's always worth considering that nothing is what it seems.

The Otherworld

Part of being a Fairy witch is either actively going to Fairy or being open to the possibility of doing so. The Otherworld is a world, or more accurately several worlds, which are closely connected to but separate from our own. One should be careful not to confuse Fairy with the astral plane, as the two are definitely separate places; the astral can be influenced by the human mind and shaped by our thoughts, while Fairy exists independent from human thought and is not open to our influence simply through focus.[2] Fairy is also a very diverse landscape that includes cities, villages, forests, mountains, and nearly anything else you can imagine.

In mythology and folklore we find references to different names for Fairy and it may be that these are names for one place or it may equally be that these are names for different interrelated places. For our purposes it really doesn't matter whether these are actually distinct worlds or not, although it is important to keep in mind that different, distinct areas, much like different countries on earth, may have their own rules and culture. The expectations in Ljossálfheim are not the same as in Tír na nÓg, for example, and both are different than what one might expect in Annwyn. And those are some of the bigger more well-known examples – there are innumerable small places with no great fame that you might run across, places that have no written folklore to guide you.

There are some basic things we can say about the Otherworld based on looking at the bulk of folklore. Time moves differently there, and while the Gentry seem able to predict and control that flow, we can't. A day may be a year here, or the reverse may be true and you could live months there only to find that little time has passed here. It is often described as a land of perpetual summer and fruitfulness, although I will say that I have seen places that are always winter or always autumn as well. Some mythology and folklore hints that the seasons of Fairy are inverse to our own, while other stories say it is always pleasant and temperate.[3] Like our world it contains plants, animals, different types of intelligent being, a diverse array of landscapes, and as I already mentioned, various forms of civilization.

We have many names for the Otherworld or Fairy and within its bounds there are many, many beings. Although we may tend to always go to the same general places it's important not to get complacent and never forget that variety exists, and that dealing with the Otherworld and its inhabitants means accepting a different mindset.

Envisioning Fairies

One of the most pervasive and potentially dangerous myths that I see among modern pagans interested in working with fairies is that if it looks pleasant and attractive it must be morally good and if it looks fearsome or dangerous then it must be morally evil. With the Good People, I might suggest that it is unwise to ever judge anything based on appearance. I admit, I find it odd that people expect the Seelie Court beings to look traditionally good and appealing and the Unseelie Court beings to look traditionally evil and disturbing. Some of the Blessed Court things look quite disturbing, even though they are relatively harmless. Like merrows and urisks, for example. Some of the Unseelie Court things look extremely enticing, even though they will eat you for lunch. Take Each Uisge or Baobhan Sithe for example, one of which appears as either a beautiful horse or handsome person and the other which looks like a beautiful woman, but both of which kill and consume people.

When you imagine what a fairy looks like, what do you picture? For most people the mental image is strongly shaped by pop-culture and artwork, and these in turn are largely products of an idealized cultural aesthetic. Although Tolkien-style elves may be an accurate representation of one type of Fairy being, the idea that all fairies are tall, lithe, and handsome is far from what we find in folklore. And while the images of small insect-winged[4] children may fit a very specific type of garden fairy, the more widespread images of winged Barbie-like beauties – wasp waisted, disproportionately large eyed, large breasted, with tiny hands and feet – is straight out of our culture's fantasies. Many modern images, such as those that depict selkies as a kind of seal mermaid with the upper torso of a human and lower half of a seal, are purely from an artist's imagination. In the same way, the recent upsurge in anime and video game influenced images – those that have extremely long pointed ears, sharp features, slim figures but exaggerated sexual characteristics – don't reflect actual folklore or mythology but an artistic view which is aimed at appealing visually to an audience used to consuming a specific aesthetic.

So, what do the Good People really look like? As with most

questions relating to Themselves there is no simple answer, because the subject is too broad and diverse. I think therefore that the best approach is to look at a range of different types of fairy known to have more human-like forms and discuss how we see them described in folklore, in order to get a feel for the ways that these beings, overall, may appear. In order to keep this article reasonably short I'm only going to give very brief descriptions of each below:

Aos Sí – Yeats described the Daoine Maithe as looking much like human people, although prone to wearing slightly outdated fashions. Described as around five feet tall, sometimes slightly taller. We see the idea of their human appearance reinforced in much of the anecdotal evidence, particularly stories of borrowed midwives, stolen brides, and musicians who spend a night inside a fairy hill. There would seem to be then at least one type of more powerful fairy, people who do or can look very much like humans and may even pass for a human to some degree.

Tylweth Teg – Like the aos sí generally described as human-like in appearance, usually fair haired.

Pixies – Descriptions can vary greatly but they are known to wear green; in one potential account of two children who may have been pixies they were said to have green-tinted skin. Pixies may range in height from a few inches tall to five or six feet, and by some accounts may take the form of hedgehogs. Briggs describes them as red haired with pointed ears, short faces, and up-tilted noses.

The Baobhan Sithe – Described as beautiful human-looking women, about five feet tall, who wear long green dresses to hide their feet which are the hooves of a deer. Said to take the form of wolves and crows or ravens.

Brownies – generally about three feet tall, a uniform medium brown colour all over and preferring brown clothing. In some areas it was said they had no fingers while others described them as having no noses.

Leprechauns – Look much like humans in the oldest stories, except they are said to only be about 12 to 18 inches tall. In later folklore they are described with a similar height and as looking like older men with grey or white hair and beards.

Goblins – three to four feet tall, ranging from almost human-like, although extremely ugly (by our standards), to very animalistic with whiskers, tails, claws, and the like.

Trows – In some folklore trows are described as very human in appearance, although they may appear old, shrivelled, or physically deformed. In other stories, however, they are described as clearly inhuman, unattractive, and twisted, sometimes appearing as a mix of human and horse. They are often described in unflattering terms as having oversized feet, large noses, flat faces, and short limbs. They can range in height from three to six feet depending on the story. They are often said to dress in grey.

Dwarves – Another type of fairy that has a wide range even within its grouping. In some cases they may appear as Tolkien described them, as short, barrel chested, heavily bearded men. In other cases they may have clear physical deformities such as animal feet or feet turned backwards at the ankle.

Púca – A shape-shifter, the Púca can appear as a variety of animals including eagles, goats, horses, bulls, and dogs. May also appear as a small man.

Kelpies – Can assume the form of a horse or of a dark haired person, usually but not always a man. As a horse he is appealing and fine-looking; as a person he would seem human except that his hair remains damp and may have water weeds in it if one looks closely.

Merrows – Like traditional mermaids they have the upper torso of a human and the lower half of a fish; merrows also have webbed hands. Females are extremely beautiful. Males are hideously ugly, with green tinted skin, and deep-set red eyes. Children born from the union of a merrow and a mortal are said to have scales.

Selkies – Selkies can take the form of seals or of dark haired human-like beings. The children of selkies and humans are said in folklore to be born with webbed hands or feet.

Glaistig – May appear as a beautiful woman with slightly damp or dripping hair; as a woman wearing a long green dress to conceal her lower half which is that of a goat; or may appear in the form of a goat.

Huldra –A kind of Scandinavian fairy that looks like a very beautiful woman but always has some hidden deformity in stories; sometimes a tail, or a hollow back. The Huldrekall (male huldra) is quite ugly with a long nose.

Elves – Elves present a unique difficulty because the English word, elf, is used to gloss several words in other languages and was also used for a long time as a generic. Because of this, we end up with a range of beings that fall under the label 'elf' but are very different in nature and description. We may perhaps divide them into two main groupings, the taller elves and the small elves. The latter are generally described as about one foot tall and can appear as old and wizened or younger. The former group is often described as more human in appearance, although they are clearly supernatural in their abilities and are averse to iron. Jacob Grimm suggest a division in Germanic mythology of taller elves into three main groups, the ljossalfar, dokkalfar, and svartalfar, each living in different domains and having slightly different appearances; lossalfar means 'light elves', dokkalfar 'dark elves', and svartalfar 'black elves'. Snorri, writing about Norse mythology, described only ljossalfar and svartalfar. In Scottish and Germanic sources the taller elves may be described as beautiful and the word elf was sometimes glossed with incubus; elves were known for seducing mortal women. However, in other Germanic sources elves were explicitly called ugly and were said to have long or crooked noses.

Giants – There are also a variety of giants to be found in

fairylore, beings who can be seven or eight feet tall or more. In English folklore these are usually named beings like the Jack-in-Irons or Jimmy Squarefoot. In other cultures these may appear as a type of being in their own right such as the Norse Jotun or Anglo-Saxon Etin, both names meaning 'giant'. Giants may appear very human but on a larger scale, or may be monstrous, such as the aforementioned Jimmy Squarefoot who was part man and part boar, or they may have extra heads or limbs.

Gruagachs – Male or female, generally human-like in looks, may appear as either young and attractive, or as wizened, old, and very hairy.

Muryans – Cornish fairies that could be as small as ants. They might be shape-shifters who could take animal forms, particularly birds, but were also associated with the Heathen dead. It was believed they had once been human-sized but had shrunk over time, eventually disappearing entirely.

This is only, obviously, a small sample of the huge array of fairies that can be found in folklore. I hope though that this has illustrated the range of descriptions we see, from human-like to monstrous, from tiny to taller, from what we may call beautiful to what we judge as ugly, from entirely human-like to animalistic, with various skin colours including green. As Katherine Briggs says *The fairy people are good and bad, beautiful and hideous, stately and comical ... one of their greatest variations is size* (Briggs, 1976, p. 368). There is also an equally wide range of fairy animals, both those that are true animals living in or from Fairy and those beings like the kelpie and púca who are able to shape-shift between humanoid and animal forms.

Personally, I have seen what we would call beautiful, but I have also seen beings we'd describe as outside that 'normal' that are within context considered beautiful by their own. Hollow backs, back-turned feet, single eyes and limbs, small, huge, horns, tails, famine-thin and very large, webbed feet or hands, immobile, non-ambulatory – Fairy has an enormous diversity to it that far, far defies our modern cultural perceptions of 'beauty'. If we are seeking to understand and appreciate the folklore, and to connect on any level with these beings then we must understand this diversity and appreciate it for what it is without overlaying our own perceptions and opinions onto it. We must understand that each group of fairies, each kind, would seem to judge by their own standards just as we do by our cultural ones, so that what a pixie considers beautiful is not what an elf (of any type) might consider beautiful, and neither may be what a human would call beautiful. I think we limit our appreciation of Fairy when we are looking at it through our own lens of beauty, height, ability, size, skill, or mobility, rather than appreciating it and Themselves for what and who they are in themselves.

As a witch on this particular path you must be prepared to see anything because you may meet anything, and whatever you see you shouldn't rush to judge by appearance. That which looks frightening may be a worthy ally and that which looks alluring may be very, very dangerous.

Fairies, Invisibility, and Old Irish Mythology

It is generally understood in modern folklore that the Fair Folk cannot be seen unless they choose to be or unless a person has some special ability or power to see them. The idea of the Good People being able to go unseen by mortal eyes is well accepted but not necessarily well understood and can often lead to discussion of the related subject of whether or not the fairies have physical forms. This seems to be rooted in the modern perception that we cannot see them because they are insubstantial or exist entirely as energetic beings, rather than that we cannot see them because they do not want us to see them. I would argue that they do indeed have physical forms, based on the amount of folklore in which they interact directly and substantially with people and the number of stories where children are produced. However, that issue aside, we are left with an assumption that the Fair Folk can become, effectively, invisible as an idea that is embedded in folklore. I think it may be worth looking at how far back that idea stretches in order to appreciate how deeply rooted it actually is and so that we can understand how it may impact us.

Although some people today may attribute this ability to newer folklore relating to fairy glamour or even see it as evidence of fairies fading from this world, when we look at Irish mythology we see the same power attributed to them. We can find evidence of the concept in Irish mythology for as long as we have evidence of the fairy folk themselves:

1. *"Oenfer sund chucund innossa a Chucucán", ar Loég ...'Acht ni saig nech (fair) & ní saig-som dana for nech, feib nacha n-aicced nech issin dúnud chethri n-ollchóiced hErend'*
   'Is fír aní sin a daltán,' for se. 'Cia dom chardib Sídchaire-sa ...'
   Tain Bo Cuailigne, twelfth century from oral material that dates earlier
   ['A single man coming towards us now, oh Cu Chulainn,' said Laeg ... 'But none advance on him and he advances on no one, as if no one saw him in all the camp of the four grand provinces of Ireland.'
   'The man coming there, oh fosterling,' said [Cu Chulainn], 'he is to me a friend from the fairy-troop ...']

2. *'Síd mór i taam conid de suidib nonn ainmnigther áes síde.'*
   'Cía a gillai" ol Cond fria mac acailli. úair ni acca nech in mnaí acht Condla a óenur.'Echtra Condla, eleventh century, material likely dating to the eighth century
   ['We live in the great fairy hill and are called the people of the fairy hill.'
   'Who [do you speak to], oh boy?' said Conn to his son. Because no one could see the woman but Connla alone.]

3. *'Lá n-and doib a n-ingenaib uilib isind inbiur oca fothrocud co*

n-accatar in marcach isa mmag cucu dond usciu ... Etain indiu. .n. Dochúaid úadib in t-óclaech iar sain iocus ní fetatar can dodeochaid la cid iarom.'

Tochmarc Etaine, fourteenth century, language dated to ninth century

[One day it happened to them that the girls on this occasion were at a river-mouth and were washing when they saw a horseman on the plain from the noble waters ... (he recites a poem claiming Etain as one of the sí and predicting war on her behalf) ... Etain at that time went from the young man and was different afterwards and they didn't know whence he came from or yet went afterwards.]

In all of these examples, from texts written between 1,000 and 600 years ago, but generally based on oral material hundreds of years older, we see people of the sí coming to interact with people in our world but remaining unseen by those they didn't want to be seen by. Cu Chulainn's friend among the sí walks through the encampment of the men of Ireland, the army who at the time was fighting against Cu Chulainn and Ulster, unimpeded and as Laeg relates unseen. Connla's fairy woman, who has come to court him and tempt him to join her in the sí, appears next to him and talks to him but only he can see and hear her until she chooses to speak to his father Conn as well.[5] The rider of the sí who speaks a prophecy about Etain appears and seemingly disappears with no one the wiser as to where he came from or where he went afterwards. There are other similar stories in other texts, including the appearance of the fairy woman Fidelm in the Tain Bo Cuailigne. In the exact same way, we find tales in later folklore of people of the fairy hills who appear to specific people but not others or who can choose who sees them in our world.

We find this power to go unseen among the Tuatha Dé Danann as well as the fairy folk, but there is some persuasive evidence that it is an ability that the fairies had first. This power seems to have come to the Tuatha Dé Danann from their connection to the Good Neighbours and particularly from Manannán's gift of the Féth Fiadha. The Féth Fiadha is a magical mist or veil, likely a type of enchantment, which hides those under its power by making them invisible or otherwise deceiving the sight of those who looked at them so they were hidden. We find a discussion of this in the story 'Altram Tige Dá Medar' where the Féth Fiadha is given to the Tuatha Dé Danann by Manannán so that they *'could not be seen'* and he also teaches them *'to carry on their mansions in the manner of the people of the fair-sided Land of Promise and fair Emhain Ablach"'* (Dobs, 1929). Manannán is also the one in that version of the story who allocated the sí to the Tuatha Dé Danann and decided who would live where. From this we can safely gather that it was Manannán who taught the Tuatha Dé Danann to live among the Fairy folk after they were forced into the sí by the Gaels. We may also perhaps conclude that it was the Daoine Sí, through Manannán, who taught the Tuatha Dé Danann how to move unseen and how to live in the sí, not the other way around.

Ultimately the evidence we have from Irish mythology shows us that the idea of the Fair Folk going unseen, or being selectively seen, can be traced back in writing at least 1,000 years. If we accept scholars' assertions that the oldest text discussed here, the *Echtra Condla,* can be further backdated based on language to the seventh century[6] then we are looking at a 1,400-year-old story of a fairy woman who was seen by one person in a crowd. The ability by the Good People to make themselves invisible is one that is not only deeply ingrained in their mythology and folklore, but even seems to be something they taught to the Irish Gods. This power then rather than a modern concept is one of the oldest and most significant magics that we are aware of the Daoine Maithe possessing.

This idea of invisibility ties directly into one of the strongest prohibitions around the Fair Folk, that of privacy. They often do not wish to be seen and it is unwise to make a show of letting them know you can see them, if you can. As a witch you may find that you become more aware of this side of reality over time and as a Fairy witch you may find that as you build friendships and alliances with those among the Good People you gain some ability to discern their presence or even see them directly. This ability should be treated with great caution, and one should always be very careful about acknowledging seeing fairies.

There is a very well-known story that has many different versions of a midwife who is borrowed for a fairy birth and given an ointment to anoint the babies eyes with. Afterwards she accidently rubs one of her own eyes and finds that the ointment grants her the ability to see through fairy glamour. Sometime later she sees the father of the child she delivered at a fair and greets him; when the fairy man realizes she can see him he blinds her eye.

The fairies take their privacy very seriously.

What's in a Name? Imp, Elf, Fairy, Good Neighbour

When it comes to the denizens of Fairy, what's in a name? As it happens, a lot, but there's also a great deal of confusion because many of the terms in English that we apply today to specific beings are rooted in generic terms that were once interchangeable. One author noted no less than 50 different names for the Lutins and Korrigans of Brittany, while simultaneously noting that those beings were comparable to beings by other names, including elves, in other countries (Vallee, 1969). The water is further muddied by the widespread use of euphemisms, designed to encourage a positive response should you attract the attention of anything Otherworldly. These terms which we now think of as exclusively applying to one specific type of Otherworldly being a few hundred years ago, or less, were used synonymously with each other and different groupings of terms had certain connotations for good or ill. What one called the beings popularly named fairies today would dictate the way they would respond, and whether that response would be friendly or hostile. This is something that witches should be aware of and also make use of; use euphemisms to your advantage. More than that though keep in mind, always, that the names we use for any type of being are at best generalities.

This Scottish poem demonstrates some of the variety of synonymous terms we see in the folk cultures:

> *Gin ye ca' me imp or elf*
> *I rede ye look weel to yourself;*
> *Gin ye call me fairy*
> *I'll work ye muckle tarrie;*
> *Gind guid neibour ye ca' me*
> *Then guid neibour I will be;*
> *But gin ye ca' me seelie wicht*
> *I'll be your freend baith day and nicht.*
> Chambers, 1842
> [If you call me imp or elf
> I counsel you, look well to yourself;
> If you call me fairy
> I'll work you great misery;
> If good neighbour you call me
> Then good neighbour I will be;
> But if you call me seelie wight[7]
> I'll be your friend both day and night]

Looking at this nineteenth-century rhyme we see an assortment of terms that can all be applied to the Good Folk, each of which either angers or pleases them. We're advised that calling a member of the Other Crowd an imp, elf, or fairy will anger them, while calling them 'Good Neighbour' or seelie wight will gain their favour. However, all of these various terms are treated synonymously rather than as unique terms for different types of being. There is no idea that these are different types of being, but rather that these are all terms that someone might choose to apply to the same being. This reflects an older understanding that saw the members of Fairy more fluidly and less rigidly categorized.

The first two terms mentioned, which are used together, are imp and elf. Imp comes to us as a term in older forms of English that originally denoted a child but by the sixteenth century had become a term for a small devilish being (Harper, 2017). Similarly, the English word elf during that period was often used to both describe a malicious creature, often used interchangeably with incubus and goblin, as well as more generically to describe any Otherworldly being (Williams, 1991). There was often a fine, sometimes indistinguishable, line between the demonic and the Otherworldly and it was not uncommon in older sources to see the same being described by one person as a demon or incubus and by another as an elf or fairy. The activities of some of these beings were also grey areas that could be considered evil as they may involve seduction, violence, or death. So, we see in the first line of the poem two terms often used to indicate potentially dangerous beings, with the warning that to call them such is to invite the danger they represent.

Next we see the term fairy,[8] with the warning that to call them that invites great misery. The term fairy is actually a complicated one, of obscure origin, which was originally used to describe the Otherworld itself – the world of Fairy – and as an adjective for beings from that world or a type of enchantment (Williams, 1991). Only later would the word itself shift to indicate an individual being. In this sense it is strongly reminiscent of the Irish term 'sí' (later sí) which in the same way is a word indicating a place and used as an adjective, but that has recently started to be used to indicate the individual beings. When it comes to the word fairy in early sources, including Chaucer, we see the beings referred to often as elves and their world as Fairy (Williams, 1991). Why this word would offend them may seem less clear to us today, however, just as the words imp and elf had strong associations with evil, the word fairy at different points had pejorative uses, including being applied to sexually loose women and later homosexual men, in both cases carrying overtones of sexual impropriety (Briggs, 1967). These associations towards people only came later, likely because of the word fairy's meaning relating to the Otherworld and enchantment which when used to describe a person implied uncanniness and improper behaviour. Since early sources do not indicate the word fairy caused any insult I would suggest that it was this pejorative association that was the source of the offense and with their dislike for the term. In a modern context fairy is possibly the most widely used generic term for all Otherworldly beings as well as a specific term for small winged beings. Many people use it regularly without consequence, although I will note that in some places such as Ireland there are still prohibitions about the word.

Next we see the term Good Neighbour, one of the more well-know euphemisms. I haven't been able to trace how far back this one goes, but I do know that the use of euphemisms has a long history. For example, we can find the term Fair Folk (Fair Folkis) in a work from 1513 by Gavin Douglas. We can see Good Neighbours used slightly later in the fifteenth and sixteenth centuries as a term for fairies in these examples: from Ancient Criminal Trials in Scotland 1588 'For hanting and repairing with the gude nychtbouris and Quene of Elfame [for haunting and repairing with the good neighbours and Queen of Elfhame]' and from the Orkney Witch Trial, 1615 '... to the fary folk callit of hir our guid nichbouris [to the fairy folk called by her our good neighbours]' (DSL, 2017). The idea of euphemisms is simple: you use a nice term for them and they respond in a nice way. This is illustrated by the poem itself, 'If Good Neighbour you call me, then good neighbour I will be'. As such we see all the euphemisms reflecting positive qualities, from Good Neighbour and Fair Folk, to Good People and the Gentry.

The final term used in the poem is Seelie wicht, a name we are assured will gain us the friendship of the Fey folk *'both day and night'* if it's used. Wicht is a Scots term, also found in related languages including Old English, Icelandic, and German, that simply means a living thing. Sometimes seen as wight in English, it is often used in combination with good as a term for the fairies; guid wichts, good wights, the fairies. Seelie is a Scots term that means lucky, blessed, fortunate. So, in effect, seelie wicht means 'lucky or blessed being'. Understandable why they'd be so pleased at the use of this term then. It is also seen in one of the more well-known Scots euphemisms for the fairies, Seelie Court, which has grown into a complex concept in itself.

So, what's in a name? Ultimately the meaning and context of the name seems to be the key to whether it pleases or offends the Othercrowd when we call them by it. They respond well to being complimented and flattered with favourable terms, explaining perhaps why the use of euphemisms became so popular, and are angered at being insulted. To offend them is to risk their wrath; to please them is to invite their blessing.

The Queen of Elfland

One figure that we see appearing in Scottish folklore in ballads, stories, and witch trial accounts is the Queen of Elfland or Queen of Fairies. In the stories and ballads the Queen is never named explicitly but only referred to by her title and usually appears alone, although, in some rare cases she was known to have a king by her side. An enigmatic figure, she travelled to the mortal world in some ballads and took young men who interested her, keeping them for a period of time, and in other stories she held court in Fairy itself. She was also known to favour some witches and to have them brought to her in her court or sometimes to visit them on mortal earth where she would teach them or give them things like elfshot. In other cases the Queen was named and would have a body of folklore attached to her that could be learned and studied. In all cases she appeared to be a powerful and influential force.

As a witch following a Fairycraft path I believe the odds are very high that at some point you will at the very least encounter one of the Queens of Fairy, whether it is the unnamed Queen or one of the many named ones. Fairy Queens may be or overlap with the liminal Goddesses of Fairycraft or they may not, but either way as you deepen your path you may find a Fairy Queen becoming a presence in your life. Even if you don't expect this to be so or feel like you have been on your path for a long time and have built up other connections that would preclude that sort of thing, you may be surprised. I certainly never expected to end up dedicated to a Fairy Queen and after 25 years on this path I felt pretty settled where I was at. I was already dedicated to Odin and Macha, deities who have their own strong connections to the Hidden People.[7] Yet sometimes the path takes a turn we don't expect and I found myself pledged to a Fairy Queen and shortly thereafter released from my dedication to Odin after a decade. It's important to understand who and what the Fairy Queens are, in case – or I should say *so that when* – one of them comes around you understand. Dealing with them is a whole different level of seriousness and what they may ask of you should never be taken lightly.

In ballads the Queen of Elfland appears frequently, often having stolen a young man, sometimes to be her personal servant and other times apparently to serve more generally in Fairy. We find a wide array of examples of this across different ballads in Scotland. In the ballad of Tam Lin the eponymous character relates to the protagonist, Janet, that when he fell from his horse as a youth the Queen of Fairies caught him and took him *'in yon green hill to dwell'* (Acland, 1997). Tam Lin has become the fairy guardian of a specific well in the wood of Carterhaugh, which seems to be his assignment for the Fairy Queen; later, after he is rescued by his mortal lover, the Queen implies that she loved him, although it's unclear whether that love was platonic or romantic. In a similar ballad with a less successful end for the human protagonist, The Faerie Oak of Corriewater, a boy named Elph Irving has been taken by the Queen of the Fairies to be her cupbearer for seven years and she says that his payment will be a kiss from her. In the Ballad of Thomas the Rhymer, a man sees a beautiful woman riding on a horse and after calling her the Queen of Heaven she corrects him and say that she is in fact the Queen of Elfland (Acland, 1997). In some versions she offers him a kiss and then declares that he must come with her to serve her for seven years, in other versions the two have sex and afterwards she seems to his sight to have become an ugly hag, but nonetheless she compels him to go with her; once in Fairy her beauty is returned (Acland, 1997; Henderson & Cowan, 2007). It's possible this ugly appearance is a test for Thomas as he faces several others in Fairy including the requirement that he not speak while he is there. It is interesting to note that a service for seven years appears in more than one story, as does the idea of the Queen kissing the man to bind him to her or pay him for his service.

It was not always young men who were taken however, as we see in 'The Queen of Elfan's Nourice' (the Queen of Elfland's Nurse). In that ballad the Queen abducts a nursing mother, with the promise that the woman will be freed when the child she is wet-nursing reaches a certain height (Buchan, 1991). We also see anecdotal accounts among some of the witchcraft trial records that discuss encounters between female witches and the Queen of Elfland.

The Queen of Elfland in the ballads has some common themes. When she is described she is usually on a white horse and wearing green. The white horse is almost certainly a sign of rank or importance as well as a colour associated with fairy animals and green is a common colour for fairies to wear in folklore, placing her appearance solidly in the realm of the supernatural. She is said to be incomparably beautiful, sometimes compared to the Christian Queen of Heaven, and her actions are best described as mercurial. A kiss as either an element of binding or as payment features in both The Faerie Oak of Corriewater and Thomas the Rhymer as mentioned, and male witches talked about sexual encounters with her in the Scottish witchcraft trial records. In all the ballads we see her able to both bless and curse people, having the power to transform what she chooses and as we see in Thomas the Rhymer, to give the gift of prophecy and true speech. She often takes people, but usually for a set amount of time which seems to have been agreed beforehand, and those who are taken can be won free with effort. She is a power that transcends humanity yet chooses to seek it out and interact with humans, for both good and ill.

The Queen also appears in the witch trial documents, as some of the Scottish witches said it was to this Fairy Queen and not the Christian Devil that they owed allegiance. Isobel Gowdie, one of the most well-known Scottish witches, described the Queen of Fairy well dressed in white and claimed she had been taken into the fairy hill and given as much meat as she could eat (Henderson & Cowan, 2007). In this case, as meat was a luxury food, it may be that what Isobel was fed was a form of payment for her services. She also said she was taught things and given elfshot to use against people. Accused witch Bessie Dunlop claimed that she encountered the Queen of Elfland while giving birth, and Alison Pearson was put on trial and accused, in part, for spending time with the '*Quene of Elfame* [Queen of Elfhame]' (Henderson & Cowan, 2007). Many of these witches claimed in the trials to have been brought to Fairy to meet with the Queen or the Queen and King of Elfland and related things they had done or seen while there. These visits, and the relationship with the Queen more generally, involved being taught knowledge of healing herbs and skills, and in some cases potentially of cursing. Another Scottish witch, Andro Man, claimed to have had repeated sexual encounters with the Queen of Elfland, or as he called it Elphin (Henderson & Cowan, 2007). This tie in to sexuality is an interesting echo of what we see in the ballads where the Queen also uses sex and intimacy to bind men to her service. Several of these witches said it was this Queen who directed them in their witchcraft and assigned them a fairy as a familiar spirit (Wilby, 2005).

The Queen of Elfland tends to appear to people in liminal times and places and during dire periods in their lives. In accounts from the Scottish witch trials she would require people to give up their previous religion and deity in favour of herself but in exchange she would offer them specific benefits, including the gift of a fairy familiar and wisdom about certain subjects.

Beyond this unnamed Fairy Queen, who we may say like the Liminal Gods goes by a title rather than a name, there are also named Fairy Queens. Many of these are known to have originally been goddesses, but they also have a lot of folklore just as Fairy Queens, which creates a complex tapestry for those studying them. An entire book could be written about these Queens but here, I want to at least touch briefly on some of them. I will also say that when the Fairy Queen I am connected to first came to me, she did not tell me her name, but only what she was so that I spent the first six months calling her 'Fairy Queen' before finally being told her actual name.

Nicnevin – Often said to be the Queen of the Unseelie Court in Scotland, her special holiday is Samhain, although this may be celebrated for her on the old date of November 11th. In 'Montgomery's Flyting' she is compared to Hecate and it's said that she leads a retinue of both fairies and witches.

Gyre Carling – Sometimes associated with Nicnevin and strongly tied to the more monstrous Fey in Scotland. The Gyre Carling has a strong tie to spinning and weaving as well as magic.

Cliodhna – Sometimes called the Queen of the Banshees, Cliodhna is particularly associated with Cork in the southwest of Ireland. She is an ancestor of the McCarthy family and serves as a Bean Si for them. She was also known to take mortal men, particularly poets, as her lovers and had a rivalry with her sister Aoibheal because of a dispute over a mortal man.

Aine – Her special place is at Cnoc Aine in county Limerick, Ireland. She has appeared in mythology as a Goddess and in folklore as a fairy woman and a Fairy Queen. In one story she curses a human king who murders her father and rapes her, while in another she appears to several girls on her hill and instructs them to look through her ring to see the fairies dancing there; she can be both dangerous and benevolent depending on how one interacts with her. Overall though she is usually viewed as kindly inclined towards humans and is the progenitor of two human families. She is celebrated on midsummer with torchlit processions on her hill in thanks for her blessing of the harvest and animals, and on Lughnasa, in her role as the consort of Crom Cruach.

Aoibheal – The Fairy Queen of Clare in Ireland. She possesses a harp whose music kills those who hear it and she can control the weather. Like her sister Cliodhna she was sometimes seen as a Bean Sidhe and was strongly associated with a mortal family, the O'Briens. Aoibheal also appears in one later poem in which she is called the 'all seeing' and 'the truthful' as a judge over mortal men when the women of her area complain they are being taken advantage of and not wed.

Una – The Fairy Queen of Connacht, wife of Finnbheara. Assumes the form of a cow in one story, and seems to have a fondness for musicians. She respects courage and stubbornness.

Dangerous Fey

I know that many people would prefer to focus on the positive and pleasant in this kind of book, and generally speaking I'd rather focus on that sort of being all the time myself. But the reality is that the pleasant things aren't things you need to worry as much about dealing with because they are less likely to show up randomly and cause you major problems. They are also the beings who, when they do show up, can generally be dealt with amicably. It is said that when you anger the Seelie Court or one of its members they always give a warning before retaliating and I have found this to be true; in contrast, the beings of the Unseelie Court do not give warnings and in some cases you don't even need to do anything to offend them to be in danger from them. It can be as simple as being in the wrong place at the wrong time, so it's best to know what is likely to present a danger to you and how to handle it.

What I have found myself is that the deeper you get into this spirituality the more you end up attracting the attention of, or even just being in a position to stumble across, the dangerous things and these are exactly the things you need to be prepared for and know how to deal with. What I'm going to do here then is look at some of the more dangerous fairy beings that I have run across or which I think you may potentially run across. Keep in mind though that you could end up running into a wide array of beings not mentioned here as this is hardly an exhaustive list. I'd suggest looking into your local folklore as well as studying fairylore more generally.

An Amadán na Bruidhne – The Fairy Fool

According to folklore there two fairies who are more dangerous than others, because their touch brings madness that cannot be cured: the Fairy Queen and the Fairy Fool. We've already looked at the Fairy Queen and her mythology, so now let's look at the Fairy Fool who is a more obscure figure. If one journeys into Fairy you may encounter the Fool at some point and it is also possible to fall foul of the Fairy Fool in our world at particular times. He is considered by some to be one of the most dangerous fairies to come across and should always be avoided when possible or treated with extreme caution if he can't be avoided.

Yeats tells us in his Celtic Twilight that '*in every household of faery there is a queen and a fool*' (Yeats, 1998). This shows us not only the importance of the Queen of Fairy but also how ubiquitous Fairy Queens were thought to be, that one could be found in all areas of Fairy.[8] Yeats's comment also demonstrates that along with the Queen there was another important figure, one who was feared not because of their status or influence but because of what they represented: madness.

The Fairy Fool is known by two different names in Irish each of which has a different character. The Amadán na Bruidhne (Fool of the Otherworldy Hall) is a greatly feared fairy, whose touch brings madness, paralysis, or death to those whose path he crosses (MacKillop, 1998). It is said by some his touch is the fairy stroke, while others say his power is unique to him. The Fool's power was feared so greatly because while other maladies caused by the fairies could often be cured by someone who knew the right remedy, the touch of the Fool could not be. The other type of Fairy Fool is the Amadán Mór (Great Fool) a more ambiguous figure who appears sometimes as a king of the fairies or leading the fairy host (MacKillop, 1998). We will be looking at the Amadan na Bruidhne here.

Yeats related from folklore, discussing the Amadán na Bruidhne, that the Fairy Fool could be either male or female; the male Fool was described as immensely strong, wild, wide, and appeared as a half-naked person or sometimes in the form of a bearded sheep (Yeats, 1962). By another account, the Fool changes shape every couple of days, appearing as a young person or as a wild animal, but always seeking to bring madness to those he touches (Yeats, 1962). Interestingly, in all the folklore accounts people seemed to have recognized the Amadán na

Bruidhne immediately when he was seen, no matter what form he was wearing.

One person out of a group might see the Fool when the others did not, or a person out alone might see the Fool, but the danger came only if you were touched by him. Those who saw the Fool and successfully averted them or fled could escape any consequences from the encounter, but those who were touched by the Amadán na Bruidhne lost their minds afterwards although they might live for many years. In most stories of the Fool his actions seem random, but in at least one story it seemed that he intentionally set upon a person in retaliation for that person's aiding a rival group of Daoine Sí. As the story goes the young man was called out to join a group of the Daoine Maithe who were fighting another group; his job was to fight with a human man among the other group. He did this and won, to the delight of his own side. However, three years later he found himself pursued by the Amadán na Bruidhne who touched him and after that, as Yeats relates it, *'his wits were gone'* (Yeats, 1962). The man and those who knew him felt that this was done because he had aided one group of the Other Crowd in winning, and the losing group was angry with him.

At any point in the year a person might encounter the Amadán na Bruidhne, but they are most active in June and it is during this month that people need to be careful to avoid crossing the Fool's path. It is always risky of course to run into any of the fairy folk but the Fairy Fool represented a particular danger, as is related by Yeats, quoting someone he had interviewed, *'They, the other sort of people, might be passing you close here and they might touch you. But any that gets the touch of the Amadán-na-Breena [Fairy Fool] is done for'* (Yeats, 1962, p. 110). For this reason extra caution is needed in the month of June, so that the Fairy Fool can be avoided.

Despite his name the Fool should be treated with great care, as one of the more dangerous beings of Fairy. As Fairy witches we should never assume that we are immune or exempt from the Fool's power and should instead treat him with great caution if we see him. There are no known treatments or cures for the touch of the Amadan na Bruidhne, remember that.

I have never seen or encountered the Fairy Fool myself but I include them here precisely because of the danger they represent.

Kelpies and Each Uisge

Fairy horses are well known in Celtic mythology and are found in two main variations, those that are animals – literally horses who are from Fairy, such as the steeds we see ridden in the Fairy Rade – and those who are intelligent fairies in the form of horses. Intelligent fairies who can take or are in the form of horses are found across the Celtic world; in Orkney, they are called Nuggles, in Wales Ceffyl Dwr. In Shetland, they are Coofiltees, and on the Isle of Man they are called Cabbyl Ushtey or the Glashtin. They are also found in parts of the Norse world; in Scandinavian folklore they are called Bäckahästen or 'Brook horses', in Norway they are Nokken and in Iceland they are called Nykur. In Scottish and Irish folklore there are two main kinds of intelligent fairy horse seen in stories: the Kelpie and the Each Uisge (Water Horse). The Each Uisge is also called Aughisky and Each Uisce (Irish Gaelic for water horse). I believe that Water Horses and Kelpies, like other European fairies, have followed the people who believed in them to new countries so that they can be found all over the world now. Different variations of water horse will have their own folklore and stories so if any specific type of water horse I have mentioned here interests you I recommend looking them up; in this section I will be focusing on the Kelpie and Each Uisge specifically.

Both Each Uisge and Kelpies are water fairies, with the Each Uisge making its home in salt water and lakes and the kelpie preferring running water, including rivers (Briggs, 1976). They both usually appear as white or black horses or ponies, but sometimes may be green or green with a black mane. They look like unusually beautiful horses and act very tame and friendly; however, an Each Uisge or Kelpie can be recognized by the seaweed or other water plants which are sometimes seen tangled in their hair and the water that drips constantly from their mane and tail. Both may take the shape of humans, either men or women, although handsome men are the most commonly described, but even in this form they can still be recognized for their dripping hair and seaweed or other water plants that cling to them. Additionally, the Each Uisge is said to be able to take the form of a large bird (Brigs, 1976). The two types of fairy horse can be difficult to tell apart and even in mythology it may be hard to tell whether a story is referring to a Kelpie or Each Uisge and sometimes a being may be given one name but seem more like the other type.

Both Kelpies and Each Uisge appear as beautiful horses to try to lure people into trying to ride them. Once a person has touched or mounted one of these fairy beings they will find they cannot let go or jump off, and the Fairy Horse will run into the nearest body of water and drown them before eating them, although it's said the Each Uisge doesn't eat the liver. There is some folklore that suggests a person would be safe riding a Kelpie as long as the Fairy never smells water and it is also said that each Kelpie possess a silver bridle which can be used to control them. Each Uisge are more sinister; besides humans they are also known to eat sheep and cows.

There is some folklore that relates stories of Kelpies who court or love mortal women. In a story from Scotland, a Kelpie fell in love with a mortal girl. He came to her in the form of a handsome man, courted her, and convinced her to marry him. They had a small home together and in time a child; they lived happily together until the day that the human woman discovered her husband's true nature. Realizing he was a Kelpie, she abandoned her child and fled. The Kelpie, deeply in love with his mortal wife, raised their child and waited futilely for her to return. In a story from Ireland, a Kelpie loved a mortal girl who discovered his true nature and used his silver bridle to bind him in his horse form into service on her father's farm. Nonetheless, after a year he was given the opportunity to choose freedom and immortality or give up his fairy-nature and choose marriage to the girl; he chose his love. In Scottish folklore we find Kelpies kidnapping women and imprisoning them; a child is usually produced and eventually the woman escapes leaving the child behind. The Each Uisge, in contrast, is known only to kill, and in stories appears in its horse form most often and carries off riders to their deaths.

Kelpies and Each Uisge are dangerous beings in any form, whether they are trying to seduce mortals or prey on them literally as a food source. They are very difficult to fight against with folklore offering few tips about how to defeat them. In one story a water horse is killed by a blacksmith and his son seeking vengeance for the death of the smith's daughter; the smith lures the water horse onto land using the body of a sheep and then kills it with iron hooks. The aforementioned silver bridle is another means that could be used to fight a Kelpie by taking control of it, if a person could obtain the item. Besides iron and the silver bridle, water horses are not known to have many weaknesses. They are, however, usually fairly territorial and likely to remain near a specific area so it is possible to escape one by leaving his territory.

As a Fairy witch you may encounter either of these beings at some point; I personally have seen at least one that I know of in a local body of water and have dealt with another in Fairy. They are intelligent but dangerous beings who should not be underestimated.

Hags

Another dangerous water Fey that should be understood is the hag. There are other types of supernatural being which are also called hags, but here I am using the term specifically to reference the water Fey kind; as was already mentioned when we discussed names for fairies, sometimes the terms we use aren't clear. So just keep in mind that we're calling them hags here but there are also other hags that are different from these.

Most hags that we know of from folklore have specific names like Jenny Greenteeth and Black Annis, however, it is possible to come across less well-known hags without common names. The ones with known names generally have a lot of folklore surrounding them and are also location specific. I have found that hags seem to be very territorial, like the kelpies and water horses we just discussed, and tend to stay in one area, something that is often (but not always) true of many types of water Fey.

Hags usually live in rivers or streams and are known for drowning people, especially children. They do this by grabbing at the legs of children who get too near the edge of the water and drag them under the surface. They are usually described as looking like withered old women with long sharp finger nails and sharp teeth. Unlike many fairies, hags may not be averse to iron as at least one, Black Annis, was described as having iron claws (Briggs, 1976).

Although I live in America I have encountered at least one hag in a river, in a place where someone else I was talking to later independently confirmed a similar experience. When you are near water and you get a really bad feeling or just a general sense of danger, always trust your gut. Hags are difficult creatures to fight and honestly your best bet is to avoid getting near the water they live in. Iron, as I mentioned, does not seem to affect them, so don't trust in that to protect you. Salt may be worth trying if you find yourself needing to fight one off.

The Slua Sí
Let's begin this with an experience my husband and I had one

night in March.

We were sitting in our living room around 10 o'clock that night when the wind picked up suddenly, so strong and loud that I turned to my husband and noted that it was a bit scary. Then just as suddenly, on the wind was the distinct sound of bells jingling, like you find on horses' harnesses sometimes, which really freaked me out, and I said, 'Can you hear that?'

He said, 'What? The bells? Yeah, what is that?'

And I honestly didn't know what to say because I knew it was probably the Slua or maybe a Fairy Rade and it was really scaring me.

But he pushed and said, 'I know you know more about this stuff than I do, what do you think it is?'

So, I told him, 'Not all fairies are nice.'

He wanted to go out to smoke. I told him in all seriousness to be careful – mind you we live in the suburbs – and if he saw anything, to come back in. He asked, saw anything like what? And I said I didn't know, like if he saw any horses. And he rolled his eyes and asked me several times why there would be a horse in our neighbourhood. So, I just kept saying if you see or hear one come back in right away.

He went out, and within 90 seconds came back in, because he saw a strange red light and could hear horses' hooves on the stone walkway in front of our house.

And a few minutes later the wind had gone and it was totally calm.

I ended up having to give my husband a crash course on who the Slua Sí are and what to do in emergency situations like that. I mentioned the Slua in my last book on Fairycraft so I don't want to repeat myself here, but I think it's important to understand that these are not abstract concepts or beings who you will only encounter if you travel to certain places. Of all the types of dangerous Fey, the Slua Sí are the most known to travel and so perhaps the ones you are most likely to encounter. They travel in the air as a group of horses, riders and usually hounds, often seen by humans as only a swirl of wind although sometimes the sound of the horses and hounds, people talking, music, bells, or other commotion can be heard as they pass. They are known to seize people they pass and take them up, to carry them great distances, to make them assist in tormenting other humans, and to bring illness and madness to those they pass by.

I started this with a story about an encounter my husband and I had with the Fairy Host, an encounter which frightened my husband enough that he refused to go out into the yard at night for months afterwards. That was my third encounter with the Slua in my life, and I think it's very important for anyone engaged in this spirituality to be aware of the Slua and to know that they are not something to mess around with.

If you feel the Slua is passing near you it is recommended to say *'Good luck to them, the ladies and gentlemen'* and if you believe they have taken a person and you want to free that person you can throw something like dirt from the road or a knife at them and say *'this is yours that is mine'*.[9] Like many other fairies they are averse to iron so it was once a common practice to always carry a bit of iron with you, such as a nail or blade. Going indoors is another way to avoid the Host, which is why I told my husband to come right back in if he saw or heard anything strange outside.

The Wild Hunt

The Slua is sometimes seen as related to the Wild Hunt, spirits found originally on the continent who travel the air and can also take people. For myself, I think that while the two may be similar they are not the same. That said, I have encountered the Wild Hunt – or Ghost Riders as they are called in America – several times so I want to mention them here as well.

Unlike the other fairies mentioned so far the Wild Hunt is less straightforward, and indeed there is debate about whether or not they are even fairies. They may be spirits of the dead or even witches, and can be led by a deity, ghost, or possibly by a fairy like Gwyn ap Nudd in Wales. Also, unlike the Slua Sí the Wild Hunt is much more ambivalent in nature representing both danger and blessing to those it passes. In some cases they may take souls or even living people up with them and they can kill, but they can also bring blessing, particularly to crops, and reward those who please them with money.

While the Slua can travel at any time of year the Wild Hunt is most likely to be seen in the fall and winter, more or less between Samhain and Beltaine in the US although in some parts of Europe they were more known for travelling out between Yule and Midsummer. Like the Slua, though, people would seek shelter when they thought the Hunt was out, especially during the 12 nights during the Yule season when it was considered unsafe to be out after dark alone.

The Wild Hunt travels in the sky as a group of riders, horses and dogs, and can sometimes be heard on the wind as a sound of hooves, dogs barking or hunting horns. I have personally heard them as the noise of harnesses and riders and also as hunting horns; both are extremely unnerving. In America I've been told that sometimes the Ghost Riders are known by the sound of geese in the sky when there are no geese during the winter.

The best protection against the Wild Hunt is seeking shelter indoors, although I will add that the time I saw them passing near Yule one year I jumped into my car and that seemed to work just as well. Dealing with them politely and cleverly is also an option (unlike the Slua Sí) but it certainly carries some risks which should be kept in mind. As a last ditch effort there is a small charm you can say, which I included in my last book but will repeat here:

Woden's host and all his men
Who are bearing wheels and willow twigs

Broken on the wheel and hanged
You must go away from here.
(Translated by S. Gundarsson)

Måran

Måran are a type of being who come at night while you are sleeping, paralyzing you, bringing fear and nightmares. The name for them, Måran or singular Mår is related to the same root word we get our modern word nightmare from, and indeed that is why we have the word – nightmare, night mare, a mare that comes at night. Mare is the Old English while Mår is the German which I use to avoid confusion with mare meaning a female horse. The word Måran is usually translated as goblins, night-goblins, or incubi but I would suggest that Måran are best understood as entirely their own type of being. Much like so many of the other beings we have discussed they are not straightforward, with some Mår obviously supernatural beings while others are human witches with the ability to intentionally or unwittingly project to people at night and oppress them. Additionally, Måran are often confused with other similar nighttime beings and occasionally with elves (Seo Helrune, 2017). It is important when dealing with them to learn to differentiate between a possible attack from another human who has the same symptoms as the Måran, malicious activity by elves, and activity by Måran.

In folklore, Måran are always seen as female beings and it is possible to capture them, usually by blocking whatever place they entered through; it was believed that unless they could go out exactly as they had come in they lost their power (Ashliman, 2005). In several stories a man captured a Mår and then married her, similar to the Selkie tales, and the new wife would act like any other human woman, even giving him children, but if she could ever get him to show her the place she'd entered that he'd blocked and clear it, she'd leave immediately. In one tale a Mår is captured when the victim stays awake and sees her enter as a cat and then nails one of her paws to the floor; by morning she has transformed to a young woman (Ashliman, 2005).

When Måran appear they generally come alone and afflict a person in their sleep by perching on their chest. They cause a feeling of paralysis and fear, and can also make breathing difficult, creating a feeling of pressure or weight on the chest. In folklore they can kill both people and animals (Ashliman, 2005). An old term for this is 'Old Hag' although nowadays it's known as sleep paralysis and scientific explanations remove spirits from the equation (Seo Helrune, 2017). Some people who are attacked by Måran also experience a sexual overtone to the experience which is partially why the word was translated as incubi and also why I think they are associated with elves, who themselves were often associated with incubi as well. It should be noted, however, that elves or in this case specifically the Anglo-Saxon aelfe were usually male and the Måran were believed to be female beings, suggesting that we may indeed be looking at two different beings here with a similar method of attack in some cases. This idea is supported by Alaric Hall in his article 'The Evidence for Maran: The Anglo-Saxon "Nightmares"' in which he argues persuasively that Måran were in fact always seen as female and the translation of incubi was an early confusion between texts, and might more properly have been given as succubi.

Because attacks by Måran where not uncommon in the past there are many methods of dealing with them. Blocking the keyhole (if the door has one), placing your shoes backwards – i.e. laces facing the bed – by the bed, and then climbing into bed backwards can protect you from attack; animals can be protected by placing a broom near them (Ashliman, 2005). Also Måran, like many fairies, ghosts and spirits can be warded off with iron which should be placed near or under the bed. A salve or powder can be made with herbs including Lupin, Betony and Garlic (Seo Helrune, 2017). Mugwort can also be burned to ward off dangerous spirits. There is also a variety of charms to protect against Måran, such as this one which uses a single hair of the person's head to mime tying up the Mår while saying:

The man of might
He rode at night
With neither sword
Nor food nor light,
He sought the mare,
He found the mare,
He bound the mare
With his own hair,
And made her swear
By mother's might,
That she would never bide a night
What he had trod, that man of might.[10]
(Black, 1903; language modified from Shetland Scots)

There is also this one from Germany:

I lay me here to sleep;
No night-mare shall plague me,
Until they swim all the waters
That flow upon the earth,
And count all the stars
That appear in the firmament!
(Ashliman, 2005).[11]

I have had an experience with a Mår once so far. I have never had sleep paralysis before in my life but I woke up in the middle of the night, unable to move or speak, surrounded by a pervasive sense of malevolence and dread. There was a strong sense of presence with this and a kind of impending doom. At first I was disoriented, because I'd been asleep but then honestly I got really angry because I'd had a long difficult day and I was so not in the mood to deal with anything supernatural. I drove the spirit off and forced it out of the house by visualizing bright light shoving it away. It took several minutes of slow effort but it worked.

In talking later with other people on social media I was surprised to find out how common these encounters seemed to be among people I knew, even casually. I think for those who deal with extra-ordinary things and Otherworldly beings it's important to be aware of the Måran and know how to combat them if they attack either you or anyone you know.

Endnotes

1. There really is not a good definition for god or deity that isn't just circular logic. For my purposes I tend to define 'deity' as an extremely powerful being who can influence all levels of reality to the greatest degree; following along with that, however, not-Gods or 'spirits' are beings with lesser degrees of influence.

2. Obviously it can be influenced in the same way mortal earth can be, by interacting with it. Magic is also a more powerful and palpable force there, so it is possible even for us to create and shape things with magic. However, the key difference here is that Fairy still operates by the same basic laws that our world does including gravity, momentum and force. You can create things, but you can't imagine them into existence. The astral is also often described as a mirror of our world, where what is done there has effects here and vice versa; this is not true of Fairy which operates independently.

3. Personally I suspect that the stories which paint Fairy as always in summer and always pleasant are reflecting later Christian influences where we see ideas of Paradise creeping into the Fairy narrative. I will not rule out the possibility that there are some places there that may be this way while others are not.

4. The idea of fairies having wings, specifically insect wings, actually comes to us from the theatre. If you are curious about the history of this idea and how it entered popular consciousness I recommend reading the article 'In Search of the Earliest Fairy Wings' here http://www.strangehistory. net/2016/12/17/search-earliest-fairy-wings/ but the gist of it is that the theatre of the eighteenth and nineteenth centuries used wings to distinguish actors playing fairies to the audience, probably drawing on sixteenth-century artwork depictions of small winged spirits. Those spirits were not fairies but rather usually angels, demons, cupids, or even depictions of the human soul.

5. Later in the story, Conn's druid is able through magic to temporarily hide her entirely from Connla so that she cannot keep courting him, but he is apparently unable to force her to reveal herself.

6. Some scholars feel the eighth or ninth century is more likely while others argue for dates as early as the seventh. See Beveridge 'Children into Swans' and Oskamp 'Echtra Condla' in Etudes Celtiques 14 for further discussion on the dating of this manuscript.

7. Odin has connections to the Wild Hunt specifically and also in certain ways to the dead which may overlap with the Fey folk. Macha has strong connections to the daoine sidhe and one of her guises is often called 'Macha of the sidhe' as it is said that she came from the Otherworld into our world to interact with the people of Ulster.

8. This ubiquitous nature of the Fairy Queens is part of why I have chosen to discuss them here but not to discuss the Fairy Kings. There certainly are Kings as well as Queens, however, we do not see them in all places or consider them as vital in Fairy as the Queens are. It is not uncommon to see a solitary Fairy Queen with no King but it is unusual to see a solitary Fairy King, for example.

9. I'm excerpting this short section on the Fairy Host from my book *Fairies*.

10. The original text is:
    De man o' meicht
    He rod a' neicht
    We nedder swird
    Nor faerd nor leicht,
    He socht da mare,
    He fand da mare,
    He band da mare
    Wi' his ain hair,
    An' made her swear
    By midder's meicht,
    Dat shö wad never bide a neicht
    What he had rod, dat man o' meicht.

11. Original German:
    Hier leg' ich mich schlafen,
    Keine Nachtmahr soll mich plagen,
    Bis sie schwemmen alle Wasser,
    Die auf Erden fließen,
    Und tellet alle Sterne,
    Die am Firmament erscheinen!

Chapter 5

The Wisdom of Ballads and Poems

Spirits white as lightning,
shall on my travels guide me
The moon would quake and the stars would shake,
when' ere they espied me.

One of our best resources for Fairy Witchcraft is obviously the old folklore, but another great resource that can be overlooked is the old folk ballads. They represent a treasure trove of beliefs and wisdom although they require some decoding to be useful. In this chapter I want to look at several poems and ballads that have been passed down to us and my interpretations of their content. Please understand, as always, that other people may have different opinions of what some of these things mean and how they can be viewed and there are entire books written just on the topic of folklore and fairylore themes within the ballads in particular. I encourage people who find these things useful to research and look into other interpretations as well as coming up with your own. This represents the ballads which I have found to be the most useful as well as my personal thoughts and understanding of them.

Advice to Fergus from Iubhdán

In the following poem from the Aided Fergusa meic Leide, Iubhdán, the king of the leprechauns,[1] is giving advice to the king of Ulster, Fergus, explaining the values of different trees and which should or should not be burned. For modern Fairy witches this offers insight into some ways to approach treating different trees in our practice as well as giving useful folklore about the different trees mentioned.

The pliant woodbine/honeysuckle if you burn, wailings for misfortune will abound,

Dire extremity at weapons' points or drowning in great waves will follow.

Burn not the precious apple tree of spreading and low-sweeping bough;

Tree ever decked in bloom of white, against whose fair head all men put forth the hand.

The surly blackthorn is a wanderer, a wood that the artificer burns not;

Throughout his body, though it be scanty, birds in their flocks warble.

The noble willow burn not, a tree sacred to poems;

Within his blooms bees are a-sucking, all love the little cage.

The graceful tree with the berries, the wizard's tree, the rowan burn;

But spare the limber tree; burn not the slender hazel.

Dark is the colour of ash; timber that makes the wheels to go;

Rods he furnishes for horsemen's hands, his form turns battle into flight.

Tenterhook among woods the spiteful briar is, burn him that is so keen and green;

He cuts, he flays the foot, him that would advance he forcibly drags backward.

Fiercest heat-giver of all timber is green oak, from him none may escape unhurt;

By partiality for him the head is set on aching, and by his acrid embers the eye is made sore.

Alder, very battle-witch of all woods, tree that is hottest in the fight–

Undoubtedly burn at thy discretion both the alder and whitethorn.

Holly, burn it green; holly, burn it dry;

Of all trees whatsoever the critically best is holly.

Elder that hath tough bark, tree that in truth hurts sore;
Him that furnishes horses to the armies from the fairies burn so
that he be charred.

The birch as well, if he be laid low, promises abiding fortune;
Burn up most sure and certainly the stakes that bear the
constant pods.

Put on the hearth if it so please thee, the russet aspen to come
headlong down;
Burn, be it late or early, the tree with the palsied branch.

Patriarch of long-lasting woods is the yew sacred to feasts as it
is well known;
Of him now build ye dark-red vats of goodly size.

(O'Grady, 1892)

From this we learn that we should not burn honeysuckle/woodbine, apple, blackthorn, hazel, and willow. In contrast we are told we should burn the rowan, briar, oak, alder, hawthorn, holly, elder, birch, and aspen. Of the ash and yew we are only told that the former makes good wheels and the latter good vats. I try to consider these things, including what to burn and not burn, in my own magical practices and daily life.

Each tree is listed with specific qualities as well which a witch could consider when making a wand. For example, the rowan is called the '*wizard's tree*' alluding to its use in enchantment and the alder is called the '*battle witch of the woods*' and '*hottest in the fight*' implying that it would be useful in cursing or offensive magic. A person can look at these to fill a specific need or look at these for a particular wood to better understand some of its folklore.[2]

The Ballad of Tam Lin

One of the most significant Scottish ballads, from a fairylore perspective is undoubtedly Tam Lin, which can be found under variant names and versions dating back to 1549. As eminent folklorist Katherine Briggs puts it *'It is perhaps the most important of all supernatural ballads because of the many fairy beliefs incorporated in it'* (Briggs, 1976, p. 449). An indication of the importance of the ballad may be its popularity over the centuries and its prolific nature. Indeed there are nearly 50 versions of the ballad that I am aware of, and probably more that I am not aware of, each with variations which can be minor or major in nature. It also survives today in as a folk song. However, the wider theme of the ballad remains consistent: a young woman goes to a well in a wood that is rumoured to be guarded by a fairy who takes a toll from all trespassers, she becomes pregnant by him, and returns to free him from the fairies on Halloween night.

It is worth looking more closely at the themes and plot of Tam Lin, but it is beyond the scope of this particular discussion to compare all of the numerous versions. I do recommend reading Acland's 'Major Variations in Tam Lin' for a better understanding of some of these if it interests you. What I will be doing here is looking at the most common and to the best of my knowledge, the oldest version of the ballad 'Child's 39A' from the book *The English and Scottish Popular Ballads* and using this as a basis of discussion. I will also look at a few important variants and additions, but not a full comparison of every version.

Below, I am going to include the version of the ballad from Child's collection, but I am updating the language slightly and translating the Doric words. The original unaltered version can be found free online. I will present the ballad followed by my commentary.

1. O I forbid you, maidens all,
That wear gold on your hair,
To come or go by Carterhaugh,
For young Tam Lin is there.
2. There's none that go by Carterhaugh
But they leave him a treasure,

Either their rings, or green mantles,
Or else their maidenhead.
3. *Janet has tucked up her green skirt*
A little above her knee,
And she has braided her yellow hair
A little above her eyebrow,
And she's away to Carterhaugh
As fast as she can go.
4. *When she came to Carterhaugh*
Tam Lin was at the well,
And there she found his steed standing,
But away was himself.
5. *She had not pulled a double rose,*
A rose but only two,
Till up then started young Tam Lin,
Says, Lady, you'll pull no more.
6. *Why pull you the rose, Janet,*
And why break you the wand?
Or why come you to Carterhaugh
Without my command?
7. *'Carterhaugh, it is my own,*
My daddy gave it to me,
I'll come and go by Carterhaugh,
And ask no leave of you.'
8. *Janet has tucked up her green skirt*
A little above her knee,
And she has braided her yellow hair
A little above her eyebrow,
And she is to her father's house,
As fast as she can go.
9. *Four and twenty ladies fair*
Were playing at the ball,
And out then came the fair Janet,
The flower among them all.

10. Four and twenty ladies fair
Were playing at the chess,
And out then came the fair Janet,
As green as any glass.

11. Out then spoke an old grey knight,
Laying over the castle wall,
And says, 'Alas, fair Janet, for you,
But we'll be blamed all.'

12. 'Hold your tongue, you old faced knight,
Some ill death may you die!
Father my child on whom I will,
I'll father none on you.'

13. Out then spoke her father dear,
And he spoke meek and mild,
'And ever alas, sweet Janet,' he says,
'I think you go with child.'

14. 'If that I go with child, father,
Myself must bear the blame,
There's not a lord about your hall,
Shall get the child's name.

15. 'If my love were an earthly knight,
As he's an elfin grey,
I would not give my own true-love
For any lord that you have.

16. 'The steed that my true love rides on
Is lighter than the wind,
With silver he is shod before,
With burning gold behind.'

17. Janet has tucked up her green skirt
A little above her knee,
And she has braided her yellow hair
A little above her eyebrow,
And she's away to Carterhaugh
As fast as she can go.

18. *When she came to Carterhaugh,*
Tam Lin was at the well,
And there she found his steed standing,
But away was himself.
19. *She had not pulled a double rose,*
A rose but only two,
Till up then started young Tam Lin,
Says, 'Lady, you'll pull no more.'
20. *'Why pull you the rose, Janet,*
Among the groves so green,
And all to kill the bonny babe
That we got us between?'
21. *'O tell me, tell me, Tam Lin,' she says,*
'For his sake that died on tree [i.e. Christ's sake],
If ever you were in holy chapel,
Or Christendom did see?'
22. *'Roxbrugh he was my grandfather,*
Took me with him to stay
And once it fell upon a day
That woe did me betide.'
23. *'And once it fell upon a day*
A cold day and windy,
When we were from the hunting come,
That from my horse I fell,
The Queen of Fairies she caught me,
In yonder green hill to dwell.'
24. *'And pleasant is the fairy land,*
But, an eerie tale to tell,
Yes at the end of seven years,
We pay a teind to hell,
I am so fair and full of flesh,
I'm afraid it will be myself.'
25. *'But the night is Halloween, lady,*
The morn is Hallowday,

Then win me, win me, if you will,
For well I know you may.'
26. *'Just at the dark and midnight hour*
The fairy folk will ride,
And they that would their true-love win,
At Miles Cross they must bide.'
27. *'But how shall I know you, Tam Lin,*
Or how my true-love know,
Among so many uncouth knights,
The like I never saw?'
28. *'O first let pass the black, lady,*
And soon let pass the brown,
But quickly run to the milk-white steed,
Pull you his rider down.'
29. *'For I'll ride on the milk-white steed,*
And yes nearest the town,
Because I was an earthly knight
They give me that renown.'
30. *'My right hand will be gloved, lady,*
My left hand will be bare,
Tilted up shall my hat be,
And combed down shall be my hair,
And that's the tokens I give you,
No doubt I will be there.'
31. *'They'll turn me in your arms, lady,*
Into a lizard and snake,
But hold me fast, and fear me not,
I am your child's father.'
32. *'They'll turn me to a bear so grim,*
And then a lion bold,
But hold me fast, and fear me not,
And you shall love your child.'
33. *'Again they'll turn me in your arms*
To a red hot rod of iron,

But hold me fast, and fear me not,
I'll do you no harm.'
34. *'And last they'll turn me in your arms*
Into the burning coal,
Then throw me into well water,
O throw me in with speed.'
35. *'And then I'll be your own true-love,*
I'll turn a naked knight,
Then cover me with your green mantle,
And hide me out o sight.'
36. *Gloomy, gloomy was the night,*
And eerie was the way,
As fair Janet in her green mantle
To Miles Cross she did go.
37. *At the dark and midnight hour*
She heard the bridles sing,
She was as glad at that
As any earthly thing.
38. *First she let the black pass by,*
And soon she let the brown,
But quickly she ran to the milk-white steed,
And pulled the rider down.
39. *So well she minded what he did say,*
And young Tam Lin did win,
Soon covered him with her green mantle,
As happy as a bird in spring
40. *Out then spoke the Queen of Fairies,*
Out of a bush of broom,
'Them that has gotten young Tam Lin
Has gotten a stately-groom.'
41. *Out then spoke the Queen of Fairies,*
And an angry woman was she,
'Shame betide her ill-fared face,
And an ill death may she die,

For she's taken away the handsomest knight
In all my company.'
42. *'But had I known, Tam Lin,' said she,*
'What now this night I see,
I would have taken out your two grey eyes,
And put in two eyes of a tree.'

There you have it, the most common version of the Ballad of Tam Lin. Let's take a closer look at the material.

The name Tam Lin, which elsewhere sometimes appears in variants as Tam-a-Line, Tam o the Lin and Tamlane is not a proper name but what we might understand as a nickname or name with epithet. Tam is a version of Tom. Lin, or Linn, has several meanings in Doric but the most likely here is a waterfall or pool of water; a Lane is a slow moving stream. Tam Lin may be read as Tom of the Pool or Tom of the Waterfall and Tamlane similarly as Tom of the stream, which of course makes perfect sense for a fairy who guards a well in the Carterhaugh woods. In some alternate versions the fairy knight is named as True Thomas, conflating this story with that other ballad of a Fairy Queen abducting a man, possibly due to both characters having similar names, Tam/Tom and Thomas.

Tam Lin initially appears as a mysterious figure who controls the woods of Carterhaugh. He expects a toll from trespassers of something valuable which is listed here as either jewellery, green cloaks, or the virginity of maidens. The mention of green is interesting, as green is particularly a fairy colour and was seen as an unlucky colour for women to wear for this reason. The mention of it here may be the first hint of fairy involvement. Janet – given different names in some other versions – has heard the warning about Tam Lin and decided to go to Carterhaugh, in alternate versions such as we see in 39C going *'By the only light of the moon'*. It should be noted here that Janet has been told that Tam Lin expects sex from maidens and is intentionally going there, which at least implies that she accepts this as a possibility. She has also dressed in a green skirt, which as was just mentioned is a fairy colour normally not worn by women. I have always personally seen this as indicating that Janet knew exactly what she was doing and intended to go find herself a fairy lover.

Janet arrives in the Carterhaugh wood at the well which Tam Lin guards and finds Tam Lin's horse, but not Tam Lin himself. The verse states that Tam Lin is at the well, however, implying that although she may not see him he is nearby. It is possible that this is an allusion to fairy glamour or enchantment. Finding the fairy horse, but not the guardian she was looking for, she picks two roses, taking them from the place that Tam Lin guards. This naturally, immediately, summons Tam Lin to her side. You have to admire Janet's directness here, as we see her intentionally invoking Tam Lin with her actions. I might suggest that this is not generally the wisest course of action, as usually disturbing or violating a place guarded by fairies results in retribution; in this case we see instead a conversation.

The interaction between the two doesn't include any sex, although we will find out later that it occurred but was not directly mentioned; in various alternate versions the sex is more obviously stated and is usually clearly consensual but not always so.[3] For example:

'He's taken her by the milk-white hand
Among the leaves so green
And what they did I cannot say
The leaves they were between.' (39I)
And:
'He took her by the milk-white hand
And gently laid her down,
Just in below some shady trees
Where the green leaves hung down.' (39J)

What we do have in 39A, however, is Tam Lin challenging Janet over her trespassing on the place he guards and her pulling of the roses. Janet's response is to tell him that she is the one who owns Carterhaugh and so doesn't need his permission. It's pretty obvious at this point that Janet just doesn't back down from anyone, including Fairy Knights, which may be why – as we see later in the ballad – Tam Lin chooses her to save him from Fairy.

As far as we can tell from the ballad Janet has no further contact with Tam Lin after returning home to her father's hall. It soon becomes obvious to those around her that she is pregnant and one of her father's knights accuses her of as much, worrying that she will get them in trouble. Here we see an illustration of why I like Janet so much in this version of the ballad. She has been publicly accused of a significant social transgression – sex out of wedlock and pregnancy resulting from it – and her response is to yell back and tell the knight, effectively, to shut up and curse him with an ill death, that whoever she has a child with it won't be him. Now that it's been brought out in public, her father also asks if she is pregnant, although we may note he speaks to her 'meek and mild'. She doesn't outright admit that she is, but says that if she is she will take the blame for it because no man in her father's hall is responsible.

Janet then admits that her lover is one of the Other Crowd, and despite having, as far as we are aware, only one tryst with Tam Lin declares that he is her true love and that she will not give him up for any mortal lord. She then describes his horse, an interesting bit of lore from our perspective, as lighter than the wind and having silver horseshoes in front and gold in back. The horseshoes are interesting, although tangential, but give us an idea of what fairy horses may be shod with since iron is obviously not an option. Why the two different kinds of metal? It's hard to say but it could represent the animal's ability to travel between the two worlds.

Janet immediately goes back to Carterhaugh after this and once again finding the horse at the well and not Tam Lin, pulls two roses to invoke him. He appears and tells her to stop but also asks her why she wants to abort the child she is carrying. Although in other versions of the ballad Janet is advised to take such an action or is pulling not roses but abortifacient herbs; in this version there has been no mention of such, implying that Tam Lin has some supernatural knowledge of her intentions. Janet questions him about whether he is truly one of the Gentry or is a mortal man and he tells her how he was claimed by the Fairy Queen after falling from his horse. It is quite likely that this is an analogy for dying, and reinforces the blurred lines between the fairies and the dead.

At this point in another version, 39I, we see the following passage which isn't present in 39A but is pertinent for our discussion here:

31. 'The Queen of Fairies kept me
In yonder green hill to dwell,
And I'm a fairv, lyth [joint] and limb,
Fair lady, view me well.'
32. 'But we that live in Fairy-land
No sickness know nor pain;
I quit my body when I will,
And take to it again.'
33. 'I quit my body when I please,
Or unto it repair;
We can inhabit at our ease
In either earth or air.'
34. 'Our shapes and size we can convert
To either large or small;
An old nut-shell's the same to us
As is the lofty hall.'
35. 'We sleep in rose-buds soft and sweet

We revel in the stream;
We wander lightly on the wind
Or glide on a sunbeam.'
36. *'And all our wants are well supplied*
From every rich man's store,
Who thankless sins the gifts he gets,
And vainly grasps for more.'

I'm including this here, as it appears in Child's notes, because I feel that it offers some essential information about the nature of fairies. In this version, Tamlane has just told Janet that he knew her as a child and that he was born a human son to the Earl of Murray before being taken by the Queen of Fairies. Yet he also explicitly tells her that he is *'a fairy, lyth [joint] and limb'*. This confirms that the fairies may take a person and by some means transform that person into one of their own kind. He then goes on to describe to her what it is like to be a fairy, including the facts that they do not get sick or know pain, can leave their bodies or re-enter them, change their sizes, and exist as either physical beings or ethereal ones (*'we can inhabit at our ease in either earth or air'*). He finally references something mentioned by both Rev. Kirk in the seventeenth century and Campbell in the nineteenth writing on fairies, that fairies will take the substance or produce of food if a person speaks ill of their own crops or stores, and that this is one of the ways that they live.

He also expresses his concern over being given to Hell as part of the tiend paid on All Hallows (I discuss the fairies tithe to Hell in depth in my book Fairies if it interests you) and tells her that she can rescue him if she is brave enough. What follows is a very specific method of rescuing a person during a fairy procession, although it is possible that this only works because Janet is very brave and because she is carrying Tam Lin's child. In other examples of this method, the person shares a blood relationship with the person they were trying to save, and I suspect that being related by blood in some manner is an essential factor, which may be why Tam Lin hadn't mentioned it earlier, although the timing of Halloween may also have played a part. In a similar story, The Faerie Oak of Corriewater, a woman tries and fails to save her brother in a similar situation, indicating that this method is certainly not foolproof and that Janet was indeed risking her life to save Tam Lin.

Janet is advised to go to Miles Cross on Halloween and wait for the fairy procession to ride past at midnight, perhaps meaning that the timing of midnight on Halloween is essential, or perhaps merely referencing that this was the usual point that the Fairy Rade rode out. In some versions it is specifically mentioned that he is riding with the Seelie Court:

> The night, the night is Halloween,
> Our seely court maun ride,
> Thro England and thro Ireland both,
> And a' the warld wide.
> 'A fragment of Young Tamlane' Hinloch MSS, V, 391(Child, 1898)

I feel it important to add that in alternate versions, including 39D and 39G, the protagonist carries holy water and uses it to make a 'compass' or circle around herself before the fairies emerge from the mound;she does this because Tam Lin has instructed her to do so. This can be seen as a protective gesture and also perhaps explain why the fairies do not perceive her presence until she breaks the circle to grab Tam Lin down from his horse. The 'compass' of holy water around her shields her from their sight and perception until she moves to grab Tam Lin.

Janet watches, in many versions, as other fairies pass by sometimes described as other courts sometimes enumerated as the King and Queen, followed by maidens, squires, footmen, and grooms. The knights follow at the rear. It is mentioned that because of his renown, Tam Lin will be riding on a white horse; the idea of white horses carrying people of significance in Fairy is something we see repeated often in different places, but it is worth noting here. The Queen of Fairies herself is said to ride on a white horse in many stories, and white animals are often messengers of the Otherworld. In the few versions where he is not riding a white horse, he is riding next to the Queen herself, mounted on a 'blood-red steed', with red also having significant – and far grimmer – Otherworldly meaning.

Once she has pulled him from his horse we see the fairies turning Tam Lin into a variety of fearsome things, finally ending by turning him into a coal which Janet must throw into a well. From the water, Tam Lin emerges as a naked man and Janet covers him with her green cloak, claiming him with this act. It is likely that there is great significance in his final forms of heated iron and a burning coal and that he must, in a fiery form, be thrust into well water. Tam Lin himself guarded a well and wells were often sacred and viewed as both powerful and healing.

Having withstood these trials and won Tam Lin, the fairies cannot take him back again, although it's unclear whether he has regained his mortality or not. For her efforts, Janet wins a bridegroom and a father for her child, but she is also cursed by the Fairy Queen who wishes for her *an ill death may she die*. Arguably Tam Lin is the truest winner here, having avoided being tithed to Hell, being returned to mortal earth, and getting a well-off wife and child into the bargain. The Queen's parting words imply that if she had foreseen these events then she could have prevented it by either literally blinding Tam Lin or, perhaps, by altering his sight less literally so that he wasn't moved by Janet's beauty, depending on how we choose to interpret her giving him the eyes of a tree. In some alternate versions she also says that she should have replaced his heart with one of stone, again implying that she could have avoided this situation by keeping Tam Lin from loving Janet. It is implied in some, and stated outright in others, that the Fairy Queen loved Tam Lin herself, although it is ambiguous as to whether this was romantic love or maternal, she having taken him in many versions when he was only a boy:

> *Out and spak the queen o fairies,*
> *Out o a shot o wheat,*
> *She that has gotten young Tamlane*
> *Has gotten my heart's delight.*
> Tamlane, 'Scotch Ballads, Materials for Border Minstrelsy', No 96A

What can we learn then from Tam Lin? It's a complicated question and a layered answer. Janet, arguably, goes out seeking a fairy lover and finds one. She does this by dressing in green and going to a well in a wood that is known to have a fairy guardian who takes a toll from trespassers, including having sex with them. She possibly goes at night, by the light of the moon, perhaps a full moon? She invokes him by picking forbidden flowers, the property of the fairies. The two talk and it is later implied (stated in other versions) they have a tryst which results in a pregnancy, putting Janet in a difficult position with her family, so she goes back to Carterhaugh and invokes Tam Lin a second time. He then gives her a means to rescue him, something that may only work because the timing is right and Janet is stubborn, fearless, and carrying his child. We learn about how to invoke fairies, and what payments they may expect. We learn as well how a mortal might become one of the Good People, what that might mean, and how he might be rescued. We see that a fairy lover can be gained, and even won away from the fairies, if one is brave.

One is left wondering about Janet's fate though, since she has clearly earned the enmity of the Fairy Queen.

The Faerie Oak of Corriewater
In sharp contrast to Tam Lin, yet sharing many of its themes

is the ballad of the Faerie Oak of Corriewater. I will include a
version of the ballad with the language slightly updated:

1. *The small bird's head is under its wing,*
The deep sleeps on the grass;
The moon comes out, and the stars shine down,
The dew gleams like the glass:
There is no sound in the world so wide,
Save the sound of the smitten brass,
With the merry cittern and the pipe
Of the fairies as they pass.
But oh! the fire must burn and burn,
And the hour is gone, and will never return.
2. *The green hill cleaves, and forth, with a bound,*
Comes elf and elfin steed;
The moon dives down in a golden cloud,
The stars grow dim with dread;
But a light is running along the earth,
So of heaven's they have no need:
Over moor and moss with a shout they pass,
And the word is spur and speed—
But the fire must burn, and I must quake,
And the hour is gone that will never come back.
3. *And when they came to Craigyburnwood,*
The Queen of the Fairies spoke:
'Come, bind your steeds to the rushes so green,
And dance by the haunted oak:
I found the acorn on Heshbon Hill,
In the nook of a palmer's poke,
A thousand years since; here it grows!'
And they danced till the greenwood shook:
But oh! the fire, the burning fire,
The longer it burns, it but blazes the higher.
4. *'I have won me a youth,' the Elf Queen said,*

'The fairest that earth may see;
This night I have won young Elph Irving
My cupbearer to be.
His service lasts but for seven sweet years,
And his wage is a kiss of me.'
And merrily, merrily, laughed the wild elves
Round Corrie's greenwood tree.
But oh! the fire it glows in my brain,
And the hour is gone, and comes not again.
5. The Queen she has whispered a secret word,
'Come hither, my Elphin sweet,
And bring that cup of the charmed wine,
Your lips and mine to wet.'
But a brown elf shouted a loud, loud shout,
'Come, leap on your horses fleet,
For here comes the smell of some baptised flesh,
And the sounding of baptised feet.'
But oh! the fire that burns, and must burn;
For the time that is gone will never return.
6. On a steed as white as the new-milked milk,
The Elf Queen leaped with a bound,
And young Elphin a steed like December snow
Beneath him at the word he found.
But a maiden came, and her christened arms
She linked her brother around,
And called on God, and the steed with a snort
Sank into the gaping ground.
But the fire must burn, and I must quake,
And the time that is gone will no more come back.
7. And she held her brother, and lo! he grew
A wild bull waked in ire;
And she held her brother, and lo! he changed
To a river roaring higher;
And she held her brother, and he became

A flood of the raging fire;
She shrieked and sank, and the wild elves laughed
Till the mountain rang and mire.
But oh! the fire yet burns in my brain,
And the hour is gone, and comes not again.
8. *'O maiden, why waxed your faith so faint,*
Your spirit so slack and slaw?
Your courage kept good till the flame waxed wild,
Then your might began to thaw;
Had you kissed him from among us all.
Now bless the fire, the elfin fire,
That made you faint and fall;
Now bless the fire, the elfin fire,
The longer it burns it blazes the higher.'
(Douglas, 1901)

In this ballad we see, like in the previous, a young man who has been taken by the Fairy Queen to be put into her service. She doesn't say exactly how she's taken him, only that she's 'won' him into her service for seven years to be her cupbearer. His payment for this service is a kiss from the Queen, something that we see often repeated; it may or may not imply a sexual relationship but one could easily read that into her later comment about sharing her wine with him. It would be in-line with accounts by male witches who claimed to have had sexual relations with the Fairy Queen as part of their pact with her (Wilby, 2007).

Another thing that we see here that is also common elsewhere is the idea of the fairies coming forth out of mounds or the earth, and of higher ranking people riding white horses. The Queen's horse is described as white as milk and Elph Irving's as white as snow and we may assume that he was given the prestige of such a mount because of the Queen's affection for him. The description of the elves and horses appearing out of the mound fits what we would expect from a Fairy Rade, a type of ride or procession that the Fey folk are fond of indulging in. Since they ride out to a location in order to dance, the entire air of the event seems festive and cheerful which is also supportive of other lore about fairies' nighttime activities when the mood suits them.

This revelry, described as wild and merry, is interrupted by Elph Irving's sister who is trying, like Janet in Tam Lin, to rescue her brother from the fairies. Unlike Tam Lin we have no idea if Elph wants to be rescued or not. The Good People seem to sense her presence based on the fact that she is baptized as a Christian, something that also causes the fairy horse to disappear when she grabbed Elph and *'called on God'*. This does the sister no good in the end, as Elph is put through a series of transformations (just as Tam Lin was) but while she holds fast when he is a bull and river, she panics when he turns into fire. When she faints at that she is apparently consumed by the flames, a fate that the Fairy Queen mocks.

Interestingly, the Fairy Queen seems to imply that a kiss from his sister would have freed Elph, perhaps as a counter to the kiss with which she'd paid him for his service. It is also likely, I think, that his sister was able to attempt the rescue at all in this manner because she shared a blood relationship with the captured person, just as I believe that Janet's pregnancy allowed her to attempt to save (more successfully) Tam Lin. In this ballad we see the contrast to Janet's success – the price of failure.

Thomas the Rhymer

One of the most famous ballads is that of Thomas the Rhymer and it contains a lot of significant fairylore that we can look at here. In its oldest prose form it is called 'The Romance and Prophecies of Thomas of Erceldoune' and it goes back to at least the fifteenth century in written form (Henderson & Cowan, 2001). It is the story of a man named Thomas who meets the Queen of Elfland one day and is taken into her service for seven years. The two journey into Fairy together and Thomas is paid for his service, ultimately, with the ability to tell only the truth which is also a gift for prophecy. Below I will include one of the standard versions:

1. *True Thomas lay on Huntlie Bank,*
A wonder he spied with his eye
And there he saw a lady bright,
Come riding down by Eildon Tree.
2. *Her shirt was of the grass-green silk,*
Her mantle of the velvet fine
At each tuft of her horse's mane
Hang fifty silver bells and nine.
3. *True Thomas, he pulled off his cap,*
And bowed low down to his knee
'All hail, you mighty Queen of Heaven!
For your peer on earth I never did see.'
4. *'O no, O no, Thomas,' she said,*
'That name does not belong to me;
I am but the queen of fair Elfland,
That am hither come to visit you.'
5. *'Harp and sing, Thomas,' she said,*
'Harp and sing along with me,
And if you dare to kiss my lips,
Sure of your body I will be.'
6. *'Fare me well, fare me woe,*
That fate shall never daunt me;'
Soon he has kissed her rosy lips,
All underneath the Eildon Tree.
7. *'Now, you must go with me,' she said,*
'True Thomas, you must go with me,
And you must serve me seven years,
Through good or bad, as may chance to be.'
8. *She mounted on her milk-white steed,*
She's taken True Thomas up behind,

And yes whenever her bridle rung,
The steed flew swifter than the wind.
9. O they rode on, and farther on—
The steed went swifter than the wind—
Until they reached a desert wide,
And living land was left behind.
10. 'Light down, light down, now, True Thomas,
And lean your head upon my knee;
Abide and rest a little space,
And I will show you wonders three.'
11. 'O see you not that narrow road,
So thick beset with thorns and briers?
That is the path of righteousness,
Though after it but few enquires.
12. 'And see not you that broad broad road,
That lies across that lily meadow?
That is the path to wickedness,
Though some call it the road to heaven.
13. 'And see not you that bonny road,
That winds about the ferny hillside?
That is the road to fair Elfland,
Where you and I this night must go.
14. 'But, Thomas, you must hold your tongue,
Whatever you may hear or see,
For, if you speak word in Elfiyn land,
You'll never get back to your own country.'
15. O they rode on, and farther on,
And they waded through rivers above the knee,
And they saw neither sun nor moon,
But they heard the roaring of the sea.
16. It was dark dark night, and there was no star light,
And they waded through red blood to the knee;
For all the blood that's shed on earth
Runs through the springs of that country.

17. Soon they came on to a garden green,
And she pulled an apple from the tree:
'Take this for your wages, True Thomas,
It will give you a tongue that can never lie.'
18. 'My tongue is mine own,' True Thomas said;
'A good gift you would give to me!
I would neither be able to buy nor sell,
At fair or tryst where I may be.'
19. 'I'd be able neither to speak to prince or peer,
Nor ask of grace from fair lady:'
'Now hold your peace,' the lady said,
'For as I say, so must it be.'
20. He has gotten a coat of the even cloth,
And a pair of shoes of velvet green,
And till seven years were gone and past
True Thomas on earth was never seen.

(Child, 1898, language modified to modern English)

We meet Thomas as he is lying on a bank and are told that he sees *'a wonder'*, or a fairlie in Doric, which it turns out is the queen of Elfland. So wondrous is her appearance indeed that Thomas initially mistakes her for the Christian Virgin Mary and has to be corrected by her. In most versions she is described as riding a white horse which has 59 silver bells in its mane, although in at least one alternate version her mount is *'dappled grey'* and she is holding nine silver bells in her hand instead (Child, 1898). It is likely that the silver bells are significant and possibly represent a means to travel between worlds. Certainly we see the idea of elven horses wearing bells in other folklore and ballads and in Irish mythology we have Manannán mac Lir's bell branch which also features silver bells and aids in passage between the worlds.

She is wearing green, a fairy colour, and identifies herself as the Queen of Elfland, although in one version she states that she is *'but a lady of an unco [strange] land, come out a hunting'* (Child,

1898). In the oldest version of the story, 'Thomas of Erceldoune', the Queen is indeed hunting and appears blowing her hunting horn accompanied by seven hunting hounds (Henderson & Cowan, 2001). In the ballad she asks Thomas to play and sing for her and in some versions immediately takes him into her service for seven years; in others, as in the one given above, she offers him a kiss saying that if he agrees she will be *'sure of his body'*. In the story of 'Thomas of Erceldoune' rather than the Queen setting the terms immediately we see Thomas propositioning her, saying he would live with her forever in return even though she claims that laying with him will ruin her beauty; the two have sex seven times in a row (Henderson & Cowan, 2001). You will note the repeated appearance of the number seven, a number that is often, although obscurely, associated with Fairy and its inhabitants.

After agreeing to serve the Queen, Thomas goes with her to Fairy and as they travelled *'living land was left behind'*. They stop along the way and in many of the other versions Thomas either asks for food or complains of hunger, trying to pick fruit which the Queen warns him is dangerous; in some versions she instead offers him bread and wine, while in others she tells him to rest his head on her knee. The Fairy Queen then offers to show him more wonders. The same term is used here for the three paths as we saw earlier for the first appearance of the Fairy Queen, three wonders, or fairlies in the original text. These new wonders are three[4] roads which lead to Heaven, Hell, and Fairy respectively. This idea of three paths is one we will also see in other ballads and I think reflects the merging of older folk beliefs which saw Fairy as one possible destination for the dead with the newer Christian beliefs about Heaven and Hell. The path to Heaven, or righteousness, is beset with thorns and narrow, while the path to Hell is broad and easy; the third path to Fairy is winding and beautiful.

Thomas is warned that he must not speak a word while he

is in Fairy or he will never be allowed to return to mortal earth. This is a distinct change from the usual pattern in Fairylore of a person being prohibited from eating or drinking while in Fairy lest they be bound there, and may indicate either that being in service to the Queen has different rules or that the Queen can set the rules herself. In the Erceldoune version, the reason for the prohibition is very clearly explained by the Queen who has suddenly regained her beauty after losing it when she and Thomas had sex;[5] the two had been lovers but she is the wife of the King of Fairy and he will be enraged if he finds out so she tells Thomas he must only speak to her while he is there (Henderson & Cowan, 2001). This is certainly worth noting as it comes from the oldest version of the story, but it is also a version that has some clear Christian overtones including the looming figure of the Christian Devil who shows up after Thomas has been there for three days to collect his tithe.[6] It is, however, also worth keeping in mind that the Queen has elsewhere warned Thomas against picking and eating fruit in Fairy telling him:

That fruit must not be touched by you
For all the plagues that are in hell
Light on the fruit of this country
And in another version:
Hold your hand, that must not be;
It was all that cursed fruit of yours
Beggared man and woman in your country.

In that case she offered him bread and wine from her own hand, again suggesting that she had some power in herself to mitigate the usual rules of Fairy, but that if Thomas took the food from the source himself there would be some dire consequence to him.

The two continue on for *'forty days and forty nights'* through rivers, perpetual twilight, darkness, and rivers of blood; interestingly we find out that the rivers of blood are created by all the blood shed on earth. They stop again and this time the Queen picks an apple from a tree and offers it to Thomas as his payment for his service telling him it will give him the gift of true speech. At first he tries to refuse, saying he would rather keep his speech his own, but the Queen insists. He is also given a new coat and a pair of green shoes. In the older version Thomas asks the Queen for a gift and she gives him the choice of a gift of harping or a gift of speech and prophecy; Thomas chooses speech which he thinks is the more powerful (Henderson & Cowan, 2001). After seven years Thomas is returned to earth; in the Erceldoune version he has only experienced three days in Fairy but finds that seven years have passed on earth, while in the ballad versions he is clearly taken into service for seven years. This is where the ballads end although the folklore about Thomas himself tells us that the Fairy Queen returned for him, sending him a sign – a doe and stag – to lead him back into Fairy where it's believed he still remains today (Henderson & Cowan, 2001).

The Ballad of Thomas the Rhymer, or True Thomas as he's sometimes called, provides us with many pieces of fairylore. It reinforces the importance of the colour green and the number seven, and the idea that Fairy exists in perpetual twilight, an idea we see elsewhere as well. Here we are told that blood shed on earth flows in Fairy, and we also perhaps see a hint that those who are taken into Fairy and returned again are not truly freed. Above all, for those of us on this path this may serve as a good guide and warning tale about dealing with and being in service to the Fairy Queens.

Lady Isabel and the Elf Knight

Another interesting ballad, which may serve in some ways as a warning to be careful what you wish for, is Lady Isabel and the Elf Knight. In it we see Lady Isabel on Bealtaine morning when she hears an elf knight blowing his horn and wishes for him as her lover. He leaps into her room and abducts her, taking her to a 'greenwood' where he tells her that she is the eighth king's daughter he has taken and that he killed the other seven. She lulls him to sleep, possibly with magic, and then binds him with his own belt and kills him with his own dagger. Below, I am including the ballad but have updated the language:

Fair lady Isabel sits in her bower sewing,
Yes as the daisies grow gay
There she heard an elf-knight blowing his horn.
The first morning in May
'If I had yonder horn that I hear blowing,
And yonder elf-knight to sleep in my bosom.'
This maiden had scarcely these words spoken,
Till in at her window the elf-knight has leapt.
'It's a very strange matter, fair maiden,' said he,
'I cannot blow my horn but you call on me.
'But will you go to yonder greenwood's edge?
If you cannot go, I will cause you to ride.'
He leapt on a horse, and she on another,
And they rode on to the greenwood together.
'Light down, light down, lady Isabel,' said he,
'We are come to the place where you are to die.'
'Have mercy, have mercy, kind sir, on me,
Till once my dear father and mother I see.'
'Seven king's-daughters here have I slain,
And you shall be the eighth of them.'
'0 sit down a while, lay your head on my knee,
That we may have some rest before that I die.'
She stroked him so fast, the nearer he did creep,
With a small charm she lulled him fast asleep.
With his own sword-belt so fast she bound him,
With his own dagger so grievously she struck him.
'If seven king's-daughters here you have slain,

Lie you here, a husband to them all.'

It is key I think, that this occurs on Bealtaine, a time when the Fair Folk are always more active and when people are warned to be extra cautious, particularly of strangers. It is also probably noteworthy that Lady Isabel was able to hear the Elf Knight blowing his horn at all, either indicating that the nature of the date allowed such perception to occur or that he was out hunting for such a victim.

Initially when she expresses her wish that she have the Elf Knight *'to sleep in [her] bosom'* his response seems almost to imply that she has compelled him in some way to go to her, saying that he cannot sound his horn without her calling on him. We may perhaps conclude from this that her words have called him to her, yet he then says that if she will not go with him to the Greenwood he will *'compel her to ride'* which he subsequently does. If indeed she had forced him to her side with her wish the tables quickly turn with his abduction of her. Keeping in mind the importance of Fairy etiquette, it is possible that Lady Isabel has opened herself to the Elf Knight's influence and abduction by saying what she did on the day that she did. In effect, we may say that by compelling him to come to her side she was open to being compelled by him to leave at his side. This is certainly something to keep in mind if one is ever tempted to wish aloud for a fairy lover.

The two ride into the Greenwood and when they stop he tells her that he has killed seven king's daughters there, an interesting thing to note since seven is a number that often appears in fairylore. Lady Isabel saves herself from being the eighth victim by using a charm to lull the Knight to sleep and then binding him with his own belt and slaying him with his own dagger. We don't know what the charm she uses is, but I believe that it is vital that she used his own possessions against him, although arguably one could say she merely used what was at hand.

The Elfin Knight

This ballad is more familiar to most people in its later song form as 'Scarborough Fair' but in this older ballad the context is clearly supernatural. Later versions slowly lose this aspect and become a simpler song: in one example, variant I, a woman tries to avoid marriage to an older man; and in others, a lover asks a person to remind another of them and asks them to complete impossible tasks. In the older versions the supernatural is clearly on display, telling the tale of a woman who wishes for an Elf Knight as her true love, who responds by giving her a series of seemingly impossible tasks to complete to win him. She in turn gives him a series of equally impossible tasks to earn her as his wife. Below I will include one of the oldest versions dating to 1670 (Caffrey, 2002). Then I'll discuss some of the variations; as with many of the ballads there are multiple versions and some have significant differences.

The Elfin Knight Version 2B

1. *My plaid[7] away, my plaid away*
And over the hills and far away
And far away to Norway,
My plaid shall not be blown away.
The Elfin knight stands on yonder hill,
Refrain: Ba, ba, ba, lillie ba
He blows his horn both loud and shrill.
Refrain: The wind has blown my plaid away
2. *He blows it east, he blows it west*
He blows it where he likes it best
3. *'I wish that horn were in my chest,*
Yes and the Knight in my arms next!
4. *She had no sooner these words said*
Than the Knight came to her bed.
5. *'You are too young a girl', he said*
'Married with me that you would be.'

6. *'I have a sister younger than I*
And she was married yesterday'
7. *'Married with me if you would be*
A courtesy you must do for me.
8. *'It's you must make a shirt for me,*
Without any cut or seem', said he.
9. *'And you must shape it knife- and shearless,*
And also sow it needle and threadless.'
10. *'If that piece of courtesy I do for you*
Another you must do for me.
11. *'I have an acre of good untilled land,*
Which lays low by yonder sea shore.
12. *'It's you must till it with your blowing horn,*
And you must sow it with pepper corn.
13. *'And you must harrow with a thorn*
And have your work done before the morning.'
14. *'And you must shear it with your knife*
And not lose a stack of it for your life.'
15. *'And you must stack it in a mouse hole*
And you must thresh it in your shoe-sole.'
16. *'And you must prepare it in the palm of your hand*
And also stack it in your glove
17. *'And you must bring it over the sea*
Fair and dry and clean to me.'
18. *'And when you've done, and finished your work,*
You'll come to me, and you'll get your shirt.'
19. *'I'll not abandon my plaid for my life;*
It covers my seven children and my wife.'
20. *'My maidenhead I'll then keep still*
Let the Elfin Knight do what he will.'
(modified from Child, 1898)

This is a complex ballad and one that stands in stark contrast to others like Tam Lin and Lady Isabel and the Elf Knight. Like the latter though, this one begins with a young woman hearing an Elfin Knight blowing his horn and wishing aloud that she had him for her own, and like 'Lady Isabel' the elf seems compelled to immediately respond by going to her. He does not seem to want to do this and we can gather his reluctance since his first comment is that she is too young for him, which she counters by saying that her younger sister was just married. In most versions the girl's age is unspecified although she does seem to at least be of marriageable age; only in version D is her age given as the very young nine years old, and we may interpret his challenge to her there as a way to put her off until she's older. In version A the Elf Knight says not only that she is too young but that *'married with me you ill would be'* and in version C he asks her *'Are you not over young a maid; with only young men down to lay?'* (Child, 1898). When she insists despite his concern over her age that she is acceptable – by referring to the marriage of her younger sister – he issues her a challenge, more kindly worded in version B above and more bluntly said in C *'married with me you shall never be; until you make me a shirt without a seam* [etc.]'.

Looking at this section several things are clear. The Elf Knight seems to have no choice in responding to the young woman when she hears his horn and wishes for his company. He also seems unable to simply refuse her advances when she expresses a desire to marry him, or at the least to have sex with him. Instead he responds to her insistence by giving her a list of things she must do to earn him as a spouse, in all versions this seems to include making a shirt that is not sown or cut, and not touched by iron. In several alternate versions there are additional requirements including:

D: ... *wash it in yonder well,*
Where the dew never wet, nor the rain ever fell
And you must dry it on a thorn
That never budded since Adam was born.

Or alternately from version C:
And you must wash it in yonder cistern
Where water never stood nor ran
And you must dry it on yonder Hawthorn
Where the sun never shone since man was born.

In both of these we see the key to the additions being the idea of washing the shirt in water that is not ordinary water and drying it on an ancient thorn tree that has either never flowered or never seen the sun for as long as humans have existed.

The girl responds to these challenges with a set of her own which in most versions are more complex than what she has been asked to do and involve plowing, planting, harvesting and preparing an acre of land in ways that are just as impossible as the shirt she has been asked to make. In some versions the land is said to *'lay low by yonder sea strand'* but in some others it is specifically *'between the sea and the sand'* (Child, 1898). We may, perhaps, assume the challenges are more difficult and numerous because the Elfin Knight is assumed to have a greater ability to achieve the impossible tasks than the girl has.

In the later variations the ballad ends with the young woman telling the Knight that when he has completed his task and is ready to present the literal fruit (or at least grain) of his labour he can return for his shirt. However, in the two earlier versions, A and B, the woman responding with challenges of her own seems to free the elf of the compulsion he was under (or at least a portion of it), as he replies to her telling him when to come for the shirt by saying he won't *'abandon his plaid for his life; it covers his seven children and his wife'*. (Note the number 7 appearing here once again.) In other words he doesn't want to give up his own bed and family for this young woman. She at least has the good grace then to reply that she will keep her virginity and he can do as he will, certainly setting him completely free at that point.

There are also variations of the refrain presented here in the oldest form of *'ba ba ba lillie ba; the wind has blown my plaid away'* which is found in variants A and B; versions C, D and E are fairly similar with the second line saying *'and the wind has blown my plaid away'* but the first line varies from *'over the hills and far away'* to *'blow, blow, blow wind blow'* except version E which uses the opening line of the refrain from versions A and B. The refrain for version F is *'sober and grave grows merry in time; once she was a true love of mine'* and marks the first version with no mention of the Elfin Knight. G introduces the famous lines *'Parsley, sage, rosemary, and thyme; and you shall be a true lover of mine'* and H blends the previous two giving us *'every rose grows merrier with thyme; and then you will be a true lover of mine'*. I returns to the older version with *'Hee ba and balou ba'* as the beginning but the reference to the wind blowing away the plaid to finish; J uses nonsense words. K's refrain is *'Sing ivy, sing ivy; sing holly, go whistle and ivy'* while L uses the variant *'Sing ivy, sing ivy; sing green bush, ivy and holly'*; finally M returns to a version of *'Every rose springs merry in its time; and she longed to be a true lover of mine'*. It is likely that the earliest refrains which rely on references to the wind blowing away the plaid are symbolic and that the plaid in this case was meant to represent either a loss of innocence or security. Caffrey, in his article 'The Elfin Knight Child #2: Impossible Tasks and Impossible Love' suggests that the plaid is meant to have sexual connotations and that is certainly likely throughout the ballad. The other versions of the refrain include a selection of herbs: ivy, holly, rose, parsley, sage, rosemary, and thyme. Ivy was used in love magic and had protective qualities; holly is favoured by fairies and also has protective qualities but interestingly was known as a plant that protected the heart against love (MacCoitir, 2006; MacCoitir, 2003). Rose, not surprisingly, has a long history as a symbol of love and also of beauty. Parsley is associated with lust and fertility; sage for fulfilling wishes; rosemary for love and lust; and thyme for love and attraction (Cunningham, 1985). All of these plants then have significance relating to the meaning of the ballad itself and for our purposes should be considered in the use of magic relating to working with or drawing the Fair Folk or love magic generally.

I think we can see from this that it is possible for a person to compel a Fairy being, particularly an Elfin Knight, if they hear his horn being blown and wish for him in that moment. However, I think that this ballad along with the previous 'Lady Isabel and the Elf Knight' make it clear that it may be either unwise or dangerous to make such a wish. You may get what you wish for but in one case the result is a homicidal lover, while in the other it is a deeply reluctant one. Many of us may wish we had an Otherworldly lover or spouse but these ballads show us that forcing Fairy beings into these relationships does not work out well.

King Orfeo

In contrast to the last two ballads which focus on a human compelling an elf, here we see a Fairy King kidnapping a human woman who then must be rescued by her husband. The man, King Orfeo, goes out hunting and leaves his lady home where the King of Fairies finds her and enchants her. Orfeo then seeks her out in the Fairy King's hall and wins her back with his skill. The original is in Norn, a dialect once found across parts of Scotland, and the Shetland and Orkney Isles. The version I am including has been modified to modern English.[9]

> *There lived a king in the east,*
> Refrain: *Early green's the wood*
> *There lived a lady in the west.*
> Refrain: *Where goes the doe yearly*
> *This king he has a hunting gone,*
> *He's left his Lady Isabel alone.*
> *'Oh I wish you'd never gone away,*
> *For at your home is misery and woe.*

'For the king of Fairy with his dart,
Has pierced your lady to the heart.'

And after them the king has gone,
But when he came there was a grey stone.
Then he took out his pipes to play,
But sore his heart with misery and woe.
And first he played the notes of grief,
And then he played the notes of joy.
And then he played the good rollicking reel,
That could have made a sick heart healthy.

Now come you into our hall,
And come you in among us all.
Now he's gone into the hall,
And he's gone in among them all.
Then he took out his pipes to play,
But sore his heart with misery and woe.
And first he played the notes of grief,
And then he played the notes of joy.
And then he played the good rollicking reel,
That could have made a sick heart healthy.
'Now tell to us what you will have:
What shall we give you for your play?'
'What I will have I will you tell,
And that's me Lady Isabel.'
'Yes take your lady, and yes go home,
And yes be king over all your own.'
He's taken his lady, and he's gone home,
And now he's king over all his own.
(Child, 1898, language updated)

As with many of the others we have discussed this appears as both a ballad and a story, dating back to the late fourteenth or early fifteenth century. We see a lot of repetition in the lines of this ballad so that it has a very rhythmic feel even when it's read. Many of its themes reflect ideas found throughout fairylore where changelings or abductions occur and the family decides to fight back and free the person. This ballad, though, has a decidedly happy ending to it with King Orfeo not only succeeding in recovering his wife but also earning the blessing of the King of Fairy who says 'yes be king over all your own' which is what comes to pass afterwards.

In the older story Orfeo's wife, Heurodis, falls asleep under a tree and has a vision of the Fairy King who tells her that he will return and take her back with him to his kingdom the next day, and this comes to pass. Orfeo dresses as a beggar and sets out after her taking his harp with him into the woods. Initially he has little luck although he occasionally sees the Fairy King, or Fairy Knights, but finally he sees his wife among a group of Fairy women who are out hawking and he successfully follows them through a stone and into Fairy. There he sees a beautiful sunny land and glittering castle; in the castle he finds the horrifying sight of a group of people dead by various means including violence, madness, and childbirth. He also finds his wife asleep. Then Orfeo played his harp for the fairy court earning a reward which he named as his wife and the restoration of his kingdom (Henderson & Cowan, 2001).

In the ballad, when King Orfeo returns home from hunting and finds his wife gone, he is told that she was abducted by the King of Fairies, who has pierced her heart with his dart, which I think could either mean a literal enchantment or imply that she fell in love with the Fairy king and ran away with him. In either case his household is in mourning and he sets off to find her, arriving at 'a grey stone', likely representing a fairy hill or similar location. King Orfeo, who it becomes clear is a talented musician, takes out a set of pipes[10] and begins playing. He then plays three types of music: sorrowful, joyful and dancing, echoing the three famous strains of music mentioned in Irish mythology of sorrowful, joyful, and sleep. Although here we see Orfeo playing dance music instead of sleep music; the idea of three kinds of song is certainly deeply rooted.

Orfeo's playing gains him an invitation into the 'stone' which he accepts, and there he plays the three kinds of music again. This time his playing gains him a reward among the Good People, who ask him to choose what he wants in payment; he asks for the return of his wife. He is in turn granted three things: his wife, his freedom to leave, and a blessing on his reign.

It is likely that the repetition of the number three in this ballad is significant, as Orfeo plays three kinds of music and is granted three boons by the Fair Folk. Had he only played one type of music he may well have earned his way in and his wife's return but perhaps not escaped again or left in safety. But as it is, the Good People are known to abhor being in debt to anyone and when they ask him about his fee for playing they seem, by their response, to have felt that each kind of music deserved its own reward.

Musicians and poets, like blacksmiths, have long held a special power when it comes to the Gentry and musicians are one group of humans who are likely to be taken into a fairy hill and returned in a timely manner unharmed. It may be this fact that aided King Orfeo in his quest to regain his wife. For us, it is worth noting the power of music and the value of remembering that we should not focus just on getting back what has been taken but also on making sure we have a way to get out safely again and to avert or avoid the fairies' wrath for taking what they wanted.

The Queen of Elfan's Nourice (the Queen of Elfland's Nurse)

The Queen of Elfan's Nourice is the story of a human woman taken by the Queen of Fairy to be a nursemaid. It gives us a unique look at one of the common reasons that the Fey folk were known to take new mothers, from the mother's point of view.

I heard a cow low, a bonnie cow low,
And a cow low down in yonder glen;
Long, long will my young son weep
For his mother to bid him come in.
I heard a cow low, a bonnie cow low,
And a cow low down in yonder fold;
Long, long will my young son weep
For his mother to take him from the cold.

Aw'ake, Queen of Elfland,
And hear your nurse moan.
'O moan you for your meat,
Or moan you for your money,
Or moan you for the other bounties
That ladies are want to give?'
'I moan not for my meat,
Nor moan I for my money,
Nor moan I for the other bounties
That ladies are want to give.'

But I moan for my young son
I left at four nights old.'
'I moan not for my meat,
Nor yet for my money,
But I mourn for Christian land,
It's there I gladly would be.'
'O nurse my child, nurse,' she says,
'Till he stands at your knee,
And you'll win home to Christian land,
Where glad it's you would be.'
'O keep my child, nurse,

Till he goes by the hand,
And you'll win home to your young son
You left at four nights old.'

'O nurse lay your head
Upon my knee:
See you not that narrow road
Up by yon tree?'

'That's the road the righteous goes,
And that's the road to heaven.'
'And see not you that broad road,
Down by yonder sunny hill?
That's the road the wicked go,
And that's the road to hell.'
(modified from Child, 1898)

The ballad opens seemingly from the human woman's point of view, as she talks about how long her son will cry over her loss. The next verse picks up with the Queen of Elfland being awoken by someone telling her that her nurse is weeping; the Queen then asks if the nurse is hungry, wanting to be paid or wanting some other small gift. The nurse replies that she wants none of those things but is crying for her baby son who she left as a newborn and for mortal earth. The Queen replies that if she nurses the Fairy Queen's son until he *'stands at [her] knee'* and *'goes by the hand'* – one may assume is walking on his own – then she will be returned to her son. Then, as we saw previously in the ballad of Thomas the Rhymer, we see the Queen comforting the nurse by telling her to lay her head on the Queen's knee and showing her a vision of two roads, one to heaven and one to hell. Obviously since they are already in Fairy she doesn't show her a third road, perhaps not wanting to show her the way to escape back to mortal earth.

It is interesting that we see here again the idea of the different roads or paths and that again they are being shown to a mortal by the Fairy Queen herself. In Thomas the Rhymer this vision was called a 'wonder' and it was also used to soothe a person who was upset. To me, this indicates that the idea of the roads has some significance worth considering. In both poems the road to heaven is described as the less attractive and more difficult and the road to Hell is more pleasant looking and 'broad'.

The Queen of Elfan's Nourice is a more obscure poem but it is valuable because it shows us another side of dealing with the Fairy Queen and fairies more generally. The new mother has been taken by the Fey folk but her unhappiness does seem to matter to them and the Queen makes some attempt to comfort her, although at no point is her freedom immediately offered. She is, however, promised that when certain conditions are met, in this case nursing the Queen's child for a specific period of time, she will be returned to mortal earth and her child. There is also the implication in the Queen's words, asking the nurse whether she is moaning about money, food, or gifts, that she was willing to pay for the services in other ways as well. Only when the nurse explains that she doesn't want those things but is upset about her baby son and her home is she offered her eventual freedom. This suggests that negotiation is an option even with the Fairy Queen.

As we have seen there is a great deal of wisdom in the ballads, sometimes subtle and sometimes quite clear. In this section we have touched on only a small selection of ballads that mention or focus on fairies in one way or another but there are certainly others to be found, and even of the ones we've mentioned, there is more to be gleaned from them than what we have discussed here. Consider this an introduction to how the ballads can be viewed and a glimpse at how I personally look at them rather than an exhaustive discussion of the material.

Endnotes

1. Keep in mind please that Leprechauns are not the image that pop culture paints of them. In older mythology they are a type of water sprite, and are a type of fairy people on their own. They are small, usually about a foot and a half tall, but they are powerful and can be dangerous.

2. Another excellent resource for tree lore is the Ogham, and so I am including an appendix focusing on the Ogham, although you will see that it goes much further and deeper than just the trees.

3. In some later versions of the ballad the sexual encounter between Janet (by any name) and Tam Lin is clearly non-consensual. This requires an entire essay of its own to unpack and I highly recommend reading Acland's 'Is Tam Lin a Rape Story?'. I agree with all the author's points and tend to favour her third argument as it relates specifically to the original ballad of Tam Lin, not the later adapted versions.

4. In the 'Thomas of Erceldoune' story, the Elfin Queen shows Thomas four roads instead of three: one to Heaven, one to Paradise, one to a place of suffering for souls who've committed sins, and the final one to Hell (Henderson & Cowan, 2001). Henderson and Cowan suggest that in this case Paradise likely means Fairy, an idea that is supported by Firth-Green in his book *Elf-Queens and Holy Friars* who discusses the sometimes blurry lines in older texts between the ecclesiastical ideas of Paradise and the folkloric ideas of Fairy. The third road to a place of suffering likely references Purgatory.

5. I strongly suspect that the loss of beauty and then the regaining of it is actually something of a test for Thomas. He asks to become her lover and promises to stay with her forever – she warns him that if they have sex she will become hideously ugly, but he is not dissuaded. After the two lay

together the Queen does indeed lose her beauty to his eyes, her body turning blue and dull, hair and clothing both awry. Nonetheless, Thomas stays with her and journeys to Fairy and only once they have arrived (but before they enter the Court) does she regain her former radiance. I think that she was testing his word and things would have fallen out differently if he had not proven true.

6. I discuss the Scottish fairies' tithe to Hell at length in my book *Fairies*. In brief, it is a belief that comes to us from a specific area of the Lowlands which says that the fairies must pay a tithe to Hell once every seven years. The general implication is that Fairy itself is a kind of rental property owned by Hell and this tithe is the rent it pays. This tithe is usually taken from the fairest and most well mannered of the inhabitants, including humans that have been previously taken by the fairies. Please note, though, that the tithe is unique to a specific area and the belief is not found elsewhere.

7. A plaid is a length of cloth that can be worn as a mantle but also serves as a bedcovering. In this context I might suggest the bedcovering meaning is intended, although one might also see it as applying to a clothing mantle.

8. In this version, also note that she does not claim that she has a younger sister who is already married but that she *'has a sister eleven years old; and she to the young men's bed has made bold'*. This does not seem to be a persuasive argument for the Elf Knight, however, who continues to put her off.

9. The original text of King Orfeo in Norn:

    1. Der lived a king inta da aste,
    Refrain: Scowan ürla grün
        Der lived a lady in da wast.
    Refrain: Whar giorten han grün oarlac
    2. Dis king he has a huntin gaen,
        He's left his Lady Isabel alane.
    3. 'Oh I wis ye'd never gaen away,

For at your hame is d'ol an wae.

4. 'For da king o Ferrie we his daert,
   Has pierced your lady to da hert.'

5. And aifter dem da king has gaen,
   But whan he cam it was a grey stane.

6. Dan he took oot his pipes ta play,
   Bit sair his hert wi d'ol an wae.

7. And first he played da notes o noy,
   An dan he played da notes o joy.

8. An dan he played da g'od gabber reel,
   Dat meicht ha made a sick hert hale.

9. 'Noo come ye in inta wir ha,
   An come ye in among wis a'.'

10. Now he's gaen in inta der ha,
    An he's gaen in among dem a'.

11. Dan he took out his pipes to play,
    Bit sair his hert wi d'ol an wae.

12. An first he played da notes o noy,
    An dan he played da notes o joy.

13. An dan he played da g'od gabber reel,
    Dat meicht ha made a sick hert hale.

14. 'Noo tell to us what ye will hae:
    What sall we gie you for your play?

15. 'What I will hae I will you tell,
    An dat's me Lady Isabel.'

16. 'Yees tak your lady, an yees gaeng hame,
    An yees be king ower a' your ain.'

17. He's taen his lady, an he's gaen hame,
    An noo he's king ower a' his ain.

10. Pipes here may refer to either bagpipes or an instrument
    rather like a tin whistle.

Chapter 6

Dreams, Trance, and Journeying Elsewhere

From the hag and hungry goblin
That into rags would rend ye,
All the sprites that stand by the naked man
In the book of moons, defend ye.

I mentioned earlier that a main aspect of the actual practice of this path hinges on connecting to and interacting with Fairy in some sense. For those who don't have what is sometimes called the Second Sight, the main way to do this is through dreams, trance and meditation or journeywork. If you do have the Second Sight then you've likely been living with the reality of these things your whole life, so none of this is new to you. Otherwise, though, you may want to study some basics of things like controlling dreams or lucid dreaming and the modern principles of journeywork. Diana Paxson has a good series of books which I think are helpful on the subject beginning with one called *Trance-Portation*. They all represent tools we have to reach out and connect to the Otherworld and its inhabitants.

Once you have established a good basic understanding of the etiquette and have started to develop a sense for personal gnosis and trusting your gut, you're ready to begin actively seeking out connections and building allies among the Other Crowd. Of course sometimes it doesn't work that way, and they come to you before you're ready and it's much more a matter of sink or swim in the deep end. But as we're talking about these things here we may as well look at the best-case scenario as well as the worst. And best-case, you get to do this in the order you want to and work up carefully and methodically. Even if you fall more into the other group and you started on this path the way I did, because it was part of your life whether you wanted it to be or not, it can be helpful to take a deeper look at some of these methods.

One thing to keep in mind as we get into this section is that there is no one-size-fits-all approach with this type of work. Certainly there are some basic safety guidelines that I highly recommend following and some basic methods and guidelines that are worth keeping in mind, but ultimately different things work for different people. I'm going to present what works for me and my thoughts on what to do and not do, but keep an open mind. I am always learning new ways to do things by listening to other people and paying attention to how others do things – even if ultimately I realize it's not for me, I've still learned something valuable.

We can reach Fairy through several means beyond the obvious – physically travelling there. We can also go there in spirit, something that is attested to in folklore as occurring both in dreams and in 'trance' (Bitel, 1991; Evans-Wentz, 1911). For our purposes, trance here will be treated as waking visions and meditation or journeywork will be distinguished from that of a more structured, focused effort. Keep in mind that not all personal spiritual efforts may take a person into actual contact with Fairy though, and it does take time to learn the discernment to tell the difference between actual contact and the inside of your own head in many cases.

When you send your spirit travelling out to Fairy the same rules apply and you should never forget that, especially if you work and journey alone.

Some other basic things to always keep in mind:

1. Time moves differently – this is a big one so I probably should repeat it, but you need to keep it in mind because it is easy to forget. Time runs differently in Fairy and even if your body is still here, if your spirit is Elsewhere you can lose track of how much time is passing. I have mentioned in other Fairycraft

books that when you perform formal ritual in a Fairycraft style it can sometimes have weird effects on time because you are, in effect, taking yourself and your ritual space out of mortal earth to some degree – or perhaps bringing a piece of Fairy here.

2. You can be hurt in Fairy – people always seem to forget or ignore this one, but it is true that you can be hurt when you go to Fairy whether it's in dreams or journeys, and if you are hurt there then it can have real world consequences here. That isn't to say that if you are cut in Fairy you will wake up here with a cut in the same place, but it isn't to say you won't either. I'll be blunt with you, I have had some seriously weird things happen and that includes waking up with bruises and scratches[1] that correlate with Otherworldly experiences and have no other rational explanation. This also includes cuts that don't bleed, bruises that exactly match places I was injured while in the Otherworld, and pain with no marks or source that line up with something which occurred Elsewhere. Please do not treat dreams and journeys as if you are playing a video game and you are impervious to harm in the real world.

3. You can be trapped in Fairy – many people assume by this that when we say you can be trapped in Fairy that means completely and physically, but things are not always that simple. When you are sending your spirit out it is possible to lose only a piece of yourself to Fairy and it is possible to lose a piece at a time. Having any part of yourself stuck in the Otherworld is not a good thing. Firstly, it leaves you vulnerable to harm. Secondly, it opens the door to the rest of you being taken. And thirdly, if part of you is in Fairy and the rest of your spirit is here then at best you will feel divided and unfocused. It is very important to make sure that all of you comes back each time.

4. Treat all interactions as real – this is another one that people seem to either intentionally or unintentionally forget, but it is very true nonetheless. I mentioned above that this sort of work is not like playing a video game and it really isn't. Even if

you don't entirely believe in the objective reality of all of this, I would urge you to treat it as real, please. As the saying goes, you don't get a second chance to make a first impression and there are many things that once done cannot be undone when one is dealing with the Fey. Words cannot be unspoken and promises cannot be unpromised. No matter how much you might want to treat your meditations and journeywork in particularly as a bit of mental exercise, I would strongly urge you to instead treat it as seriously as you would any mortal world experiences.

5. Always have an out – whether you are dreaming or journeying it is important to always have control going in and control leaving. It will happen that you may need to leave quickly and you should be prepared and able to do that. This isn't so much difficult as a matter of practice. I encourage everyone to learn both safe slow ways to carefully return to one's self after a journey and also emergency immediate ways to do the same. Then practice both until they are reflexive.

Fairy Food: 'Bite No Bit, and Drink No Drop'

And what you've not to do is this: bite no bit, and drink no drop, however hungry or thirsty you be; drink a drop, or bite a bit while in Elfland you be and never will you see Middle Earth again.
The Ballad of Childe Rowland

It's important at this point to take a closer look at one specific area that shows up often in folklore and can present a danger for witches dealing with the Fey who travel to the Otherworld in any context. Fairies are well known for taking human food, both the substance and the essence of it, but a quick glance at Celtic folklore shows a clear prohibition against humans eating the food of Fairy. As the above quote from Childe Rowland illustrates, to eat fairy food is to be trapped in Fairy; we see the same sentiment related by Lady Wilde in a story of a girl brought to a fairy banquet who was warned by another captive: *'Eat no food, and drink no wine, or you will never see your home again.'* And yet in other cases to refuse Fairy food carries heavy consequences. So, how then is a person to know when it is safe to eat and when it is dangerous?

In the *Echtra Condla* we see the Fairy woman who comes to woo Connla away from mortal earth giving him an apple; it becomes his only food and no matter how much he eats, the apple remains whole (Daimler, 2017). After a month of this the Fairy woman returns and takes Connla back with her into Fairy. In some versions of the popular Fairy Midwife stories the midwife is offered food after she refuses to stay with the fairies, but a new mother by the fire, who is herself a human captive, advises the midwife not to eat or drink anything or she won't be able to leave (Ballard, 1991). Similarly, Yeats relates a tale of a stolen bride whose groom tracks her down with the group of fairies who have taken her; she directs him away from offers of food and drink to play cards instead so that he will not also be taken (Yeats, 1902). The idea seems to be that to consume food in Fairy binds a person to Fairy either by changing their nature and making them part of Fairy or by binding some essential part of the person to Fairy. One person from Sligo in 1909 described it thus: *'Once they take you and you taste food in their palace you cannot come back. You are changed to one of them, and live with them forever'* (Evans-Wentz, 1911).

Yet this is not a hard and fast rule and we do also see cases where a person is offered or given food and walks away unharmed. In one anecdote, a pair of men was walking and heard fairies inside a sí churning butter; they wished aloud for a drink of the buttermilk and to their surprise it was given to them. One took it and the other refused; the one who refused had bad luck afterwards (Bruford, 1991). Thomas in Thomas the Rhymer is paid by the Fairy Queen with an apple that he eats and which gives him the ability to speak truly, but the apple does not bind him to Fairy, he is returned to mortal earth after his service is done (Acland, 1997). The difference may be that the men were given food they asked for and Thomas is explicitly given the apple as payment, in exchange for his service to the Queen for seven years. In the same way we see Isobel Gowdie, a Scottish witch who dealt with the Queen of Elphame, saying that the Queen gave her meat to eat although Isobel was not taken into Fairy but remained on earth. The normal rules of food may not apply when that food is given as part of a clear exchange or payment of a debt owed by the fairy or for services rendered. It may be unwise more generally to refuse gifts from the Queen of Fairy, and this includes food; indeed we see the Fairy Queens and also Fairy Kings, like Finnbheara, offering food to mortals with no apparent consequences to the mortals. In these cases the food seems to be a token of friendship or favour. The Good People are also known to give food as gifts, in which case no debt would be accrued and the person would not be bound in any way (Gwyndaf, 1991).

There are some exceptions to this of course, as we see with the goblin fruit, for example, in the Goblin Market which is paid for by the human but is nonetheless a death sentence. In that case we are dealing with the Unseelie Court and it may be that they do not follow the more polite rules of the Seelie Court on this subject, perhaps all food from their hands is dangerous. Or it may be that the person is aware of what they are buying when they buy it, given the fruits' dangerous reputation.

In most of the stories where the food is a kind of trap it is offered as part of hospitality or offered to the person when they have done nothing to pay for it. It is simply offered and taken, usually in a social context. It is also offered, most often, when the person is either in Fairy or in the company of a larger group of fairies, indicating that this may also be a factor. It should be remembered as Hartland explains: '*Almost all over the earth the rite of hospitality has been held to confer obligations on its recipient, and to unite him by special ties to the giver'* (Hartland, 1891). This may be in part why when we give food to the fairies it must not be given directly but must be left for them or given separately – as we see in Yeats's recounting of a woman of the Sí who joined a family for a meal but insisted on being served alone in a different room. They will steal food from humans and they will take food that is given if it is not given in a way that would put them under obligation to us. When in fairy, or dealing with fairies, we should be cautious about joining in communal meals or taking food in any context where we might inadvertently put ourselves in their debt or else find that we have accepted a place among Themselves without realizing it. In the stories where the food is not dangerous to take, the circumstances are generally different: the person has asked for food, the person was owed a debt by the fairy, or the person was explicitly in service to a fairy monarch. So, it would seem that like so many other things on this subject it is neither simple nor clear cut, that there are some cases when eating fairy food is dangerous and others where it is not.

If you ever find yourself in a situation involving fairy food, I'd suggest remembering that it's unwise to take what isn't owed to you.

An Dara Sealladh – The Second Sight

I have always seen spirits and Otherworldly beings as far back as I can remember.

The Irish call it an Dara Sealladh, the Second Sight, the ability to see both what will come to pass and spirits in our world. Seeing through fairy glamour, perceiving what is around us all the time from the Fey folk to ghosts; these are some aspects of the Second Sight.

Some people are born with it and some people are given the ability through various means including through ritual and from the fairies themselves. The stories of midwives borrowed by fairies often involve the use of an ointment that is put on the baby's eyes to grant it this special sight, for example, and a woman named Elspeth who was tried for witchcraft in Scotland claimed to have been given a ritual by two fairy men that granted her the Second Sight (Henderson & Cowan, 2001). It is also possible to gain the Second Sight or something similar to it with the aid of an item, such as Biddy Early's blue glass bottle or the Brahan Seer's holed stone. Rev. Robert Kirk in the seventeenth century claimed that the Sight was more common in men, although I believe it is actually evenly distributed between the genders.

If you have or acquire the Second Sight you must always be cautious with it. It is not a carte blanche to act on, or even respond to, everything you see. One of the challenges of having the Sight is often keeping silent when you see things. It is not uncommon for those with this ability to be told or otherwise know that they should not speak first to any fairy they see but should wait until the fairy speaks to them, as to do otherwise may cause offense or anger. The Fey folk guard their privacy fiercely and do not like people who are able to see through their illusions pointing that out to others.

You do not, of course, need the Second Sight to see fairies – they can choose whether or not a person can see them at any point. The Sight itself is as much a curse as a blessing and it is a difficult thing to live with. You are seeing things which other people cannot see and that marks you as different from other people, and that will inevitably make other people uncomfortable. It is worth considering that before you rush out and make any effort to gain the Second Sight. Life may well be easier without it.

When I was about five years old my room was on the second floor of our house in the front; there was a street light across the road and at night the light would shine in and cast shadows on my walls. Shining through the branches of the oaks outside, the shadows would crawl across my walls, moving in the wind, dark jagged mouths and claws and fingers. I knew they were only shadows but they terrified me and I would lie awake at night crying and afraid. On those nights when I was most afraid a woman of Fairy would come to me and comfort me, and she taught me three very valuable lessons: not to fear shadows; that my Sight could be a comfort as much as a burden; and that we can have connections and friends among the Other Crowd.

The Reality of Dreams

Dreaming is a far more important thing than many people credit it as being, yet it is also something that is widely misunderstood even in paganism. We dream, and after waking we seek meaning in our dreams. We look for interpretations, we try to decode symbols, we puzzle out each incident and occurrence, every word and conversation, seeking deeper meanings either from our subconscious or from higher powers using our sleeping mind to speak to us. And yet, at least from a Western perspective, this idea of decoding dreams is largely new, a filter that comes to our culture from modern psychology. There was a time before when dreams were seen as their own reality, and what happened in dreams was given the same weight and significance as what happened in the waking world.

In Old Irish the word *aislinge* means both dream and vision, and it used to be that the two concepts in most cultures – pagan and Christian – were not as sharply divided as we might find them viewed today. A dream and a vision were two possible terms for the same experience, and both were things that occurred when the spirit went somewhere or communicated with something while the body slept. In records we have of visionary experiences, often the person relates being taken somewhere and directly seeing or participating in events which may be portentous or divine (in the case of Christian visions) or may involve the person being taken to Otherworlds (in the case of pagan dreams and later the dreams of the common people). The common thread that unites these narratives is the idea that what was seen and experienced was real and valid on its own merits and that this reality was tangible, i.e. it could have physical effects in the waking world. People might correctly predict an event based on what was seen in a dream-vision or they might wake with a physical token of their nighttime experiences, be that marks on their body or an actual item brought back from their wanderings.[2]

It was not uncommon for a person, while dreaming, to travel to Fairy or to be contacted by Otherworldly spirits, or even for a person's spirit to travel out in this world. There was an implicit belief that what occurred to and with us while we slept was just as real as what occurred while we were awake. We find stories in mythology like the Aislinge Oenguso of a woman who appears to the deity Oengus at night while he dreams but has a noticeable physical effect on him and who has an unquestionable reality. In folklore there are stories of people who might spend years in the Otherworld while only moments passed here and they appeared to onlookers to be sleeping or in a trance. In one such story a man who seemed to sleep for a few minutes in a field experienced several years living in Fairy, enjoying a pleasant time there until he broke a taboo and was banished, finding himself sent back to the time and place he left. We also have stories of medieval witches who would be seen sleeping in their beds while they were simultaneously seen by other people elsewhere awake and active. It seemed that the soul was as busy at night as it had been during the day, the only difference being whether it made use of the body or not.

The erosion of the value of dreaming would eventually begin with Christianity's attempt to control the powerful messages gained through dreams. This was done by creating a hierarchy wherein ecclesiastical dreams and visions were direct connections to God but the dreams and visions of the common people were delusions relegated to vulgar spirits, demons, and witches. Dreaming became a dangerous thing during the witchcraft persecutions; dreams were seen as a time when we could be opened up to unsavoury influences and attacks, and when we ourselves might be out harming others and unable to offer any defence if accused of doing so. We see dreaming as a double-edged sword, a weapon of the Church for control and an unsafe activity of those outside Church bounds. Dreaming slowly lost its sacredness entirely on the altar of rational thought and became nothing more than another aspect of the mind to be dissected. This desacralization of dreaming began the descent of the dream from something profound to something almost meaningless and difficult to interpret, an individual language which only the dreamer spoke, a puzzle to be solved.

If we look at dreams and dreaming we might perhaps find that it is not dreams that have changed but only our own understanding of them. Our culture has trained us now to see dreams as trivial things, as the mind talking to itself and as the body's response to imbalance. Dreams can be a way for our mind to talk to itself and work out problems, of course, however, dreams are complex and diverse and sometimes they are a way for our soul to connect or move outwards. Certainly not all dreams are journeys Elsewhere, but sleep is still the liminal gateway for our soul to travel out that it has always been. Dreams are still an opening for different spirits to communicate with us, a time when our minds are still and receptive in ways they often are not while we are awake. This idea of communication with spirits during dreams is very old and something we see in folklore with everything from ancestors to landspirits to the Good People to Gods.

I have always personally believed in the reality of dreaming, and I think there is value in other people evaluating this concept more generally, especially within this spirituality. Dreams are more than just stories our minds tell ourselves while we sleep, at least sometimes. Sometimes what we dream is as real as what we do in our waking life, and that matters because it means that we need to take dreaming a lot more seriously. It can be a gateway to Fairy, and other worlds besides, and what we do there can impact us here. We need to remember to protect ourselves, and that the same rules apply for safe travel in dreams as in meditations or spirit journeys. Because if dreams are real then we can be hurt in them, we can swear oaths in them, we can make mistakes in them that follow us back here; and we can earn blessings as well (it's not all bad after all).

I mention this because there can be a tendency to treat dreams in a lackadaisical fashion and overall less seriously than other types of spiritual experience, but we should remember that dreams have a reality and substance. If possible, it is best to try to have some control within a dream but if not at least try to always keep track of what has occurred in dreams, especially if the dreams seemed to have an Otherworldly setting or theme. Details like conversations, symbols, and actions should be noted as they can be important in our waking life. It is possible as I mentioned to take an oath in a dream and that would be viewed as just as binding as if you had made it while awake. You can also be taught or given valuable information in dreams that would be useful in waking life and you may find yourself connecting to or establishing friendships with fairy beings in dreams. Certain types of spirit have been known to reach out to people in dreams and these include land spirits and a person's fetch. I have also had experiences in dreams that involved the Wild Hunt and fairy beings I was allied with.

I have found that much of the time with dreaming I am not the one choosing to go there but rather that I am being brought there or otherwise interacted with. I believe that when we are sleeping our spirits are more open to contact than we may be while we are awake and this may be why contact occurs as it does in our sleep. If you are having unwanted dreams or dream interactions there are ways to protect yourself while sleeping, including some charms and prayers. You can use elder, either the wood or the berries, to ward off evil influences and protect yourself while sleeping, for example. You can also place iron over or under your bed, or hang Saint John's Wort[3] above it. Before sleep this charm, which has been modified from a more Christian[4] one from the *Carmina Gadelica*, could be said (or any similar one):

> *I am placing my soul and my body*
> *In your sanctuary this night, O Gods,*
> *In your sanctuary, O ancestors,*
> *In your sanctuary, O kindly spirits who protect me,*
> *The you who would defend my cause,*
> *Who will not turn your backs upon me.*
> *You, Gods, who are fair and just,*
> *You, ancestors, who live even in death,*
> *You, Spirits of power,*
> *Keep me this night from harm;*
> *The Three who would protect me*
> *Keep me this night and always.*

Waking up after an intense Otherworldly dream experience can be both disorienting and sometimes jarring. Unlike regular dreams which may seem insubstantial or unreal, these dreams are often particularly intense, real in their emotions and sensations, and detailed. In other words, one can usually distinguish them because they don't feel at all like other dreams but seem exactly like a waking experience. They can also involve long periods of time that do not line up with the amount of time that has passed in our world. To give you an idea of what this is like there is an example from folklore in which a man fell asleep out in a field and went to Fairy where he lived for several years, experiencing each day in an Otherworldly city and was only returned when he broke a prohibition there about not touching the water in a specific fountain; upon returning he woke to find that mere minutes had passed here (Briggs, 1976). I have been through something like this where I felt as if several months had passed in the Otherworld while I was there in a dream, and this included all the usual daily things like eating, sleeping there, walking around, and such, yet woke up here to find out that very little time had passed. It is a good idea after this sort of thing to thoroughly ground yourself and work to re-orient to the here-and-now in this world. Time is a more fluid thing than we like to believe it is and, particularly, the time shifts between worlds are unpredictable and jarring to deal with. Don't assume this is any less true in dreams.

Because dreams can be an important source for personal gnosis I have established a habit of writing my dreams down as soon as possible after I wake up. I keep a special journal for this purpose because it's an excellent resource, not only to keep track of what I am getting but also to keep notes on things that I've verified or information I've gathered about something given to me in a dream. One weakness of dreams as a means of connecting to Fairy is that our dreaming mind is a different sort of thing than our waking one and even after all these years of using this as a method, I still find that the most significant of dream experiences can slip away into the ether of the forgotten after a few hours of wakefulness. While I have certainly had a few dream experiences that stayed with me so sharply that even now I can recall them as if they just happened, most others quickly fade. Writing everything down soon after waking up is a great way to safeguard the knowledge gained from them.

Trance
People who were known to have a strong connection to the Gentry were also known to fall into trances where they would remain conscious and could relay information to others but where they might also fall out of external contact with our world for hours

or days at a time. These trances are neither a dreaming state, precisely, nor are they what we in modern terms understand as meditation or spiritual journeys. The person is still conscious and aware of what is going on around them in many cases and is able to respond to people talking to them. People in these trances in anecdotal evidence could engage in conversations and answer questions about what they were seeing or describe Fairy or fairy people but were also clearly not all 'here' as it were.

We may perhaps define two types of trance: one where the person goes into a trance to see or speak to fairies and another where they go into a trance to send their spirit out to interact with beings Elsewhere while remaining conscious here.

The first type of trance seems to occur with people who are inclined to see and interact with fairies anyway, but who require some concentration to do so; those who were not born with the Second Sight but learned it may need to go into at least a light trance to use it, for example. In this type of trance the person is making an intentional effort or focusing in order connect to Fairy or fairy beings.

In the second type of trance the person is still at least somewhat conscious here and able to respond to questions but is clearly not entirely 'here'. The spirit seems to be divided in a way so that part of it is sent outwards into Fairy while the other part remains here, something similar to what occurs during journeywork but with a more obvious and sharp division and with consciousness on both sides. This type of trance is arguably harder for people to learn to do if they are not naturally prone to it. We see it discussed in anecdotes in the Fairy Faith in Celtic Countries as a common feature of people who have a strong connection to the Good People or can communicate with them. Such people were often thought to be a little bit mad and this kind of trance can be described as a kind of fit, and may not always be voluntary.

Trance is along the lines of the more classic examples of what the Irish call being 'away with the fairies', that is where a part of yourself is not present but is Elsewhere but enough of you remains here that you can still function. Operating with a divided consciousness is not easy and cannot be easily hidden, so people around you will notice that you are not acting like yourself. It's harder to focus on things here and to pay attention to tasks at hand. There are, however, advantages to this method particularly because you can communicate with both people of the Otherworld and people of the mortal world at the same time. There are points where this is helpful and even necessary.

Journeying to the Otherworld

There will be different opinions on the ideas of spiritual journeying and what follows are simply my own personal views. These are based on my experiences and things I've noted based on other people's stories and shared experiences, but as usual I encourage people to consider other viewpoints and opinions as well. I am not trying to offer this as a definitive guide to the subject but rather want to share how I think about this as I practise it.

I believe there are two distinct and different types of spiritual work that involve a person going into a fuller type of trance than what we have just discussed. The first are meditations where a person goes into a trance state and stays within their own mind but connects to something outside themselves. The second is where a person goes into the same sort of trance and journeys out in spirit to other places. The main way I use to tell the difference is the amount of control you have in the experience to influence your surroundings and what is happening. In both of these full trances a person would sit or lie down comfortably, close their eyes, and go through a basic process to enter the trance, after which they may find it hard or impossible to interact with the outside world without breaking the trance.

Generally speaking, when you are in a meditative state you can easily shift and change your surroundings and affect the

167

experience you are having. If you are in your own head, so to speak, and you want flowers to grow, or a gazebo to appear, or specific animals, then that will happen. You control what is going on. Also in these types of meditation you are more likely to hear what you want to hear or see what you expect. That is not to discount the value of the experience or the messages you may receive; they are still important even if they are in your head. As a certain well-known movie notes, *'just because it's happening in your head doesn't mean it isn't real'*. I am only pointing out that it is different than those experiences that happen outside the mind, and I would suggest somewhat safer.

Journeys, in contrast, are those trances where a portion of the spirit is sent out Elsewhere and leaves the body. Journeys are not as safe because we have less inherent control of the experience. If you find yourself in the middle of a rain storm you can't make the rain stop or make a shelter suddenly appear or anything like that. Fairy, like our world, has its own rules to follow and that includes limits in what we can and can't do there. After all if we could effectively have omnipotent control over the Otherworld then we would be Gods there and the beings who exist there would have a far different relationship to us. It is true that Fairy has more magic than mortal earth does and more things are possible there – you can learn to shapeshift and influence things – but absolute and immediate control of the world around you, no. One way that I often use to test whether I am having a meditative experience or a journey experience is to make a simple trial of seeing what I can influence around me: if I can change the colours of the flowers or create something from nothing then I tend to think meditation (i.e. inside my own head); if I can't make my external environment do what I want with some focused thought then I tend to think journey. Unexpected things happen in journeys and you can meet a whole array of beings you may not even know exist before you meet them. You will see some very strange things and should be prepared for interactions that, like those in the mortal world, can be unpredictable.

Both meditations and journeys can be done while following a script, usually spoken by another person, to have a specific experience. In my last book I included a couple of such scripted meditations/journeys, so I won't repeat them here but they are good ways to have a structured in and out and a clearly defined experience while there. Meditations and journeys can also be done without guidance, simply by going to wherever you want to go. I might suggest that visiting Fairy within the mind represents visiting an echo or inner connection to the actual Otherworld in contrast to the type of visiting done in journeying. Both have value in different ways and neither is necessarily better or worse than the other.

For some people journeying is done very easily with little or no preparation work or external aids; for others things like drumming, singing, chanting or herbs can be used to aid in the process. There are even some kinds of moving trance and meditation that are done using dance or walking. Since there is no one right way with this you need to find what works best for you and not worry about what other people do. If dance is what gets you outside yourself – or inside as the case may be – then go with that. If drumming is what works for you then invest in some good drum music. If you are the type who can drop off into trance under any circumstances you actually have the harder road in my experience because you will have to teach yourself not to go into trance unless you want to and that can be more difficult than learning how to go into a trance through one method. But self-control is important and however you do it, easy or hard, you should be in control going in and out.

As with dreams, I keep a journal to record my meditations and journeys. I find this can be very helpful especially in keeping track of experiences I have had over the years with beings I have known for a long period of time. I have found these methods are the most essential for me in nurturing friendships and building allies among Otherworldly beings over the long term and writing down each individual experience is an important tool in that process because it lets me go back over things that may have happened more than a decade ago and refresh myself on the details. This has been particularly helpful in cases where I was given advice to do or not do something, or where I made an agreement and years later need to be sure of the exact wording.

Dreams, trance, and journeywork are complex topics but ones that are essential to Fairy witchcraft. I have found that over the years they have played key roles in my practice and I believe that anyone on this path will gain from employing them. They are also more personal than some others and as such they are something that, like our allies and friends among the Others, we must find for ourselves. There are good books out there to help guide us along the way but I have also gained a lot from experimenting and learning through trial and error what did and didn't work for me. I found out that with guided meditations I rarely go where I'm being guided but almost always inevitably wander off somewhere else, and I learned to accept that it was okay. With journeying I found out that I can trance easily while walking but not dancing, that herbs and other substances make it harder not easier for me to connect, and that otherwise I can go out fairly easily with very little formal structure. I have friends, in contrast, who do very well using things like Damiana or Mugwort (for example) to trance or who journey best to drumming, or who connect best with guided meditations. None of these is better than the others and none of us is superior in what or how we do things. Ultimately all that matters is that we do them and we do what works for us to connect to those things and beings outside ourselves we are seeking.

Endnotes

1. I realize that there is an argument for these as psychosomatic and honestly I'm not going to get into that here. If you

believe that the mind is producing these marks in line with experiences you are having then I would argue that they are still 'real' experiences in some sense. You can of course also argue for the object, although unprovable, reality of these same experiences. In either case the experience is happening and the physical mark is also appearing, and that should be considered.

2. I'm not going to address here the various scientific attempts to explain these phenomena.

3. Saint John's Wort is most effective when it is gathered on Midsummer; if possible you should try to at least obtain yours on this date if not harvest it then. It is believed that the herb will have the greatest power when it is picked at the height of the sun's course. St. John's Wort can also be burned on Midsummer for protection and blessing.

4. I have modified this charm based on my own personal beliefs so that it is calling on powers that I personally deal with and am comfortable calling in. Other people may feel differently. The original charm from the CG is 'Sleeping Prayer 29':

> I am placing my soul and my body
> On Thy sanctuary this night, O God,
> On Thy sanctuary, O Jesus Christ,
> On Thy sanctuary, O Spirit of perfect truth,
> The Three who would defend my cause,
> Nor turn Their backs upon me.
> Thou, Father, who art kind and just,
> Thou, Son, who didst overcome death,
> Thou, Holy Spirit of power,
> Be keeping me this night from harm;
> The Three who would justify me
> Keeping me this night and always.

Chapter 7

Shifting Shape and Glamour

I slept not since the Conquest,
Till then I never waked,
Till the rougish boy of love where I lay
Me found and stript me naked.

There are a certain set of skills that witches have been known in folklore to have used and which we today may try to emulate in our own ways. Beyond things we may have already discussed these include different methods of shape-shifting and that fairy-staple of glamour. I have found that these can be done in various forms but also that they tend to be less widely discussed or accepted among modern witchcraft at large.

I'm not sure why this is, unless these two particular skills fall into areas that people in our modern times prefer to disbelieve. I can remember, for example, when the movie 'The Craft' came out in the 1990s. I remember the way that some people mocked the scene where one of the characters used magic to change her friends' perception of first her eye colour and then her hair colour. I liked that scene myself because it was clearly an example of glamour by causing people to perceive something differently than it actually is. There are limits to this ability of course, especially when used by humans – I don't know about a brunette making herself look like a platinum blonde for example – but it definitely can be done and we see it in both Irish folklore among the fairies and Norse magic as practised by seidhr workers. In the same way, shape-shifting may not be the movie example of the person literally turning into a wolf, or even the folklore example of the witch changing to a physical hare, but that doesn't mean that shifting one's shape can't be done magically specifically in meditations and journeys.

Shape-shifting Witches

I mentioned in the last chapter than one way I use to differentiate between a meditation and a journey is how much control I have over my external environment in the experience, well shape-shifting – indeed influencing the self more generally – is an exception to that. There are things you can do in journeys and in Fairy that you cannot do here and that doesn't mean you aren't actually in Fairy. I said the Otherworld has rules and it does, but not all those rules are the same as the ones we have here. While it's true that you can't control what's outside yourself, you do have much more control over yourself, or I should probably say your self. And that means you can change your own appearance and you can change your shape. I have found that shape-shifting, especially in journeywork, is a very valuable skill.

One of the things that witches in Ireland and Scotland were known for was shape-shifting, particularly into the form of hares, although some other shapes were noted in folklore as well including weasels, cats and even hedgehogs; all of these are also shapes taken on by fairies. From a modern perspective there is a tendency to interpret these stories literally, and indeed some of them clearly indicate a literal transformation, such as we see in the 'Witch and Hare'[1] where a witch takes the form of a hare and is pursued into a building where she regains her human form. However, many are vaguer and could be interpreted as a practice of mental projection into an animal, rather than the human witch physically transforming into the shape of one.[2] It may also be that these stories represent a projection of the witch's spirit which would appear as an animal, rather than a literal animal. Such shape-shifting appears to have served a variety of purposes from allowing the witch to travel abroad unnoticed, to casting magic, to theft of other people's property. It was also done simply for the joy of changing form and experiencing being other than human, as we can see in an account from 1673 where a Scottish witch talked about singing while her companions *'danced in several shapes, first of a hare then of their own then of a cat, sometimes a mouse and several other shapes'* (Wilby, 2005, p. 89). For modern witches who study traditional practices or who are interested in some of the skills attributed to historic witches this shape-shifting is certainly worth consideration, particularly for that last reason I mentioned.

Possibly the most common form witches were known to take when shapeshifting was of the hare and we have a variety of stories that mention witches assuming this shape, often to steal milk from cows. As Lady Wilde tells us: *'Hares are considered unlucky, as the witches constantly assume their form in order to gain entrance to a field where they can bewitch the cattle'* (Wilde, 1888). In her confession while on trial for witchcraft in Scotland, Isobel Gowdie claimed to take the form of a hare. While it was considered unlucky to see a hare, especially one that was acting unnaturally, it was also considered very unlucky to kill one, because if it was in fact a witch or fairy shape-changed there was no telling what ill would come from killing it.

Cats are also associated with witches and the Cat Sí especially, a type of large black fairy cat with a white spot on its chest. These cats are generally seen as malevolent and they may be true fairies or in some cases they may actually be shape-changed witches. In particular the witch was believed to be able to transform into a cat nine times, but legend says on the ninth time the witch would have to remain a cat forever (Old Farmer's Almanac, 2012). Jane Manning has a lovely children's book called *Cat Nights* based on this legend that both of my girls love, about a young witch who has adventures each night as a cat for eight nights and then has to decide if she wants to stay a person or transform one last time. One source mentions August 17th in connection to the Cat Sí as transformed witches, and says that it was on this night that a witch might make the ninth transformation into permanent cat form (Old Farmer's Almanac, 2012). Besides this more explicit association between witches, fairies and cats, all together witches were also associated with taking on cat forms separate from the folklore around the Cat Sí. For example, in the Scottish witchcraft trial records, accused witch Marie Lamont, in 1662, said that she and several other local witches took the form of cats in order to join together and practise magic and in that form three of them snuck into another woman's home and stole some fish[3] (Wilby, 2005). In another account an eye witness claimed to have seen a group of a dozen cats shape-shift into men and women who the person said were a mix of witches and the dead (Henderson & Cowan, 2007).

Looking at folklore sources and witchcraft trials we might surmise this was a type of mental or trance practice, where the person learned how to project their spirit out into either an existing form or into the image of an animal (literal or figurative). Claude Lecouteux in his book *Witches, Werewolves, and Fairies: Shapeshifters and Astral Doubles in the Middle Ages* discusses at length such a practice, wherein the witch appeared to be sleeping but the witch's spirit was wandering abroad, sometimes in human form, sometimes not. During these nocturnal expeditions the witch might gather information, meet with other witches or spirits, work magic, or simply wander freely.

From a modern perspective there is no reason to think witches can't still engage in this type of trance practice, although it may be easier, and easier on a person's ethics, to learn how to project one's spirit out in animal form rather than learn how to take over another being's physical form. This would not be a basic or beginner skill but something to look at doing once you are fairly comfortable with the basics of sending your spirit out from your body safely (and returning safely), spiritual journeying in general, and how to handle any emergencies that might come up while in a human form. This is important because trying any of that in a new shape is going to be harder and inherently have more risk attached to it, and you need to be confident that if anything goes wrong you know what to do to fix it.

Looking at one of the only existing chants we have today from a historic witch, Isobel Gowdie, who claimed to deal with both the Devil and the Queen of Elfhame, we see the ambiguous nature of the practice. This template also gives us a good idea of what we might want to base a structure for such a chant on as well. Some people may not see the value in this sort of thing but for a practice like this having a set ritual approach to it can add a layer of safety by providing the mind with a key, if you will, to going into and out of the shape.

Isobel claimed during her trial that to go into the form of a hare she would chant:

> *I shall go into a hare,*
> *With sorrow and such and much care;*
> *And I shall go in the Devil's name,*
> *Ay while I come home again.*

And to return again to her own form she would say:

> *Hare, hare, God send you care.*
> *I am in a hare's likeness now,*
> *But I shall be in a woman's likeness even now.*

Similarly she had chants to assume the form of a cat or crow, as follows:

> *I shall go into a cat*
> *With sorrow and such and a black shot;*
> *And I shall go in the Devil's name,*
> *Ay while I come home again*

And:

> *I shall go into a crow*
> *With sorrow and such and a black ground;*
> *And I shall go in the Devil's name,*
> *Ay while I come home again*[4]

To return from these forms the same chant would be used as for the hare except modified as appropriate for the animal shape being assumed. For myself, as I do not have anything to do with the Devil, I have modified these chants and substituted the name of the Fairy Queen I honour; you can easily in my experience use whatever name as a higher power that you prefer to call on, although I'd recommend experimenting to see what you get the best results with. You can also, of course, modify this for any other animal you'd like.

Keep in mind though that it was a dangerous practice that risked injury to the person, and the many folktales of witches who were harmed in animal form and then had the same injuries in their human forms show this. While we can, of course, interpret this as another indication of literal transformation we could also view this as a way in which the mind influences the body; the mind or spirit being injured in one form convinces the physical body it was also injured. From a metaphysical perspective this holds with the principle that what happens to us Elsewhere affects us here, while from a psychological perspective it reflects the power of the mind to influence the physical body. Many of us may be familiar with the more positive aspects of this which we see in things like placebos healing people because people believe they will, but as with everything there is another side of that as well; what we believe hurts us can indeed hurt us. For those of us in a modern context who choose to practise shape-shifting it is best to remember that injuries can happen and to be careful with this and like journeying more generally, don't take it too lightly.

Shape-shifting is a skill that witches have claimed and has been claimed of them for a long time. It is also something that modern witches can, through different means, still practise today. We have focused here on one potential method for witches to shape-shift, as a suggestion for those who are looking for either more advanced topics to study or new skill sets to branch into. As with so many things done by the traditional witches of the past though, this was not a safe thing and it came with no guarantees. Keep that in mind if you do decide to study this further.

I have found shifting shape in meditations and journeys to be both enjoyable and educational. The more you practise the skill the easier it gets and you will probably find, as I have, that you have favourite forms to take on and others that you don't like as much. For those who want to begin practising shape-shifting I recommend initially focusing on adjusting your human form in small ways, and then bigger ways until you feel as if you have a good grasp of what it means to control your form as a spirit projection. Then I might look at starting with animals that are close to your form to start or that you feel a strong kinship to – so perhaps jumping right into a bird form which will inherently be more difficult isn't the best idea, but something like a hare or cat would be better. Keep in mind that as with any other skill, not everyone may necessarily be good at shape-shifting and that's okay. I mention it here because it's something I enjoy doing and it's a classic skill of traditional witches that I feel deserves to be brought forward, but it's not in any way a requirement.

Glamour

Just as we have the practice of shape-shifting as a means by which the form, or at the very least the spirit form, is transformed and changed into something else we also have the practice of glamour. It is something that we see attributed to both fairies and witches and just like shape-shifting is a skill that bridges between the two beings. Glamour is also another skill, like shape-shifting, that is often underrated or ignored today but in which I find immense value.

At its most basic, glamour simply means 'enchantment, magic' but in the context of fairies and witches it tends to be used specifically to mean a type of magic that fools the senses. As Briggs explains it:

> *Originally a Scottish word, a variation of 'gramarye' or 'glaumerie'.*
> *We find it in undoubted use first in the 18th century ... It generally*
> *signified a mesmerism or enchantment cast over the sense, so that*
> *things were perceived or not perceived as the enchanter wished. ...*
> *[W]itches and, above all, the fairies had this power ...*
> (Briggs, 1976, p. 191)

To understand glamour as witches can use it, I think we need to better understand glamour as it's used by the Good People. It is glamour that fairies used to make a humble cave seem like a palace, or a collection of flotsam and jetsam seem a feast, or a handful of withered leaves appear to be gold coins. This kind of magic is never done capriciously but always with a purpose, often to kidnap a desired person or sometimes to get a person to do what the fairies wanted (Henderson & Cowan, 2007). Glamour does more than just fool the eyes when used by the fairies, it fools all the senses so that a person sees, feels, tastes, even smells the illusion as reality.

I personally think that glamour is also at least partially what allows the Fey folk to pass invisibly, as they use it to blind the senses or to make humans see only what they expect to see. And I might surmise that in some cases it is also this magic that can make them seem small when they are large or otherwise distort their appearance in order to manipulate the viewer. This is supported by some accounts from folklore and anecdotal evidence. For example, interviewing a man in Sligo one hundred years ago W. Y. Evans Wentz was told:

> *They are able to appear in different forms. One once appeared to me and seemed only four feet high, and stoutly built. He said, 'I am bigger than I appear to you now. We can make the old young, the big small, the small big.'*
> (Wentz, 1911)

We could certainly take this more literally as an ability by the fairies to physically effect these changes but we can also read this passage as an affirmation of the power of glamour, which causes the person's senses to be fooled into perceiving things as they are not. In many stories this may be the case, although it is also worth noting that actual shape-shifting (as previously discussed) does occur. When the Fairy Queen puts Tam Lin through his series of forms trying to get Janet to release him in the ballad of Tam Lin we may want to see this as glamour, but when the Fairy Queen puts Elph Irving through the transformations to get his sister to release him in the 'Faerie Oak of Corriewater', the sister is immolated when she loses her nerve and tries to drop her brother in the form of a fire.

Glamour is not without its weaknesses. People with second sight can see through glamour, or maybe we should say can see the reality beneath the illusion. There are also charms like a four leaf clover or peering through a holed stone that allow a person to see past glamour. The fairies themselves have an ointment that can be applied to the eyes which grants the ability to see truly and we see it mentioned in many stories, often involving a child who is born in Fairy of a union between a mortal and one of the Good People. Such a child apparently needs this ointment to see around the glamour that disguises most fairy activities, but such vision is guarded carefully. Should a mortal not meant to have the vision end up with it and give themselves away they will either be blinded or struck mute (Henderson & Cowan, 2007).

Humans using glamour generally do not do so as thoroughly as the Fey folk; human glamour in stories seems to focus on vision more than anything else. Looking to the Norse we can find an example of this in Eyrbyggja Saga were a woman named Katla who practises magic (seidhr) uses her skill to protect her son from men trying to kill him by deceiving their sight. The men come three times searching for her son and each time she makes them see him as something else including a distaff, goat, and boar.[5]

I have been using glamour for a long time and find it to be a useful tool, although not something that is often needed. I can't deny when I was younger I probably misused it because I was young and I could. I don't necessarily encourage other people to use glamour recklessly or for foolish reasons,[6] but it can be used in important situations, like helping to keep you safe by diverting attention away from you when needed. In my own experience glamour works best when we focus on slight pushes to other people's perception. I mentioned earlier the example from the movie 'The Craft' where one character changed people's perceptions of her eye colour and that is about in line with how I think glamour can be used in the modern world. And yes I am serious. I have had the most luck with it in this context by subtly altering people's perceptions, so that they don't realize I am there or don't see something I prefer to go unnoticed, like a bad hair day. I've also used it to draw attention to things about myself, so it works both ways.

When I use glamour I do so by focusing my own energy and attention on what I want other people to see, or not see as the case may be. I keep my attention on what I am trying to project for as long as I need to project it. You also have to follow through by acting confidently in line with what you want people to perceive. Confidence is an important aspect of glamour.

Shape-shifting and glamour are old skills that have fallen out of mainstream practice in modern witchcraft, yet they still have their uses. They are methods that we can teach ourselves after studying the folklore and the practices of traditional witches and cunningfolk and then implement in our own lives. When we go out in spiritual journeys or meditations we can experience the joy of shifting our shape into something new; when we are walking in our daily life we can use glamour to influence how people perceive our appearance. No matter how old school these things seem they have not lost any of their value to us, and for those of us on a Fairy path studying them can also bring us closer to understanding the Fey folk.

Endnotes

1. The story of the Witch and the Hare, from Hartland's *English Fairy and Other Folk Tales*:

    An old witch, in days of yore, lived in this neighbourhood; and whenever she wanted money she would assume the shape of a hare, and would send out her grandson to tell a certain huntsman who lived hard by that he had seen a hare sitting at such a particular spot, for which he always received the reward of sixpence. After this deception had many times been practised, the dogs turned out, the hare pursued, often seen but never caught, a sportsman of the party began to suspect, in the language of the tradition, 'that the devil was in the dance,' and there would be no end to it. The matter was discussed, a justice consulted, and a clergyman to boot; and it was thought that, however clever the devil might be, law and church combined would be more than a match for him. It was therefore agreed that, as the boy was singularly regular in the hour at which he came to announce the sight of the hare, all should be in readiness for a start the instant such information was given: and a neighbour of the witch, nothing friendly to her, promised to let the parties know directly the old woman and her grandson left the cottage and went off together; the one to be hunted, and the other to set on the hunt. The news came, the hounds were unkennelled, and huntsmen and sportsmen set off with surprising speed. The witch, now a hare, and her little colleague in iniquity, did not expect so very speedy a turn out; so that the game was pursued at a desperate rate, and the boy, forgetting himself in a moment of alarm, was heard to exclaim: 'Run, Granny, run; run for your life!' At last the pursuers lost the hare, and she once more got safe into the cottage by a little hole in the door; not large enough to admit a hound in chase. The huntsman and all the squires with their train lent a hand to break open the door, yet could not do it till the parson and the justice came up; but as law and church were certainly designed to break through iniquity, even so did they now succeed in bursting the magic bonds that opposed them. Upstairs they all went. There they found the old hag bleeding, and covered with wounds, and still out of breath. She denied she was a hare, and railed at the whole party. 'Call up the hounds,' said the huntsman, 'and let us see what they take her to be; maybe we may yet have another hunt.'

On hearing this, the old woman cried quarter. The boy dropped on his knees, and begged hard for mercy, which was granted on condition of its being received together with a good whipping; and the huntsman, having long practised amongst the hounds, now tried his hand on other game.

2. For those of you who read Terry Pratchett, you'll be familiar with this concept as he writes about his witches doing it. It's what Granny Weatherwax does that they call 'borrowing'.

3. In several trial accounts, Scottish witches claimed to transform into shapes, including those of crows or rooks, for no other reason than to steal food (Wilby, 2005). It is worth remembering here that these witches where often, although not exclusively, poor and in need. For them the ability to go in animal form and gain extra food was probably more

valuable than many other kinds of magic.

4. The originals from Isobel's confession are as follows:
   I sail gae intill ane haire,
   With sorrow and sych and meikle care;
   And I sail gae in the Devillis nam.
   Ay quhill I com horn againe.

   Haire, haire, God send thee caire;
   I am in an hairis liknes just now;
   Bot I salbe in a womanis liknes ewin now.

   I sail gae intill a catt,
   With sorrow and sych and a blak shat;
   And I sail gae in the Devillis nam,
   Ay quhill I com hom againe.

   I sail gae intill a craw,
   With sorrow and sych and a blak thiaw;
   And I sail gae in the Devillis nam.
   Ay quhill I com hom againe.
   (Rogers, 1869)

5. Each time the men leave they realize they were tricked and return only to have Katla trick them again. The fourth time though they bring a magic-worker of their own who helps them defeat Katla's magic.

6. Before anyone judges me too harshly here I should probably say that, for example, I used glamour to get on casino playing floors when I was 17. Which isn't a sterling use of magic but didn't hurt anybody either.

Chapter 8

In Practice

I know more than Apollo,
For oft when he lies sleeping
I see the stars at mortal wars
In the wounded welkin weeping.

There's a quote I like a lot from the movie 'The Matrix': *'There's a difference between knowing the path and walking the path.'* When we read books, including this one, we are gaining knowledge of the path but it's not the same as walking it. Even reading about or hearing about shared experiences someone else has had are not the same as actually living those things in your own life, and what I'm talking about here is more than just going out under a full moon or dark sky and pouring out offerings or even learning the different methods of doing things. What I'm talking about here is really the way that walking the path changes you as you go along. Because actually living this spirituality does leave its mark on you and it changes you in ways that are subtle and not so subtle. You learn new ways to look at things and you also learn new ways to do things and slowly over time it changes who you are.

Reshaped Living

As I moved deeper into working with the beings of the Otherworld I hadn't expected the way that it would impact unexpected parts of my life. I suppose I assumed that as I learned and moved deeper into the work I was doing there would be a cost but it would be something straightforward like blood or physical effort; and there has been that too. But I didn't expect the way that Themselves would come in and start re-shaping my life in practical ways, including what I could eat and drink and things I could or could not do.

There's something really, deeply alienating in this, or at least I found it so. It's hard enough, to start with, being on a spiritual path that many people don't understand that is disconnected from mainstream modern paganism because of its emphasis on traditional folklore and beliefs. When you add in a variety of restrictions in how you have to live, particularly with diet for me as I already had a few food allergies going on, it ends up making a person feel very at odds with the rest of the world. I'm also a stubborn person and I fight hard against the urge to resist when I am told not to do things.

I can't eat most processed foods (think frozen dinners and dried fruits, for example) or breads, pasta, or cereal (because of additives I have issues with). Outside of that though I was good, and my preferred diet before was heavily weighted towards coffee, soda, and convenience foods. So, when the specific Good People who I deal with told me, about five years ago now, that I needed to change that entirely and focus on fresh fruits and vegetables, dairy, limited white meats and fish, nuts, drink water and fruit juice, limited seasoning and salt and cut out all caffeine, I was not thrilled. This represented a seismic shift for me, especially the caffeine.

Here's the thing though, about getting into this sort of spirituality. If you choose to do this kind of work then there's an understanding that you are agreeing to all the terms, including the ones that haven't been specified beforehand. And if you try to get around something they are emphasizing as important, often enough, they may give you a bit of time to toe the line voluntarily then they will step in and influence things themselves.

Case in point – the caffeine. I fully admit to being a coffee addict and I don't say that lightly. When the no caffeine edict came down I was not happy, and initially I really struggled with it. It took me years to cut out caffeinated soda, and then

I found myself stuck on coffee. Finally, I reluctantly switched to decaf. And then, I suppose predictably, I began drinking a half-dozen cups or more of decaf a day, defeating the entire purpose of it since decaf coffee does have some caffeine. So, one Bealtaine morning when I poured my usual cup and added the cream, the cream disappeared; stirring it revealed that the in-date, unspoiled cream had curdled and was massed in a lump at the bottom of the cup. Not to be daunted – or to take a hint – I poured a fresh cup and added milk. It curdled as soon as it hit the surface. And I admitted defeat. I didn't touch a cup of coffee for moths afterwards, although I still craved it. Eventually, with some negotiation, I reached a compromise that would allow me a limited amount of decaf a day but I found that the taste was unpleasant and stopped drinking it again.

Initially I had no frame of reference for any of this outside of my own personal gnosis, nothing except the knowledge that they wanted certain things done or not done. Finally though, I ran across this in a book by Yeats and it made me feel less unusual in what was being asked of me:

Those we speak of have for their friends the trooping fairies—the gay and sociable populace of raths and caves. ... The fairies are, of course, visible to them, and many a new-built house have they bid the owner pull down because it lay on the fairies' road. Lady Wilde thus describes one who lived in Innis Sark: — 'He never touched beer, spirits, or meat in all his life, but has lived entirely on bread, fruit and vegetables. A man who knew him thus describes him—"Winter and summer his dress is the same—merely a flannel shirt and coat. He will pay his share at a feast, but neither eats nor drinks of the food and drink set before him. He speaks no English, and never could be made to learn the English tongue, though he says it might be used with great effect to curse one's enemy. He holds a burial-ground sacred, and would not carry away so much as a leaf of ivy from a grave. And he maintains that the people are right to keep to their ancient usages, such as never to dig a grave on a Monday, and to carry the coffin three times round the grave, following the course of the sun, for then the dead rest in peace...."' 'Witches, Fairy Doctors', *Fairy and Folk Tales of the Irish Peasantry,* Edited and Selected by W. B. Yeats (1888)

Reading this passage was very important for me because, above all, it made me feel less alone and at odds. Here was a historic account of someone who died long before I was born, but their life as it's described here resonated with me. Not every detail, of course – I eat some meat and don't eat bread, for one thing – but the broad strokes really spoke to me. I don't drink alcohol, as a rule, and my wardrobe is rather monochromatic, as it were. Despite the pressure of modern magical ways it's the older practices that speak to me, and about which I find myself compelled to speak out. And of course there's the bit about seeing the Daoine Uaisle, who I certainly try to stay on friendly terms with, for my part.

For a long time I didn't talk about these things, especially the diet, except to a very few people, not only because it seemed an awkward thing to discuss but also because I felt like they were such strange things to have restrictions on. Reading this, as well as a chapter in the book *Trojan Feast* that touched on people's food intersecting with non-human beings, and seeing that other people who were connected to the Good People had also historically been known to have restrictions, or to live in ways that were at odds with those around them even if there's no direct indication it was at Their direction, made me feel better.

I also want to be clear that while these dietary things may have some health benefits – particularly given how unhealthy modern processed foods are – that was not the reason behind them, at least not for me. I have never had a sense that the Gentry were particularly concerned with my physical well-being, unless I was doing things that actively and immediately harmed myself, then they were always pretty clear that I needed to stop for that reason. What their motivation was in asking me to eat or not eat certain things wasn't initially clear, although I began to suspect it had to do with getting me into a more, shall we say, psychically receptive state. This suspicion would later be reinforced after talking with a couple friends.

A friend at one point had mentioned that my diet as it was being shaped was strongly reminiscent of a Sattvic diet, an approach to eating found in the Ayurvedic system. A traditional Sattvic diet, broadly speaking, includes fruit and fruit juice, above-ground vegetables and carrots, nuts, seeds, dairy products, honey, and grains (Cutchin, 2015). Not knowing anything about the subject I asked another friend who was fairly knowledgeable about it and he not only agreed with my first friend's suspicion but mentioned that Sattvic diets are often used by people seeking higher spiritual states because they open a person up to connecting more easily to spiritual energy (I'm paraphrasing here). This idea was echoed in a book I read recently, the aforementioned *A Trojan Feast* which discusses, in one section, the Sattvic diet its odd and apparently unconscious predominance among modern people who experience contact with non-human beings, and its reputed ability to raise psychic awareness or clairvoyance (Cutchins, 2015). I am by no means claiming that my food do's and don'ts are Sattvic, as I do not follow nor know very much about Ayurveda, however, I did find the connection interesting. Cutchins suggested that there may be a connection between the concept of sattva and its emphasis on freshness in food and the idea of the toradh or foyson, the essence, of food that the Good Folk were reputed to consume when given food offerings. By his theory, it is the toradh of food that can be equated to its Sattvic quality, making this diet perhaps the closest to what one might hypothesize the Daoine Maithe themselves might consume.

If you were wondering about the salt restriction, I might note that salt is often a protection against the Good People and other spirits. There is also this interesting quote I stumbled across while researching this book which is worth mentioning here: *'They [the Gentry] never taste anything salt but eat fresh meat and drink pure water'* (Wentz, 1911). So since they do seem to have some issue with salt in their food, I would at least keep in mind not to add it to any food being offered to them.

I cannot say that like Lady Wilde's friend of the fairies I have had these preferences all my life, or that from childhood I was guided to seek out or avoid certain foods. But for the last five years or so, as I have stopped resisting the growing dominance of the Good People in my life and have instead embraced it, I can say with certainty that their influence has touched on unexpected areas, including my diet. This has been a hard change, and I fully admit that I fight against it as often as I go along with it, but ultimately I do think there is a purpose to it, and that the purpose has value not only to Themselves but also – I hope – to me.

Fasting

I want to be abundantly clear from the off that fasting should never be undertaken unless it can be done safely and nothing I say here should in any way be taken as advice for anyone else's personal practices. Consult a professional before undertaking any fasting as it can present real health risks if you have underlying medical conditions. Fasting should never be done, in my opinion, as a way to punish yourself or in a way that makes you ill or uncomfortable.

Fasting is not something that I personally choose to do, but it is something that I sometimes feel compelled to do in relation to my spirituality. I suspect, like the other changes in my diet, fasting for periods of time has an effect on me that is purifying or else makes me more open to spiritual connection.

Many different religions either use fasting as a part of their practices or else are open to the concept. It is often viewed as a way to purify the self and sometimes as a way to demonstrate spiritual dedication. There are two kinds of fasting that I am aware of: only drinking water, and drinking water along with an amount of other liquids. The amount of time a fast lasts can vary from 12 hours to several days. Some fasting may extend over a longer period of time but only last for a portion of each day, such as the Muslim practice of fasting during Ramadan, where fasting is done from dawn until dusk during the month of the holiday.

When I feel guided to fast I usually replace regular meals with juice and milk instead of doing a full water-only fast. I tend to follow whatever I feel guided to do when it comes to time, although I have had personal gnosis suggesting for me that periods of either three or seven days are best.

Offerings

I make offerings all the time because I see them as something that underpins my spirituality. Offerings are one way to create and continue reciprocal relationships with the Good People. I make offerings on holy days but I also make an offering to the Fey folk on a regular basis, once a week. There seems to be some confusion about why we make offerings to the fairies, what should be offered, and how to treat it.

Firstly, why do we make offerings? The main reason in folklore is twofold: to continue giving them what was their due or to offer them willingly a portion to either gain blessing or avert harm. In the first case, it goes back to a story called (in English) 'The Taking of the Sidhe' about what happened after the Tuatha De Danann were defeated by the Gaels. In that story the crops failed and the cows stopped giving milk until the humans reached out to the Dagda and an agreement was reached that a portion of each harvest, milk and grain, would be given to the Gods as their due. This idea over time shifted to the Daoine Uaisle who, later folk belief tells us, were due a portion or tithe of the crops at harvest (McNeill, 1962). The second part of the idea is that if we give to them willingly a small amount of what we have then they will be obligated by their own sense of honour to either give us a blessing or at the least not to visit any mischief on us. There are also those who traditionally would offer, especially milk or cream, once a week to the Fey in their home or immediate area in appreciation for their effort around the area and to ensure no ill luck about the place. There has long been an idea that the Fey are entitled to a portion of what we have and that it is less that we are giving them some special gift as that we are giving them what is rightly theirs.

Another aspect of this is that if we are taking something from one of their places, visiting where we don't usually go, or feel we have been given a gift by them or – in my opinion – feel we owe them in some way, we should give something back. Think of yourself as a guest in someone else's place and try to have good manners. You may also need to make an offering if you went somewhere you were unwanted, just to appease whatever was there.

When choosing what to give I look at what would have been a traditional offering and in the case of fairies that usually means milk, cream, butter, honey, cakes or sometimes bread. I also trust my intuition though, so I have on some occasions literally given a piece of jewellery I was wearing. Sometimes I give things like poetry or songs because the Good People appreciate those things if they are done well, or my own effort or energy with something, if it seems like that is an appropriate thing to give. I have a friend who makes offerings by cleaning up rubbish at sacred sites. Another option includes alcohol, although I personally wouldn't recommend this as a regular offering if it's being poured out in nature because it can be bad for plant life. When in doubt I have found good, clean water is always acceptable.

I find that sometimes when something needs to be given I'll just get an idea for what it needs to be, and as often as not it's something I'd rather keep that I have a sentimental attachment to. Over the years I've learned that trying to keep something that needs to be given is a waste of energy. As the quote goes 'resistance is futile' and I've found that when I get the feeling that I need to give something, the more I resist it the stronger the feeling gets and the more little omens and indications I'll get that I need to make the offering. Recently, for example, I had a feeling before going somewhere that I was going to need to give one of my favourite necklaces, a larger stone that was a cabochon of an amethyst naturally growing within clear quartz set in silver. My friend had called it a fairy stone when she'd seen it and I'd been quite enamoured of it. Although I wanted to keep it, I did bring it with me when I travelled and very quickly it became apparent that there were situations going on that were going to call for a bigger offering. I tried other things first of course, because I'm stubborn, but finally I gave what they wanted and after that things shifted into a more positive sense. I've had the same thing happen before over the years, and I try to be philosophical about it.

You may sometimes feel called to offer something with metaphysical significance such as your own blood or an oath and in that case you need to really seriously think about all the implications before you do it, especially if you have no familiarity with blood magic or with the power of oaths. When in doubt 'don't do it' is always a good way to go, and try to find a substitute; if you really feel you must, try to talk to someone more experienced first if you can.

I will add this though on the subject of regular offerings to the Other Crowd: it's a commitment that you shouldn't start unless you're willing to follow through with it. There are weeks where I am literally spending the last of my grocery money – or dipping into my gas money – to get the cream to give the Good Neighbours, but they always get theirs, sure enough. I learned my lesson on that one years ago when finances made me decide to stop giving them milk and I had an entire gallon pulled from my hand; as my grandfather would say; if you don't give them their due they'll take it. And in my experience, they really will. There is also an old belief which I and some of my friends have been following for years, before we even knew it was an established folk practice, that any food that is dropped is desired by the fairies and should be given to them. It's funny because my son started doing this as a toddler, picking up dropped food and announcing that it was for the fairies, without any prompting or guidance (his sisters do not do this).

Where you leave offerings is really going to depend on your own circumstances and preferences. Traditionally there is no set place and in anecdotes and folklore we find mentions of food and drink for the fairies being left in the home on the hearth, on windows, and on tables among others, while outside they might be put near fairy trees, fairy forts or even poured on the ground. I follow the school of thought that it is the essence of the item that is being consumed, what Campbell called the toradh or Rev. Kirk called the foyson, if it's food or drink this happens within the first 24 hours of it being offered and after that the physical item itself can be disposed of. I leave offerings on my altar for a day then throw them out, or put them outside. In some cases I put them directly outside, but if you choose to do this, consider whether the item is safe for any animal that might eat it. Milk, cream, honey or alcohol are either kept on the altar for a day or poured directly outside. Flammable items like paper, butter, ghee or herbs, I burn, because of the old Celtic belief (recorded by the Romans) that what is burned with intent in our world appears in the Otherworld. Solid items like silver, jewellery or weapons, I give to earth or water, again because of archaeological evidence that this is how historic offerings were made in the pagan period.

Offerings should never be taken lightly, and even when they are part of the daily round of our spirituality should never become routine. What you give should be the best quality you can afford to give and should also be something you believe is wanted, not what's on hand. Although with the Fey folk you don't want to make too big a deal of the giving itself, you want the item you are giving to speak for you.

This should be common sense but we all know the saying about that. If you are visiting a historical, archaeological, famous, or natural site please do not leave a tangible offering there unless there is a policy in place allowing it. It's bad form to leave items, even what you might consider small things like crystals or coins at sites, that might be excavated for study at some point, and it's extremely bad form to leave any sort of trash or litter anywhere. Candle wax, food wrappers, bottles and such are trash and they shouldn't be left at public sacred sites for other people to clean up. When in doubt, pouring out a bit of water is usually a respectful and safe option. You can save the bigger offerings for other private settings later, or ask someone local (if you are travelling) how best to handle what you need to do. There have been some very serious issues at historical sites with the site becoming damaged by people taking things, leaving things like candle wax, crystals, coins and plastic in trees, and even taking stones and stacking them into cairns. If you want to do something meaningful at this sort of place feel free to clean up the rubbish you find, and trust me you will find it; when I was in cairn T at Sliabh na Caillí in 2016, I found lollipop sticks, plastic and paper bits *inside* the cairn itself. Be respectful: bring nothing, change nothing, take nothing.

Cáca Síofra – a Recipe from a Dream

I have previously talked about the value of knowledge gained from dreams but I realize I haven't given many concrete examples of what that practically looks like for me. I have found a lot of value in the lessons and messages I get this way, but generally I find these things are too personal too share and sometimes they would be hard to explain outside the context of my own life. Not always though. What follows is something I was explicitly told to share, for anyone else who might want to use it as well and it follows from the discussion of offerings.

I had a dream one night and in the dream I was shown how to make little offering cakes for the Other Crowd. I found myself somewhere that wasn't here, if you know what I mean, with a woman of Themselves who was between an open fire and small rough clay oven. She had a large wooden bowl and as I watched she added eggs and then honey and began mixing them. Looking up as she added flour and meeting my eyes she said 'oat flour' then held her hand out and let some fall through her hands to the ground. She mixed that in as well and then poured the mixture into several small cake pans, which were bigger than a cupcake but smaller than an 8-inch cake. When the cakes were set she put them in the oven and then pulled them out fully cooked, although I had a sense of a certain amount of time passing. She poured more honey over the tops of the three cakes she'd made then held one out and said 'cáca síofra' (fairy cake). Then I woke up.

Below, I am including the recipe and instructions for making them. In the dream I was shown how to make them for the most part and the only thing I was told in words was the oat flour and the name of the cakes, so the first time I tried to cook these I was guessing on the temperature and timing. I don't bake (or cook particularly well) so bear with my terrible attempt to convey how to do this from what I saw in the dream. They didn't look like modern cakes but were more dense and flat when they were baked.

Cáca Síofra

3 eggs
1/2 cup honey
1/2 cup oat flour
Stir up eggs until blended then add in honey, then slowly add

flour. Pour into buttered or greased cake pan or divide into several smaller ramekins.[1] Cook at about 350 degrees F (176 C) for about 35-40 minutes for larger cake size, 30 minutes for larger ramekin, 20 minutes for smaller. Take out of oven when the centre seems done. Drizzle more honey on the top when cooled.

I'd mentioned this on my social media and several people who actually can cook have suggested cooking them on a griddle like pancakes. I've tried both ways now, and this is how they came out. I tried them as griddle cakes and as little cakes in two sizes of ramekin. The batter is slightly thinner than a box cake mix (which is my usual go-to for baking) and seems runny but it cooks well.

On the griddle they need to be cooked at a lower temperature than normal pancakes would or they burn. I found that a medium-low worked well after some experimenting. They cook very quickly.

In really small ramekins they only need 20 minutes in the oven at 350 degrees F (176C). In the slightly larger size, which was the size I saw in the dream, it was 30 minutes.

After cooking them I tried eating some to make sure they were fit to offer, as I intended to make them as offerings. Without honey they are ridiculously delicious. With honey on top they are too sweet for me, but that was how I saw them so that was how I made them to offer. Obviously my preference isn't the issue for offering cakes, but I did verify that they are edible, and in fact really good. They are also nice and simple to prepare, although they take a lot of honey.

I'll be making these for offerings to the Daoine Eile on holy days from now on and having offered them several times, I have found they are very well received.

Oaths

Oaths are a pretty serious business, or they should be and you may find in time you will either feel drawn to make an oath to a member of Fairy or you may be asked to make one. This is never something that should be treated lightly or rushed into and it's important for someone following a Fairycraft path to have a deeper understanding of oaths than you might otherwise think. Making an oath binds to you to your promise but breaking an oath has consequences, even if the oath wasn't to a member of Fairy.

An oath is a promise to do or not do something or calling on something to verify your truthfulness. The first kind of oath usually invokes either a higher power to witness it or offers something as a surety if the oath is broken. The idea with a surety is straightforward – you agree to offer something in payment if you break your word. In the story of 'How the Dagda Got His Magic Staff' for example, the Dagda gives the sun, moon, sea and land as securities against his promise to return the staff to its original owners. The idea of a divine witness is a bit more complicated but generally seems to be that you are calling on the deity, spirit or such to hold you to your word or act to prove if what you are saying is false.

In the Tain Bo Cuailgne, Cu Chulainn swears an oath by saying '*I swear by the God my people swear by*' and in the same tale Fergus swears by his sword as a sacred thing of the goddess Macha. The Romans recounted that the Gauls made oaths by the sea, land and sky, saying that should their oath be broken the sea would rise up and drown them, the land open and swallow them, and the air smother them. What you swear by matters and we will take a closer look at that in a minute. For now the point is that swearing an oath was something that often invoked divine retribution or even the retribution of the elements.

Oaths were not something to be taken lightly. Once made, an oath was not supposed to be broken, and a person's honour rested on their ability to keep their word. Even the Gods were held to this standard, something we see in the story of how Oengus mac ind Og won the Bru na Boinne as his home. In the story he got the Bru's original owner – some say Elcmar, some say the Dagda – to promise him the use of the place for a day and a night. But when the original owner returned the next day to reclaim his home, Oengus replied that since all time was measured by a day and a night he was entitled to keep the Bru. Rather than be foresworn, the owner gave up his home to Oengus. If an oath was broken a person's reputation was negatively impacted and often they would have to take some reparative action to compensate for it.

If you make an oath to a member of Fairy understand that they will expect you to hold to that oath, under all circumstances, forever. And their forever is a lot longer than ours. They are also masters of semantics so you must choose your words very carefully and be certain that you are promising something you can do. Give nothing you can't afford to lose and offer nothing that you aren't willing to give up. When in doubt keep silent and promise nothing.

This is one of those things that's a lot more serious than most people seem to treat it as being. An oath is a big deal. Failing in an oath has consequences, whether that oath was a promise related to an action or an affirmation of truthfulness. Failing in a regular oath or promise to another person weakens your honour and the strength of your word. But swearing an oath to the Fey folk and breaking it opens you up to their anger and that is a very dangerous place to be, as they have been known to punish people severely, even bringing madness and death if they are angry enough. Under no circumstances do I recommend lying to the fairies and I would never, ever swear an oath that you are telling the truth if you are lying.

I cannot answer the question of what will happen if you break an oath to a fairy or spirit because I believe it depends a lot on which fairy or spirit we are talking about. I can say, looking at folklore, that breaking an oath to the Fair Folk is a profoundly bad idea, and I don't recommend it; ever. Under the best circumstances some éraic, some weregild, some compensation will be expected of you one way or another and they will decide how you will pay. Under the worst circumstances, as I already mentioned, they will respond violently.

Who Do You Swear By?

On a related note to the power of swearing oaths is another subject to consider. As a witch, who or what do you swear to and by? How do you handle making oaths? There is something of a running joke in my house with my children, whenever someone slips into the cultural expression of saying 'oh my god' or 'I swear to god' whoever is around them will ask, 'which one?', and 'what are you swearing?'. It seems silly but it has taught my children pretty quickly to think about what they are actually saying and to be more careful with their words. I want them to understand that words do matter and oaths shouldn't be taken lightly; not when you believe in powers with agency and independence and in a magical system where the strength of your word impacts the strength of your magic.

As for me, I try not to make oaths unless I think it's essential to, as you may have already gathered. When I do, I am fond of oaths as they are made in the old ballads. In 'The Well Below the Valley' the woman *'swore by grass'* and *'swore by corn'*; although knowing that corn was a general term for grain and loving alliteration I tend to prefer saying grass and grain. As an animist, swearing by grass and grain has just as much weight for me as swearing by land, sea and sky did (I imagine) for those historic Gauls, and as making a solemn oath to any God. I certainly do not want the grass and grain rising up against me for breaking my word. I will also sometimes swear by the liminal Gods or by my Fairy Queen, with the same logic, that I don't want to break my word and have them turned against me but I really prefer to avoid that.

Oaths are a serious business, and one, I think, that we as Pagans and Polytheists should put more thought into. If you haven't before, perhaps take a moment to contemplate what significance oaths have for you. When you make an oath are you prepared to pay a price for breaking it? Who do you swear to and by? These are important questions I think, and worth considering.

Practical Magic

Folk magic is the backbone of the magic practised in Fairy witchcraft. This has countless expressions and iterations but here I want to offer, as I have in my other books, a few samples of things I use and have had success with. These are spells, charms and the like which I have written down in my own book and that I recommend. You will probably notice that they tend to focus on protection and healing, and while those are not the only sorts of magic that I utilize they are certainly the ones I use most regularly.

A Charm against Wounds and Poison

The poison of a serpent, the venom of the dog, the sharpness of the spear, doth not well in man. The blood of one dog, the blood of many dogs, the blood of the hound of Fliethas—these I invoke. It is not a wart to which my spittle is applied. I strike disease; I strike wounds. I strike the disease of the dog that bites, of the thorn that wounds, of the iron that strikes. I invoke the three daughters of Fliethas against the serpent. Benediction on this body to be healed; benediction on the spittle; benediction on him who casts out the disease. (Wilde, 1888)

A Charm against Elves and Nightmares

alb vnde ł elbelin
Ir sult nich beng' bliben hin
albes svestir vn vatir
Ir sult uz varen obir dē gatir
albes mutir trute vn mar
Ir sult uz zu dē virste varē
Noc mich dy mare druche
Noc mich dy trute zücke
Noc mich dy mare rite
Noc mich dy mare bescrite
Alb mit diner crummen nasen
Ich vorbithe dir aneblasen
(Münchener Nachtsegen, fourteenth century)

Elf, or also little elf,
you shall remain no longer
elf's sister and father,
you shall go out over the gate;
elf's mother, trute, and mare,
you shall go out to the roof-ridge!
Let the mare not oppress me,
let the trute not pinch me,
let the mare not ride me,
let the mare not mount me!
Elf with your crooked nose,
I forbid you to blow [on people] ...
(Translation modified from Hall, 2007)

A Charm for Safety

Pluck ten blades of yarrow, keep nine, and cast the tenth away for tithe to the spirits. Put the nine in your stocking,

under the heel of the right foot, when going a journey.
(Wilde, 1888)

To Ward a Space

Salt and fire are both very useful for warding. You can walk the
boundary of a place carrying fire to bless the space, for example,
or sprinkle salt along the same area. There is also a variation in
some forms of folk magic called black salt where salt is mixed
with ashes to give the salt additional properties for banishing
and protection.

Protection against Fairies

It does happen sometimes that you may need to focus on
specifically protecting yourself or an area from fairies either
because they are malicious by nature or because you have angered
them. I always recommend trying appeasement first, such as
offering milk, before you jump to protecting against them as
that can sometimes anger them more; however, when necessary,
protection is an option. As has been previously mentioned iron
and salt work well, as do herbs like Saint John's Wort, Broom
and Mugwort. Bread is also used for protection in folk charms,
something that has been mentioned as far back as Rev. Kirk
writing in the seventeenth century. As this seventeenth-century
poem says, '*For that holy piece of bread; charms the danger and the
dread*' (Briggs, 1976).

Power over Fairies

There are times when you may need to look at gaining power
over a fairy, particularly for protective purposes. I am not
recommending running out and trying this but in an emergency
you should be aware that it is possible. There are several esoteric
means to do this including learning a fairy's name, which
gives you some power over them.[2] This is not easily done but
Katherine Briggs suggests that even giving the fairy a nickname

may be enough to drive one off as they dislike the naming itself (Briggs, 1976). Possessing an item of the fairies' clothing that you acquired by stealth – think of the selkie's seal skin for example – will also give you power over them. We may immediately think of the fairies forced to be brides in these cases but it is also true in folklore of others, such as the redcap who can be controlled if you can get his cap, or mermaids who you can gain power over if you take their combs (Briggs, 1976).

The grimoire tradition of the seventeenth and eighteenth centuries also offers more formal and complex rituals that can be done to gain power over a fairy. These are by their nature heavily Christian but offer a glimpse of the method used at least. I will include one below in the original language which is meant to be used to drive a fairy from a place, with the caveat that this sort of magic will certainly earn enemies among the Hidden People:

A discharge of the fayres and other spirits or Elphes from any place or grounde, where treasure is laid or hidd. First shall the magus: 'say in the name of the father, the son, and the holy ghost, amen. And then say as followeth – I conjure you spirits or elphes which be 7 sisters and have these names. Lilia, Restilia, foca, fola, Afryca, Julia, venulia, I conjure youe & charge you by the father, the son, and the holy ghost: and holy Mary the mother of our blessed lord and savior Jesus Christ: and by the annunciation nativity and circumcision, and by the baptisme; and by his holy fasting; and by the passion, death, and resurrection of our blessed lord Jesus Christ and by the Comeing of the holy ghost our sacred comforter; and by all the Apostles Martyres confessors: and also virgins and all the elect of god and of our lord Jesus Christ; that from hensforth neither you nor any other for you have power or rule upon this round; neither within nor without nor upon this servant of the liveing god: [your name]: neither by day nor night; but the holy trinity be always upon itt & him or her. Amen'. Amen.
(Briggs, 1976)

Another reason that we may at some point need to have power over a fairy relates to the ability Themselves have to possess people.[3] We can find different charms to break this power, but again they come to us for the most part through the lens of Christianity. For example, this charm for exorcism which would have been written down and carried by the person:

Adiuro to satanae diabulus aelfae. Per deum unum ac uerum. Et per trementem diem iudicii ut refugiatur ab homine illo qui habaet hunc a Cristo scriptum secum. In nominee dei Patris et Filii et Spiritus sancti.

[I adjure you Devil of Satan, elf, through the one true God and through the fearful day of Judgement, flee from the man who has this letter from Christ with him. In the name of God the father and the son and the Holy Ghost.]

(Jolly, 1996)

Besides this written charm, which for someone practising pagan witchcraft would have to be modified while being kept effective, there are also some other options. An ointment made from various herbs is also mentioned in the Anglo-Saxon Leechbooks, the purpose of which would be to drive out fairy spirits. The herbs used do vary but are often in groups of either three or nine. Herbs which are commonly included are: Betony, Lupin, Leek, Fennel, Feverfew, Garlic, Pennyroyal, and Rue (Jolly, 1996). Mugwort has also been used traditionally to drive out spirits and break fairy enchantments, and can be burned for this purpose.

Curing Elf Shot

Using Elf Shot is one of the many ways that witches and fairies overlap and it is truly a fearsome power. It may come to be as you travel further into this spirituality that you are taught the use of elf shot or given some of it to use, but because of its ability to bring such harm or even death it is not something I will teach anyone, and certainly never in a format like this. I will, however, teach people how to remove or cure elf shot as that is equally useful.

Firstly, there is this protective charm against elf shot:

I charm you for arrow-shot, for door-shot, for window-shot, for eye-shot, for tongue-shot, for liver-shot, for lung-shot, for heart-shot, all the most, in the name of the father, the son, and the Holy Ghost, amen.

(Henderson & Cowan, 2007)

For my purposes, I always replace calling on the trinity and amen with something more appropriate for my own spirituality, but otherwise it's a good, useful charm. Carrying rowan berries is also thought to avert elf-shot and baneful magic in general. The herb Agrimony is mentioned in relation to curing elf-shot and I would use this by burning it or by making a paste of it and placing it on the body wherever I think the shot entered.

Spirit Traps

This is something that was given to me in a dream which I later researched and found out does exist as a concept in witchcraft and the occult more generally. The idea is to use a bottle to lure in a spirit and then create a situation where the spirit cannot get back out again. In the particular dream I had relating to this I was told to make two and place them near the entrance to my home, and to change them out at intervals.

To make these I use old wine bottles, or something similar. I get a long piece of rough twine and thread it into the bottle until it loops and curls and fills the bottle fairly well. Into that I place a piece of parchment with a symbol on it to draw spirits; this looks like a sideways uppercase letter A, legs pointed to the left, with a half circle on the left-hand side curving across the top of the A. Leave some of the twine hanging out of the top of the bottle and loop that around the neck several times before letting the end trail down.

Witch Bottles

One of my favourite traditional methods of protection in witchcraft is a witch's bottle. It's fairly simple to make, yet easily added to or adapted, and once made is set in place requiring no maintenance. It's effective, yet subtle. And it's something that anyone can do, no matter what the skill or experience level.

A witch's bottle is a type of folk charm which is designed to attract and trap any negative energy or malicious magic sent your way,[4] so that it is prevented from causing you any harm. Witch bottles were a common folk charm used throughout the sixteenth and seventeenth centuries to protect people from negative magic; more than 200 witch bottles have been found buried throughout Europe, but most are broken by the time they are uncovered (Viegas, 2009). An example of an American witch bottle was found in Pennsylvania dating to the eighteenth century, and the practice was common enough in America that preachers spoke out against its use, although it was also recommended by other contemporaries, including Cotton Mathers, as a good protection against witches (Becker, 2009). During a period when many people feared witchcraft, the witch bottle offered a sense of security and protection and allowed people to proactively defend themselves when they felt they may be the victim of a curse. In modern practice a witch's bottle is still an excellent tool to use to protect yourself from any possible negative magic, rather like a magical electric fence.

Examining a witch bottle found in Greenwich dating to the seventeenth century shows the contents to be similar to those that are still used today: urine, sulfur, nail clippings, nails and pins (Viegas, 2009). Many examples of witch bottles also include a felt, cloth or leather heart pierced by a pin as well, although the exact purpose of this is unknown (Becker, 2009; Viegas, 2009). It was believed that the pins and nails would turn the magic back on to the caster, while the urine and nail clippings would draw the magic intended for the person to the bottle instead; often the ingredients would be boiled together first (Becker, 2009). Historical examples are found buried, often top down, in front of a house with the intent of protecting the home or a specific inhabitant from malicious magic (Becker, 2009). The bottles used were the type commonly seen in those areas for drinking and could be stoneware, ceramic or glass, with a specific type called a 'Bellermine' often used. The Bellermine was named after a Catholic cardinal whose face appeared stamped on to the bottles.

In modern practice the bottles would be made and used in much the same way as they were historically. To make one you need a glass or ceramic bottle that can be corked or sealed at the top. For a basic bottle add your own urine and nail clippings, some hair, sulfur, nails and pins; if you want you can include the felt heart as well. The bottle can be modified with other materials such as herbs – Agrimony or Blessed Thistle work well for anti-curse magic, or for something stronger Mandrake or Belladonna could be used, for example, broken glass, mirrors or peppers. Add the urine first – on a practical note I recommend using a cup to collect it and then pouring it into the bottle – then add the other items. Traditionally, the mixture would be boiled before being added to the bottle. Once the bottle is full, seal the top and if you'd like to, say something to charge the bottle with its purpose. When complete bury the bottle near the front of your home where it won't be found or disturbed; although some people who live in an apartment or otherwise have no land to bury it in might choose to keep it hidden under a sink or bury it in a potted plant inside the home. If you move do not disturb the old bottle (although if it's under your sink don't leave it there!), rather make a new bottle for your new home.

Endnotes

1. I didn't know what these were, but I was looking for smaller cake pans and stumbled across them in the grocery store and they were the closest in size to what I had seen. I should also add here that I wouldn't recommend cooking these on or in anything made of iron.

2. It is worth noting here, by the way, that if you do have friends among the Fey folk or gain allies as you practise and they at some point give you a name to call them it will not be their True Name and will not have real power over them. Fairies guard their names as fiercely as humans should and will not tell anyone what that name is, usually, and they are very difficult to trick.

3. It's not really something to get into here as it would be tangential but you definitely should be aware that fairies are capable of possessing humans in the same way that we think of other spirits doing so; this is something noted in folklore and for which we have traditional remedies. It is usually associated with fevers and sometimes seizures. I discuss it in more length in my book, *Fairies*.

4. Many modern sites talk about using witch bottles for different purposes, along the lines of a charm. This may work well for others, but I stick to the traditional use – if I want a charm for money or love I'll just make one for that instead of using a witch bottle.

Chapter 9

Wild Witchcraft

The moon's my constant mistress,
And the lonely owl my marrow;
The flaming drake and the night crow make
Me music to my sorrow.

At its heart Fairy Witchcraft is wild witchcraft. It is not tame or domesticated and it is predicated on stepping out into the dark trackless woods and finding a way through. While it does have some similarities to other forms of modern witchcraft, it also has differences and those differences can be deep and critical. Fairy witchcraft has been woven together in pieces and parts from the Fairy Faith, from traditional witchcraft, and from modern witchcraft and it is both more than the sum of its parts and also in some ways intrinsically defined by them. It is grounded in the ideas of certain witches working with dangerous spirits, of connecting to the Unseen where you are, and the overarching theme between the two of some kinds of witchcraft as a wild and untamed practice. It is not safe and it is not comfortable and just when you think it might be either it will remind you of its wildness.

I'll emphasize at the start that this is only one kind of witchcraft. Let's be blunt here: there are hundreds, if not thousands, of different kinds at this point and they are diverse. Not all witches practise in the same way, or believe the same things, or even agree on the most basic details, so there really is no one-size-fits-all this-is-witchcraft commentary that can be made. While the idea of working with spirits of any type might be entirely inappropriate for some witches, for whatever reason, it is the backbone of practice for others, and likewise while some may be very much about community and conformity, others thrive on the opposite of that. No single approach is the right way for everyone, or is the 'real' witchcraft or anything like that. So, understand that what I'm talking about here is just one particular way of doing things (because I'm not going to keep specifying that) but it's not everyone's cup of tea and that's perfectly fine. I am not trying to define what witchcraft is for everyone or what witchcraft in general is, but to explain what the witchcraft side of Fairy Witchcraft is now that we have pretty well discussed the Fairy side of it.

When we look at what we know of historic witchcraft in certain European cultures, particularly Irish which is obviously my main focus, it's clear that witches were known to truck with spirits, often fairies, and those spirits were not considered safe by conventional standards. In Ireland – and often Scotland as well – it wasn't demons that witches dealt with but fairies, although to the Christian mind at the time there was at best a fine semantic line between the two. In fact, fairies and witches in Ireland have a long and rather convoluted connection to each other, with both the more positive bean feasa (wise woman) and negative cailleach (witch) being known to get their knowledge from Otherworldly beings, although what separated them was what they did with that knowledge. In Scottish witch trials we find confessions from some witches who claimed to have met not with the Devil but with the Queen of Elfhame and to have acquired things like elfshot[1] at her bidding from the Fey folk. In the same way, the historically famous witch's familiar in some cases[2] was not a demonic spirit but a person of the Good Neighbours.

The Other Crowd were never seen as safe which is exactly why we don't, as much as possible, call them 'fairies' but rather we use euphemisms like Good Neighbours, Mother's Blessing, Gentry, Fair Folk and so on. The idea being that speaking of them can draw their attention and if we do, it's better to not offend them at the off but try to remind them of their own potential good nature. There can be and are rewards for dealing well with them, but there's always a risk to it and there are countless stories of people who angered the Good People and suffered for it. Although modern views may like to paint them as twee and harmless – and of course there are some who are, because they are as diverse as people are – many of Themselves are quite capable of harming us if motivated to do so. Those who walk on this path must do so understanding that they are choosing to engage with beings who can be dangerous, even if, ideally, that danger is mitigated or avoided with caution and care in how they are dealt with.

As fairy witches today, we are drawn to this path because we find an appeal in this older approach, in the idea of seeking out these 'dangerous spirits' against all common wisdom and learning from them. Making allies among them and studying the old folk ways to learn how to safely deal with them, both the friendly and unfriendly ones. There is no safety net in doing this, no guarantees, no certainty. It is dangerous and you learn as much from making mistakes and having to deal with the consequences as you do from handling things correctly. But this way of doing things is the way it used to be done and I think there is a lot of value in it, for those willing to take the risk.

The Otherworld is all around us all the time, often barely separated from our own, and sometimes not separated at all. There are ghosts and echoes of past times and things layered over our present. There are also points of entry between our world and others, both the Irish one which I frequently reference and many more besides. But beyond all of this there are spirits here and now, invested in things and places and objects. This animism forms a huge part of my own belief, because it means understanding that everything around me has a spirit, not just the Otherworldly things like elves, and aos sí and the like which I talk about sometimes, but also the spirits of streams and stones and my car.

I live in a place that has been occupied by Europeans for about 400 years; before that, of course, it belonged to several tribes which now have reservations here. The Otherworldly spirits are varied and diverse, they are native to this land and they are things that have moved in over the last four centuries. But the spirits of the land are constant. The spirit of the river is the spirit of the river. The spirit of the swamp behind my house is the spirit of that swamp. The spirits of the trees are what they are, living and growing and dying like any other. How I relate to them is based on my own personal filter, and that is true for us all, but the spirits themselves are there as they have always been.

I have long advocated for witches, and pagans and polytheists generally, to make a real effort to connect to the spirits around them, where they are here and now. People are so quick to talk of travelling to sacred places or of needing to go somewhere old and wild to connect to spirits, but why? If you believe in them then you need to start where you are, where your feet are planted. Connect to the spirits in your own home – they're there. Connect to the spirits in your yard, your neighbourhood, your town. Get out and make an effort to get to know the world around you, and if you can't do that for any reason then work on getting to know the spirits where you are in your home. Whether you live in the country or suburbs or the city doesn't matter. Connect to what's around you, because it's those connections that matter most in your actual daily life and workings. Especially if you practise magic, and really especially if you are a witch in my opinion. You need to have allies among the Otherworld but you also need to have a strong connection to your spirits of place and to the spirits of the world around you as well. Think of them as your neighbours.

A final point that I wanted to touch on is the idea of breaking free from past religions or traditions that may still have power over us. In several cases from the Scottish witchcraft trials we are told that when a fairy came to someone or when a person was brought before the Queen of Elfhame one of the things that was required of them to become a witch was the formal renunciation of their religion, including rejecting their Christian baptism. This may of course be one reason why dealing with fairies was viewed as the same as dealing with Hell and why fairies more generally were seen as demon-like, but I suspect there was a reason for it. From a metaphysical perspective, belief does have power and it could be that the fairies wanted to erode any foreign belief that would interfere with what they would then teach the person.[3] It might also have been about simple loyalty, with the Fairy Queen wanting the person to swear fealty to her first and foremost, above all others including any foreign religions. I will say that even as a pagan I had a similar experience when approached by a Fairy Queen, and I believe that while they have much to offer a person – if a person is willing to pay their price – they do require loyalty. Finally, though, I think that there are practical reasons as well for this request, in that fully renouncing one's past ties frees the person completely to move forward into a new path.

Even for those of us today who find ourselves in this situation, it is worth considering the need to fully break ties with our former religions. There is an example in Paul Huson's book *Mastering Witchcraft* (excellent book by the way) of reciting the Lord's Prayer backwards in front of a mirror. As someone who wasn't raised Christian, I don't personally see the shock or power of this, but I'd suggest if the idea outrages or upsets you, as a pagan witch,[4] then you probably should do it. Why? Because if you feel shocked or outraged by the mere idea of reciting something like that backwards then the religion it comes from, in my opinion, probably still has power over you. When we become aware of things from the past, things we thought we had let go of or outgrown, which are still holding onto us we need to find a way to free ourselves from those things. Sometimes that means doing something extreme that our old self would never do, like recite a prayer backwards. And as witches, we should be free from those ties; we should not, as much as possible, allow anything unnecessary to hold us back. If you want to practise this type of witchcraft do some real soul searching and look at anything from the religion, or ways you were raised with, that still has power over you: things that make you feel guilty or uneasy, or that you won't do or don't like to do because you were previously told they were wrong. Give some thought to whether your new pagan religion and your witchcraft practices embrace the things you were told not to do.[5] If so, then go out of your way to do them, or otherwise find ways to break their power over you.

This witchcraft is not meant to be something tame and bound in the ideas of wider acceptance. Trucking with spirits isn't a game played so you can brag to other people about it – in fact talking about what you do is often not a good idea – it's something that has tangible real world consequences that can be life altering and if you think I'm just taking the piss or being melodramatic then trust me this isn't the sort of witchcraft you want to get into; which is fine, there are plenty of others to choose from. This witchcraft is about risk and being okay with the idea of magical practices that aren't safe, or more to the point, require a lot of care to practise. Traditional witchcraft as we see it in history and folklore was messy, and dangerous, and wild in the literal sense of going beyond conventional bounds, uncivilized, unrestrained. There are some modern approaches to witchcraft that are the same and Fairy witchcraft is one of them.

If one were to say that most approaches to modern witchcraft can be likened to walking on a well-worn trail in the woods, and a few are like making your own trail, then I might say that this Fairy Witchcraft is like pushing through the thickest part of the forest at night – it's as much instinct and feeling your way as it is knowledge and experience. And like the above analogy, how people like to adventure in the woods is a deeply personal sort of thing, as it should be, and the method that one person finds profound and spiritual, another may well find meaningless. If there's one thing I've learned so far, it's that we can't force our feet into other people's footsteps just for the sake of trying to follow the way we think we should be going, or we'll be unhappier for it.

So, what do these three things have in common, dealing with dangerous spirits, connecting to local spirits and following a wilder path? They are all aspects of one approach, all interwoven and linked together. We deal with dangerous spirits of the Otherworld, but the other side of that coin is connecting to local spirits where we are here and now. And sometimes those two things are the exact same. We push boundaries and do the messy dangerous things, walking deep into the wild woods where there is no path. And usually there's a purpose to that and that purpose may well have to do with fairies or spirits one way or another. I don't think one can really be separated from the others, and each builds on the others to form a Witchcraft that is unique from many others today. And that's a good thing, I think, because as our community grows, I think we need the diversity and we need the people who look back at the older ways of doing things as much or more than looking forward.

Rooted Magic

Speaking of magic, another aspect of Fairycraft that makes it wilder and less civilized, at least by most modern measures is an emphasis on using what we have at hand when it comes to both spirituality and magic. Some of this is purely practical and some of it is rooted in esoteric theory. The two work together though and strengthen each other, making it important for us to connect to our local resources, which is another way to connect to both the spirits around us and also become aware of and connect to the world and environment around us. We grow best where we have the deepest and strongest roots.

On the purely practical level using what we have around us, both in our magic and spiritual practice, is the most pragmatic option. It's a lot more cost effective to use what you have on hand than to be paying for expensive imported items, when that's an option.[6] It's also a lot faster and easier to use what's around you than to search for specific things that have to be found or ordered. When I need stones or crystals I look to the earth I live on and the rivers, streams, and ocean nearby. When I need shells I go to the shoreline. When I need herbs or parts of trees I look at the land around me and see what's there to work with. Whereas most spells in modern books give a person a list of ingredients to assemble to achieve a goal, I start by thinking of what my goal is and looking at what I have on hand – or can find around – that can be used to get that result. Things that I know are useful for specific important purposes I try to keep on hand, like mugwort and rose, and when I can find good local sources I stock up.

In traditional Irish folk magic, and by extension the Irish-American folk magic that I practise, when charms or spells require ingredients it's usually either things that are already commonly found nearby or things that are more general than specific. Herbal charms are based on herbs that grow wild or can be grown in gardens, not on exotic things that must be bought or ordered. Everything around me has a use and a purpose in my magic, and I have never had a need that I could not meet with an herb, stone or tree at hand. Ivy, Clover, Yarrow, Rose, these are some of my go-to herbs. And where I live, Raspberry, Nightshade and Honeysuckle as well. My local trees, the Maple, Witch-hazel, Cedar, as well as my Birch, Hawthorn, Oak and Ash lend themselves to my magic when needed. Stones have uses based in their colour, where they are found or in some few cases by what mineral they are. The wild earth is my first resource for supplies, before I resort to anything else.

From an esoteric perspective there's an advantage to

connecting to the magic of the place we're in as well. First of all we're working with a magical energy based in the living world around us, not in places that we may have no connection to at all. There is some argument for having tokens and material from a place we have a spiritual connection with,[7] and that's another issue, but having crystals and herbs we don't even know the sources of is something else. It's not that they won't work, of course, just that what comes from the land around us is stronger and not only, in my experience, works better magically but also has the added benefit of increasing our connection to where we are. These things help us get in sync with the magical and spiritual tides of the place we live in.

Secondly, we just talked about the power in connecting to spirits of place and to the spirits of the land where we are, and in my experience working respectfully with the materials of the earth around us aids in that connection. It teaches us to understand what's around us but it also perforce connects us to the energy and spirit of the land. People who want to work with the Good Neighbours are best to start with their house spirits and with the spirits of the land around them, in their yard, in their neighbourhood, in the places they frequent outside their home. Whether you live in an urban or rural area, the spirits are there and the possibility of connecting is there. Learning to work with local materials is a good first step and even for more experienced people, it allows for a deeper connection.

The only time in my opinion that it's not an option is if you're making an offering to a deity or spirit that has a specific requirement, or if you're doing something – magically or spiritually – that is specific to the point that it doesn't allow substitution. If you feel like the Queen of the Wind absolutely has to have dragon's blood incense, or a fairy you are dealing with wants limes and they don't grow locally, or you're using a charm against nightmares that calls for betony and it doesn't grow around you, then by all means go with that. Sometimes deities and fairies like to challenge us by asking for specific things, I think, to make us prove we will put in some effort for them. There are also a very few cases where there may be a specific stone or herb that just can't be substituted effectively, and in that case, as well, you want to go with what is going to work best. Use your own common sense to decide when you can't substitute and when you can easily use something similar or that accomplishes the same purpose.

I like the pretty, fancy things as much as the next person. But I also like magic that works and works well. I like magic and spirituality that is always at my fingertips and is woven thoroughly into my life and the world around me. Working with my landscape, with herbs, trees, stones and materials from the place I live connects me strongly to the energy and spirits of this place. And I truly believe my witchcraft and my spirituality is stronger for it.

Simple Magic, Butter and Salt

Segueing directly from that idea into one that flows logically from it, I think. There was a time when my magical practices were fairly complicated, and I suppose sometimes they still can be. I won't deny that I like my fancy candles and herbs as much as most witches do, even if I locally source them, and I am fond of a variety of woods and natural materials. There is something visceral and satisfying in working with these tangible things, in, for example, making my own incense and watching a variety of herbs ground slowly into one united purpose. It's fun to have a range of tools in the metaphysical tool kit to draw on.

But I can also appreciate a simpler approach. There are times when simple isn't just more convenient but also more powerful. You aren't being distracted by the need for a long or complex process, or trying to focus on something that may be involved or detailed. There's a purity in minimalism that can add instead of detract. That in many ways is the beauty of folk magic that we find in some old texts where it was a matter of a chant and maybe a simple action to go with it. For a while I forgot this.

When I was first starting out in witchcraft I was very young and so very limited in what I had access to for supplies. Some generic incense. Inexpensive candles. Yarn. Salt. Cornmeal for offerings. And yet with these basic things I was able to practise my spirituality and magic just fine; I never felt as if my humble tools limited my ability or success. To give you an example: at one point when I was in high school, one of my uncles who I was very fond of had a heart attack and I wanted to do a healing spell for him. Since I had nothing to work with I used a piece of notebook paper and cut out a poppet from that, believing that it was the image itself that mattered for the spell not the quality of the material used. The old witches, after all, used what they had on hand.

But like many people, as my means increased so did my desire for fancier and more elaborate things. The books I was reading in the 1990s and early 2000s tended to leave me with the impression that fancier was better, with spells often including a list of exotic ingredients, from herbs and oils to crystals and manufactured tools. I'm not criticizing those things of course – they work and they work well. But eventually I realized that so do the plants growing in my yard and the stones I can find in the earth and streams around me, provided I know what they are and how to use them. It was my deepening practice of Fairy witchcraft that led me to that and my study of the older folk magic that we have preserved, the magic of the common people who simply didn't have access to anything else.

As time has gone on I've noticed, both in myself and in some other people, a refining of the go-to magical tools. In some cases as I mentioned above it's a turning back to more locally sourced supplies. In other cases it may include that but also go even further, a refining to the simplest approaches, of something for blessing and something for banishing. For some people these tools refine down to fire and water, or perhaps earth and light. For me, it's salt and butter. I've found that in almost any circumstance one or the other can be used, either salt for banishing, protection or cleansing, or butter for offering, blessing and healing. I always carry a bit of salt and butter on me as a kind of emergency magical kit and I have found it extremely useful under a variety of unexpected circumstances.

There was a running joke when I was in Ireland in 2016 that I was buttering my way across the country because that was my go-to offering, something that was easily obtained and in my experience, always accepted. I also carried salt in my bag and used it at several points to ground and for protection. Travelling and with limited access to magical tools, I handled everything that came my way on that trip, from an unexpected fairy ring to what should have been an expected fairy gateway, from offerings when I'd lost my way to protection for someone who was hearing the Good People calling him into the woods at night. Salt and butter were enough to get me through and that made me realize that as nice as all the other things are and as much as I enjoy the fun of the pomp and circumstance, when it comes down to it simple is powerful and effective.

Magic can be complicated and many magical processes and spells can also be complex. Yet magic can also be straightforward, especially folk magic. Singing a chant. Speaking a blessing over an object or person. Offering butter to spirits. Salting a boundary. Gathering herbs from your yard. Hanging up a hag stone. Simple actions, yet when done with intention and focus, they can be very powerful. The further you walk into this wilderness, I think, the more you appreciate that lesson.

Curse-work and 'Real' Witches

I realize I talk a lot about hexing and there's a reason for that. The subject of hexing is one that is argued in witchcraft communities on a regular basis, not only whether curse-work and hexing in general are acceptable, but also the potential consequences of engaging in the practice. Not at all surprisingly, in modern witchcraft there is often a strong thread of disapproval towards the practice and also a very public outcry proclaiming that 'real'[8] witches don't hex. Period. The end. A variety of arguments are put forth for why 'real' witches don't use baneful magic but generally it boils down to; 1) it's naughty and naughty magic only really hurts the person casting it; 2) hexes don't work anyway or 3) a 'real' witch is wise enough to know better than to do naughty magic, for reasons that are never clearly explained.

Hexing and curse-work were always done by historic witches, and that kind of magic always served a purpose. It's important to understand that and also to appreciate that whether or not you personally choose to engage in hexing, the concept itself is not inherently evil and offers a tool for those who otherwise lack power and ability to defend themselves or achieve justice.

I'm not going to speak about whether or not I'm real. I think a lot which I'm given to understand is one criterion of reality, but for all any of us know, we could be a dream within a dream or characters in a story. So, let's table the question of reality. I am sure that I'm a witch, though, and I do hex. I've talked about it publicly before and I'm not ashamed of it; I don't think it should be done if you aren't willing to own up to doing it. So real or not real, I'm a witch and I hex. I guess that entitles me to an opinion on the subject. I've written about hexing before in other books because it's a subject that I feel strongly about. I am not, however, out to convince anyone that they should or should not do it. I believe that it is up to each individual to decide for themselves whether curse-work is something they are comfortable doing. What I do want, though, is to work towards removing the stigma around it that says anyone who hexes is a terrible, morally corrupt person; this is no more or less true than saying a member of the military or a martial artist is inherently violent and dangerous just because they have the skill set to cause harm and an ability to use it if necessary.

Curse-work is a specialty. It requires study just as much as healing or prophecy magic does, and I'd argue that to do it well you have to make it your focus, at least for a time. It isn't something you play with. It has its own rhythms and rules, its own flow and form. It's not for everyone, and not every witch needs to do it, just like anything else. Some people are vegetarians and some are omnivores; some are pacifists and some are fighters; some let energy work itself out and some hex. Different witches have different ethical approaches and beliefs that shape the acceptability of curse-work and any kind of magic that directly impacts other people's free will. For some people it will always be out of bounds and for others it will be acceptable within certain contexts. I certainly don't know anyone who does serious hexwork who takes it lightly or sees it as a game, for what that's worth. Rather, the other people I know who do it approach it very soberly, and often as a last resort when other options have been exhausted.

Hexing is not inherently dangerous and it isn't a practice that dooms the practitioner to suffer terrible consequences. It is no more or less dangerous to the person doing it than healing is, and just like healing, the risk only comes in if the person makes a mistake, which can happen just as easily with blessing magic as baneful magic. I've been at this a long time and I've done more than one hex in my time – and done them knowing exactly what I'm doing and how to do it – and I have never once experienced any negative repercussions on myself, nor has my magic failed to achieve my goal, although it may work faster or slower or stronger than I intended which is exactly why it has to be done with care. The narrative that anyone who hexes will be awash in bad energy, usually described as karma but in the Western sense of instant consequences, is not something I have ever personally seen as true. And I say that as someone who has been practising witchcraft since the early 1990s who admits to hexing, binding and banishing when necessary. Yes, everything we do ultimately affects us but it is far more nuanced and subtle than: do good = get equivalent good, do bad = get equivalent bad. And as I like to remind people, good and bad are matters of perspective and we must always be careful in judging what is which, especially when it comes to our own actions.

I've also seen a lot of anti-hex arguments that say that positive magic works but negative does not. By this logic healing spells work, but curses do not, because somehow what helps us and is judged good (remember what I said about judging) is effective but what is judged bad or harmful is seen as impossible or ineffective. It can't be both. Either they both work or neither does. We can't acknowledge the power of one and deny the power of the other, whether or not we, ourselves, participate in it. To me this just smacks of a way to reassure one's self that good magic works but naughty magic doesn't, as if the Universe only allowed goodness. I think it should be pretty self-evident that nothing works that way. I'd also point out as an aside that no type of magic is any more or less addictive than any other, as that has also been mentioned as a reason not to hex. Absolute power may corrupt absolutely but this isn't some fictional Dark Side of the Force we're talking about here, where even one slip into practising it will mean your light sabre turning red forever. This is reality, where people are nuanced and complicated and can be good people with functional ethics who still believe it's okay to bind a stalker or punish a rapist using magic without plunging into uncontrolled all-Evil-all-the-time-ness.

The third main argument I've seen is that a 'real' witch is wise enough to know better than to hex or curse. Um, in all seriousness why? What exactly is so wrong in hexing or cursing that being 'real' enlightens you so much that you won't do it? Ignoring for a moment the enormous implied insult here that everyone who does hex is not only "not a 'real' witch" but is also unwise or uneducated, I genuinely don't understand this argument. I'm impeding someone else's free will. Okay. I'm also impeding their free will when I get a restraining order or use mace to defend myself from a mugger, but I'm going to do both of those things if necessary too, and I don't see how defending myself against someone else's aggression isn't the best course. I suspect this ties back into the assumption that hexing is just done to be mean, but let me tell you something here, the hexing that I've done that falls into the bounds of curse-work has usually[9] been done because I had exhausted all my other options and I was desperate. I or people I cared about were usually in physical danger, or other serious situations were occurring that needed an immediate response for which I had no options.

If you want to argue against hexing then argue against it from a moral standpoint, make it clear that you are discussing your own morals, or explain your own reasoning for not doing it, but don't use scare tactics that make the practice seem like magical Russian roulette. It isn't. If done with skill and knowledge, hexing and cursing are powerful tools and can be useful to achieve goals that otherwise may be unachievable, especially relating to justice and some types of protection. I'm not saying it can't be misused just like anything else, of course, but it can and often is done well and safely for the practitioner. And effectively. And keep in mind that anything which is judged good or bad is based purely on our own perspective. There's nothing wrong with choosing not to hex because it goes against your own morals or makes you uncomfortable. That's fine. But there's also nothing wrong with deciding that you are morally comfortable with hexing.

I like to hope that someday we can get beyond this divisive 'real witches don't hex' stuff. Yes, some 'real' witches do. And some don't. There is no one single type of witchcraft, no single ethic that unites all witches, no agreed witchcraft code that defines who and what witches are based on what magic they do. What makes a person a real witch isn't whether or not they adhere to one particular moral viewpoint. Even within Fairy witchcraft there is room for different viewpoints on this and different comfort levels; no one is required to hex if they don't want to – but no one is going to be told they are naughty if they choose to do it. As adults we must all seek our own way on this, and certainly looking to the past and to folklore will show plenty of examples of hexing used by both witches and the fairies. And cursing and hexing, whether anyone likes it or not, are deeply ingrained in historic and traditional witchcraft, and in some forms of modern witchcraft as well. Witchcraft is dazzlingly diverse in its variety and scope of practice. Let's try celebrating that, even when we don't agree with what other people do in their personal traditional magic, rather than condemning and trying to limit other people to conform to our own expectations and comfort zone.

I am a witch. I hex. And I'm proud of the knowledge and skill it takes to do that well.

Practising Safe Hex

Since we just discussed my view on hexing, let's stay with that for this next section if only because it's not a topic that gets much air time in most books. This isn't about the ethics pro or con, but purely offering some safety tips for people who may feel motivated to hex and who are not well versed in the practice. Like any other magical specialty it is a niche practice that requires its own study – in my opinion – to do well. And like most magical specialties, if done wrong a person can potentially cause themselves some serious problems.

First let's clarify some terms. Technically hex just means to use magic but it's taken on connotations of harm that make it in common usage synonymous with cursing, i.e. to use magic to inflict harm or punishment on someone. I use the two terms interchangeably in English. In many views both binding and banishing magic falls under the purview of hexing/cursing because they involve forcibly altering another person's freewill.

Binding means magically controlling someone's actions, often by limiting what they can do; banishing means sending them away from an area or keeping them away from a person or situation. Hexing in general terms can be a diverse practice that may involve a wide array of methods intended to affect a person in a negative manner, often as a means to achieve justice.[10]

So, with that in mind some general tips on how to hex safely:

If you are calling on deities of justice or associated with justice, be 100 per cent sure you are innocent in the situation. Generally speaking, just because you invoked them doesn't mean they won't weigh your actions as well. Justice is their thing after all.

If you are invoking other types of spirit that historically expect to get paid make sure you pay them something. Most spirits don't work for free, unless you go the route of calling them and binding them to your service which is a whole other conversation. Spirits will help you out but they expect something in return, so offer it to them up front.

If you invoke, you dismiss. Don't just open that metaphysical door and leave it swinging in the wind. Make sure you show your guests out and close and lock that door when you are done. This is especially true if you are calling on spirits or beings you don't usually work with.

-   Keep your wording consistent. If you are using positive language like 'may he be destroyed, may he lose his prosperity' or whatever then stick with that throughout; if you are using negative language[11] like 'may she be without rest, may she be without peace' stick with that. Don't mix and match the two, it muddies the waters. Clarity is very important in any kind of magical work because you need to keep your energy focused. Your words are a main way to do that.

- Keep your intent consistent. Focus matters. Don't try to cram in a variety of goals in a single working, just stick with a single strong intention and be clear on exactly what your intended outcome is.
- Be really clear with your symbolism and know what you are using, what it represents, what it's associated with, and any possible deeper layers of meaning that could apply. If you don't know what a symbol means, don't use it.
- Don't use foreign symbols or items that you don't understand or know the meaning of. As long as you believe you know what a symbol means or you have a strong association with it that's fine. Many symbols have multiple meanings and it's alright if you are only focusing on one of those, just be clear with what that focus and meaning is.
- Although there is a lot of historic precedent for using languages you don't speak yourself, I don't personally recommend it. If you don't know what you are saying, don't say it.
- Be specific in naming your target. This is a big one and reiterates the idea that you don't want to be vague in any of this. If you are uncomfortable naming anyone then don't do the spell.
- Do not use your own name, especially if you are invoking spirits. This is what magical pseudonyms are for, and no, I don't mean your True Name – you guard that like your ATM pin number – I mean that magical name that you share around like free candy. The one that has no real meaning for you. That one. If you don't have one, make one up. Think of it as a hexing code name. We already discussed the power of names in depth so I won't get back into that here, but really, it's important.
- If it's a binding be aware you are tying yourself to the person, thing, or situation. Consider whether that's your best option. If it's any other type of hex be willing to accept

whatever consequences result from it. While we can do everything right in any type of magic we cannot always predict exactly how a spell will play out; sometimes things are stronger or weaker than we intended. In my experience, magic seeks the path of least resistance in manifesting its purpose.

- Always cleanse afterwards and double down on your own protections.

A basic classic hex[12] would go along the lines of: 'Spirit of ---- I call you to punish (person's name) who has (done X) and caused me (this specific harm). May they suffer (lack of sleep and lack of peace, etc.,) until (item is returned/they are sorry/justice is done/ etc.). In the name of --- I offer (specific offering) let (person's name) be brought to justice.'

We also have a wide array of maledictions and satire to look to for examples of traditional hexes in Celtic culture. These usually combine physical actions and spoken charms. Similarly, the Norse culture offers an array of cursing options we can look to for examples of how it's done in that tradition. These all help provide guidelines for ways to hex safely.

Fairy Witchcraft Ethics in the Context of a Gaming Alignment

Out-worn heart, in a time out-worn,
Come clear of the nets of wrong and right
W. B. Yeats

There's a running joke among my friends – or at least it started out as a joke – that I consider myself 'Chaotic Neutral'. It grew out of my adopting the gaming alignment term for my particular approach to ethics within my practice of Fairy Witchcraft (specifically, because Druidic ethics would definitely be more Lawful Good). If you're guessing at this point that I have previous experience playing role-playing games (RPGs) you would be correct. I had started to refer to myself as Chaotic Neutral because I found some aspects of the gaming alignment actually fairly descriptive of both situational ethics and fey ethics and also because I thought it was funny. Over time people began to ask me, quite seriously, what it meant and it shifted from something that was purely a jest to something more solid; which is oddly a very Chaotic Neutral thing for it to do. But let's back up a bit for people who don't know what Chaotic Neutral is.

This is the standard gaming definition. At its core Chaotic Neutral is neither good nor evil by the traditional definitions of the terms, but neutral; they do not generally seek to actively help others out of altruism nor do they seek to actively hurt for the sake of malevolence. Neutrality in this case isn't a lack of choosing sides, but a lack of commitment to either ultimate purpose, which is where the chaotic aspect comes in, because someone who is Chaotic Neutral can choose to act in either direction, to do good or to harm, if the situation seems to warrant either. There is an emphasis on balance and the need for both good and evil in the world. Chaotic Neutral emphasizes following your own whims, indulgence, and the value of the self. Independence, self-reliance, unpredictability, randomness and freedom are key aspects of this alignment.

As to Fairy ethics and Fairy Witchcraft ethics (excerpted from my book *Fairycraft*):

Ethics in Fairy Witchcraft, as with so many things Fairy, are tricky, and may best be described as situational ethics, where there are few hard and fast rules but rather the situation dictates the correct moral response. Generally speaking a person should strive to be kind, take responsibility for their own actions, be generous, compassionate, brave, and honest because these are qualities fairies respect. However, in some cases it is also good to be clever even if that involves deception, if you can pull off being tricky in an honest way, because fairies also admire people who can outsmart their adversaries.

In any dealings with the Otherworld it is essential to be completely honorable; fairies expect that a debt will be repaid and oaths will be kept. They abhor liars, however, they admire cleverness and deception is an art form in Fairy where it is entirely possible using semantics to lie by telling nothing but the absolute truth. Fairies love beauty and this includes beauty of spirit; therefore they love people who are generous, kind, helpful and compassionate. However, they themselves are also beings of unmixed passions, as Yeats would say, who love or hate completely and react to anything in ways we consider extreme. Those they approve of are often rewarded with extreme generosity while those who anger them are punished in ways that seem excessive or even cruel to us. Although they do admire determination in us, it is unwise to try to imitate this behavior ourselves as the negative end of the spectrum tends to typify the things fairies themselves dislike in us. In other words trying to act like you might believe a fairy would in anger is more likely to anger them than win their approval.

It can be difficult for us to understand the fairy people and the fairy Gods when their behavior seems unethical to us, because there are many aspects of their nature we will never be able to fully understand. What we can know though is what they expect of us and what behavior they want to see from us, and that is what we should strive to do. Living an honorable life and being generous and honest is important for anyone following this path.

Now, for me it was fairly obvious that the two concepts, fairy ethics and Chaotic Neutral alignment, overlapped. Both emphasize a degree of unpredictability and of transcending the usual understanding of 'good' and 'bad'. Chaotic Neutral and Fairy reject the idea of following human society's expectations of behaviour or doing something just because it's expected. A fairy bride, for example, might cry at a wedding or laugh at a funeral, and a chaotic neutral character might appear to runaway only to return and help unexpectedly. The point being that they are not bound by the rigid requirements of society at large. Both also admire trickery when it's done within a specific context, usually to achieve a particular end and within very set boundaries (for example, without lying). And both fairy ethics and Chaotic Neutral emphasize the value of personal fulfilment and indulgence while avoiding actions that are committed to either one extreme or another. Both also often confound people who want an easy to understand and predictable response to any situation. Sometimes a fairy will help you, sometimes they may hurt you and often people find the nuances that decide the reaction, helping or hurting, hard to predict simply because they go into the situation expecting human responses. Sometimes a character with a Chaotic Neutral alignment[13] will help you or hurt you, and this also often feels unpredictable, not because it is but because we tend to ignore the actual indicators of behaviour and instead look for what we'd like to see from that person. In the same way the ethics of Fairy Witchcraft, because they are situation based, are not a clear-cut easy to define thing, but rather a matter of seeking to achieve the best outcome possible in the situation, and that will always be a matter of personal perspective.

My personal approach to Chaotic Neutral as a real-world concept is pretty straightforward. I see it as an easy and humourous way to describe my approach to life, and particularly ethics. Being Chaotic Neutral, ultimately means doing what you feel you need to do, or want to do, while simultaneously understanding that you bear the full responsibility for the consequences of all your actions, positive or negative. Freedom is important in our actions, and it is up to us to choose how we react in a situation; we understand that we are not bound by a system of divine reward or punishment so much as we are obligated to deal with a system of consequences for what we do, so, then it is up to us to choose our actions and accept those consequences, whatever they may be. If we were to have a Chaotic Neutral Rede it would be something like: *'Do what you enjoy, if you are willing to pay the cost'*. Okay, in fairness it would really be more like *'Be serious when needed, otherwise shenanigans'*.[14] That's the chaos aspect of it, the balance between serious and pleasure, between fun and grim, and sometimes the two overlap and occur simultaneously; that is also very, very Fey in its own way. There are rules, and ethics, and guidelines to follow – as mentioned above – in how to be a good person, it's just that we worry about our own definition of what a good person is and not what society or other people think makes a person good or bad. A key aspect of it is understanding that perspective is hugely significant in judging whether something is 'good' or 'bad' and that one person's good is almost always another person's bad. The wolf eating the rabbit is terrible for the rabbit but great for the wolf, for example, and yet ultimately this action – terrible and great – is also necessary to preserve a much wider and important balance. And that is Chaotic Neutral.

Endnotes

1. Elfshot, also known as fairyshot or elf arrows, are small stone arrows which are thought to be used by the Good People as well as witches to cause illness, madness and death to those struck by it.

2. Emma Wilby discusses this in her book *Cunningfolk and Familiar Spirits*.

3. I will note here that while the Fey folk wanted this it was not a hard and fast requirement. Scottish witch, Bessie Dunlop, adamantly claimed that she refused to renounce the church and yet she still had a fairy familiar and was given much herbal knowledge by them.

4. Unless you're a Christian witch, or similar, but understand I'm discussing pagan witches here specifically. One can, as it happens, follow Fairy Witchcraft and also continue to adhere to another faith, to be dual tradition as it were, and it is not for me to tell anyone what religion they should or should not be. As I mention in the above footnote, Bessie Dunlop successfully dealt with the fairies despite refusing to renounce Christianity, so it certainly can be done.

5. Common sense here of course, I'm talking about things similar to saying a prayer backwards, or maybe eating a specific kind of food, getting a tattoo, cutting your hair, those sorts of things. Obviously, don't break the law please.

6. For the most part in Fairy witchcraft, using what is local is entirely possible and ideal. There are, occasionally, times when you may need something that you can't personally get any other way than by purchasing and that is alright. Just because local and wild sourced is best doesn't mean it's required. If you can't get an herb any other way than by buying, that's okay. I certainly had little choice but to purchase my cauldron and knife, and because I wanted a wand from a blackthorn I also had to buy that (we don't have any blackthorns here). I'd suggest trying to look for things that were hand-made and that you can identify the sources of, rather than mass market produced but ultimately it's whatever works for you.

7. As someone who has a strong spiritual connection to Ireland, for example, I have found a lot of significance in having items that are also connected to that place. We shouldn't discount the value, psychologically and spiritually, of having tokens we can touch and hold and see that come from places we don't live in but have more complex connections to. There's nothing wrong with that either, as long as it doesn't become unbalanced.

8. I'm putting *real* in quotes here to convey sarcasm. I know

that doesn't always read well but I can't type *real witch* in any seriousness. If you consider yourself a witch then of course you are real.

9. Usually, as with everything in life it isn't always simple or clear cut and I'm sure that some of what I've done could be judged as a bit heavy handed. One of the reasons that I do suggest taking curse-work seriously is because of how easy it is to justify it to ourselves.

10. Historic, mythic and folkloric examples of hexing often are predicated on attempts to restore social order or avenge harm done to people who have no other recourse. Often, but not always.

11. Some people prefer to avoid negative phrasing altogether but there is some precedent for it, for example, in Irish satire practices.

12. Based on curse tablets found in healing springs.

13. Pop culture examples of Chaotic Neutral characters: Captain Jack Sparrow from Pirates of the Caribbean, Q from Star Trek Next Generation, the eponymous character on House, Riddick, Ferris Bueller.

    For those that don't get the pop culture examples – to be more straightforward: cats. Cats are Chaotic Neutral. Might cuddle with you and make you feel better. Might claw your hand and draw blood. Dealer's choice.

14. Shenanigans is a term that is often misunderstood, so, to be clear. Shenanigans = devilry, trickery, intense mischief.

Chapter 10

Advice from the Fairy Courts

With a host of furious fancies,
Whereof I am commander,
With a burning spear and a horse of air
To the wilderness I wander.

Walking this path is more than just believing and practising. It is also about experiencing and listening. I've talked about the reality of dreams and I've talked about the power of visions and of travelling out to Fairy. In practical terms these things aren't just ways to entertain ourselves or pass some time; we do these because we learn from the experiences themselves and we learn from the beings we encounter. What exactly we learn, as with so much of this spirituality, will be different for each person. What I want to do in this chapter is share some of the things I have been told or taught which I feel were or are meant to be shared. These are things that are truisms in some ways but are also lessons that were given to apply just to Fairy and those within it, yet I have found also work well in the human world.

Although I do think dividing or categorizing the Fey folk is something of an exercise in futility there are times when it is necessary. For the purposes of this chapter, I think it's important to divide the advice I've been given into roughly two groupings based on who was giving it, the Unseelie Court or the Seelie Court, because I do feel that the source reflects on the content somewhat. And although I always advise greater caution when dealing with the Unseelie, I wanted to show that they should not necessarily be avoided entirely all the time and that there are good lessons to be learned from them.

Lessons from the Unseelie Court

The Unseelie Court comprises those who are generally more malicious or inclined to harm humans. If one wishes to deal with a member of this Court one really needs to be very careful and to keep in mind that these are not beings who have any particular concern for your welfare. There are lessons to be learned from them, and those lessons are more than simply to avoid them entirely, but you still need to be careful not to get too cocky. Unlike their counterparts in the Bright Court, they don't give warnings or second chances.

So, over the years I have learned several valuable lessons from the Unseelie:

- Nothing's nature is truly set – all things are changeable and one would be wise to never see anything as fixed in stone. When you get into a mindset of expecting behaviour from anything based on a set expectation then you are bound to have a problem: either the other being will do what you don't expect or your own expectations will shape how you act in a negative way.
- All things can be either fierce or gentle – this was told to me by someone who might be termed a guide. I was struggling with an ingrained view of spirits as either good or bad, at the time, and this came in a larger context of a discussion about the way that beings that seem meek can fight to defend themselves while beings that seem aggressive can be kind. It ended up changing my entire view on things, and breaking me out of an either/or mindset.
- External beauty is an illusion, trust the beauty inside a thing if you would use that as a judge – we see a lot of emphasis in stories on physical beauty as a reflection of inner goodness, and I honestly expected the Fey Folk to have a similar opinion on the subject, but for what it's worth I was told that external appearances are fluid and untrust-

worthy. Only the qualities within can or perhaps should be used as a measure. This dovetailed with something else I'd had revealed in a separate experience, that I shouldn't use human standards of beauty, ability or character as a measure for anything else. It basically boiled down to 'humans aren't the measuring stick for all sentient beings'.

- Good manners are the line between earning blessing and earning grief – this one applies to every interaction we have I think, but especially in the context of the Other Crowd. Being polite is at the least the best way to begin interactions. Often enough with the Fey Folk, politeness will gain a better outcome even in a difficult situation than rudeness, while rudeness has consequences.

- Nothing comes without a cost – this was advice given to me in the context of being careful not to assume that something which looked good and beneficial to me didn't have any hidden catch to it. Effectively, the fairy version of always read the fine print, but I've found it a good motto to live by. With rare exceptions Gods, spirits, humans, all expect something in return for something. Knowing that means not (hopefully) making any bad bargains or accidently writing any metaphorical blank cheques. It may sound cynical but truly it isn't, it just means knowing that everything has a value and I need to know going into a situation what that value means to me, what I am willing to pay for something. Or not, as the case may be.

- Always know the measure of your own strength – this falls into the good advice given in a dream category, but it has served me well in life. It's probably not surprising that this advice would come from the darker Fey, I suppose, but the key in dealing with dangerous spirits is to know your own limits and abilities and exactly how far you can push before you need to call in help, whatever that means to you. Don't overestimate yourself, obviously, but don't underestimate yourself either. Know what you can do and how much. It's no guarantee that you won't still get into situations you aren't prepared for or that are beyond you, but it means you'll recognize those situations when they happen and be better prepared to deal with them.

These are only a few of the things I've learned over the years from the Unseelie Court, messages I've taken and incorporated into my practice. Some of these may seem obvious or common sense, but receiving these in the context of spiritual experiences, of dreams or meditations, has been impactful. It offers me a way to feel more deeply connected to my religion but also for these ideas to be more than just ideas because they aren't something I read somewhere but things that I believe were directly communicated.

Lessons from the Seelie Court

The Seelie Court comprises those who are generally more kindly inclined towards humans and more likely to help us and willingly interact with us. Their lessons naturally reflect what you might assume is more in line with their nature, although it's always worth bearing in mind that they are not 100 per cent safe to deal with. Like their darker counterparts they can be moved to do harm as well as to help, they are just less inclined towards it.

Keep in mind that the two Courts are not inverses of each other, as some might imagine, but more like complementary concepts with overlapping features. Sometimes the lessons learned from one can be similar to the lessons of the other, while other times the lesson may be very different. I have found that it is important to try not to have any expectations when going in of what you think you may get from one or the other – they often surprise you. If you go into any experiences without expecting anything then you can take the experiences for what they are without any bias or filter colouring your perception (well, hopefully).

So, what I have learned from the Seelie:

- Embrace joy when and where you find it – all of the Other Crowd are sometimes accused of being shallow or lacking human emotions. I think that's more of a cultural difference than an actual lack on their part, personally, but it is true that they love a good party and embrace things that we would describe as fun: good food, good music, good company. They enjoy any pleasurable experience fully and then move on to the next. From a human perspective we might call this *carpe diem*, but I think that would be misunderstanding their approach, which isn't so much about seizing the day or living life to the fullest – they are immortal or nearly so after all – but rather about appreciating the good things in life when they are there to appreciate.[1] This is one of the first messages I was ever given from the Seelie Court, although arguably it's the one I have the hardest time following through on.

- Even the broken is beautiful – I would have expected this to come from the Unseelie Court, personally, but it didn't. It was relayed in a dream from a source that was definitely a member of the Blessed Court. The point I gathered here was that they value things (and people) who are unique and so see a special value in items that have been broken. It makes that object one of a kind. In the same way, I suspect this is why they are often drawn to people who are eccentric or defy social norms, although that is only my supposition. Being told this has given me a new appreciation for the value of items that I might otherwise have thrown away and a new perspective on the value of things that are different or damaged.

- Do everything with purpose – of all the things I've learned from the Summer Court, this may be the most valuable. For a long time I tended to view any activity that didn't accomplish something as wasted time, or a means to a greater end; however, during a meditation I had a conversation, the crux of which was this message: '*Do everything with purpose*'. And that means everything, including relaxing, napping, eating, walking. In a way it ties into the first point, the idea of embracing joy, but in a larger view it is simply about making all of our actions intentional. Give purpose to even casual moments and you will learn to value things our culture usually doesn't see value in, like relaxing or walking across a parking lot.

- Beauty is a weapon – you may have thought this would be another Unseelie Court thing, but this particular bit of advice, if you want to call it that, came from a Seelie Court being. My own experience, for what it's worth, has been that it is the Seelie Court that really enjoys the power and value of illusion and deception through appearance, so thinking about this one for a bit afterwards, it made sense to me that it came from the source it did. I don't utilize this in my life, but it is a valuable lesson to always keep in mind, especially in a world where we are often inundated with cultural messages that tell us that beauty = goodness.

This is just a small selection of things I have learned over the years from dealing with the Seelie Court in dreams and meditations. As with the things from the Unseelie Court, I have found these bits of wisdom surprisingly profound and impactful. Looking at the way these direct lessons have influenced me has definitely shaped my approach to my spirituality as well as my appreciation for the value of listening to the beings we say we honour and deal with.

Endnotes

1. They can be just as single-minded about warfare, competition, or vengeance, for example.

Conclusion

Walking On

By a knight of ghosts and shadows
I summoned am to tourney
Ten leagues beyond the wide world's end —
Methinks it is no journey.

This path is not an easy one to walk.

It is often less of a path than the hint of a way in the deep forest, the place beneath the trees where the underbrush is less and you think you can almost see the ground to set your feet on. Almost.

I would leave you with these bits of advice which have served me well over the years.

This path is built on the basics. Although we don't often like to admit it, many people don't keep up with the basic practices that they learn early on. The things that may be seen as boring or routine tend to slowly erode from daily and then weekly practice until we have long-time practitioners who don't know how to do very basic things, not from ignorance but from lack of practice. Grounding, shielding, warding, cleansing, these should be staples for any witch. For the Fairy witch you can add in trance-work or journeying. Like any other skill, to be good at witchcraft and ritual requires effort and practice, not once in a while or when a situation calls for it, but constantly. You can't be good at anything if you aren't doing it on a regular basis.

Why do we let the basics slip so easily? I think in the end it comes down to one simple thing that I see as a very widespread occurrence throughout the pagan and witchcraft communities – people feel as if moving forward means moving on, and they treat their practice like classes in school where you finish one and move to the next without worrying too much about keeping up with what you just learned. We need to start emphasizing the importance of maintaining the basic practices as we add to them, not looking at them as things to graduate from so we can stop doing them.

This is a lonely path, and that's just the truth. Learn to love to be alone in your spirituality. People want books and classes to learn from and that's fine to a point because we all start somewhere. In the beginning, especially, those lesson plans and books are our stepping stones and guide posts. We need them to find our way. We need teachers who can show us what to do and how to do it. But the problem is that a time comes when the training wheels have to come off, when other people can't take you any further, and you have to start doing for yourself.

The nicely maintained road ends and only the trackless woods remain, and it's up to you, by yourself, to forge on anyway. And many people don't like getting sweaty and dirty. They don't like the lack of certainty, the dark unknown, the unanswerable 'what now?' that looms ahead of them. People want a life that is neatly ordered and organized, and especially in witchcraft, at least my witchcraft, there is none of that. You may realize that you have come to that point now yourself where you are leaving behind the crowd and forging ahead for yourself. You may be reaching a place where the spirits and fairies call to you more, resonate with you more, than most human people. It's hard to let go of that need for community acceptance and that desire to be part of something – and indeed you don't have to move into a hut in the forest and stop speaking to other people. You can still have friends and celebrate with others and belong to groups. But you will find as you go further down the path that other people understand you less. You begin, I think, to edge a little at a time into the Otherworld in ways that start to be perceptible to other people. Be prepared for that.

This is a dangerous path. I can teach you the rules of safety but I can't promise you'll be safe – in fact I can almost guarantee, if you are actually out there doing then, you will stumble and fall and get hurt sometimes. I can describe the experiences, but you can't experience it with me, any more than telling you what dirt under my fingernails feels likes can really make you understand the sensation of it. You have to get out there and get dirty, dig your fingers into the earth, make your own trail, have your own experiences. No one else can do that for you. And the truth is that the experiences you have as you go along will be unique to you. They won't be like mine, nor should they be.

So go out, my friends, and get your hands dirty. Walk into those woods, where the trail ends, and make your own way. It won't always be easy and it won't always be fun – although you may be surprised how often it is – but it will be worth it.

Appendix A

Bedlam Boys

I've begun each chapter throughout the text with a verse from the traditional folk song 'Bedlam Boys'. Here I'd like to offer the full text of the song which includes more than the few verses seen so far. I find the song inspiring and also believe, like the ballads we discussed in Chapter 5, that there is some valuable folklore to be dug out here. Unlike the previous ballads we discussed though, I will leave it to you to decide what you see in here and what meaning you find.

> For to see Mad Tom of Bedlam
> Ten thousand miles I'd travel
> Mad Maudlin goes on dirty toes
> To save her shoes from gravel.

> Chorus: Still I sing bonny boys, bonny mad boys
> Bedlam boys are bonny
> For they all go bare and they live by the air
> And they want no drink nor money.

> I went down to Satan's kitchen
> To break my fast one morning
> And there I got souls piping hot
> That were on the spit a-turning.

> There I took a cauldron
> Where boiled ten thousand harlots
> Though full of flame I drank the same
> To the health of all such varlets.

My staff has murdered giants
My bag a long knife carries
To cut mince pies from children's thighs
For which to feed the fairies.

No gypsy, slut nor doxy
Shall win my mad Tom from me
I'll weep all night, with stars I'll fight
The fray shall well become me.

From the hag and hungry goblin
That into rags would rend ye,
All the sprites that stand by the naked man
In the book of moons, defend ye.

With a thought I took for Maudlin,
And a cruse of cockle pottage,
With a thing thus tall, Sky bless you all,
I befell into this dotage.

I slept not since the Conquest,
Till then I never waked,
Till the naked boy of love where I lay
Me found and stript me naked.

I know more than Apollo,
For oft when he lies sleeping
I see the stars at mortal wars
In the wounded welkin weeping.

The moon embrace her shepherd,
And the Queen of Love her warrior,
While the first doth horn the star of morn,
And the next the heavenly farrier.

Of thirty years have I
Twice twenty been enraged
And of forty been three times fifteen
In durance soundly caged.

On the lordly lofts of Bedlam
With stubble soft and dainty,
Brave bracelets strong, sweet whips, ding-dong,
With wholesome hunger plenty.

When I short have shorn my sour-face
And swigged my horny barrel
In an oaken inn, I pound my skin
As a suit of gilt apparel.

The moon's my constant mistress,
And the lonely owl my marrow;
The flaming drake and the night crow make
Me music to my sorrow.

The spirits white as lightening
Would on my travels guide me
The stars would shake and the moon would quake
Whenever they espied me.

And then that I'll be murdering
The Man in the Moon to the powder
His staff I'll break, his dog I'll shake
And there'll howl no demon louder.

By a knight of ghosts and shadows
I summoned am to tourney
Ten leagues beyond the wide world's end—
Methinks it is no journey.

With a host of furious fancies,
Whereof I am commander,
With a burning spear and a horse of air
To the wilderness I wander.

The palsy plagues my pulses
When I prig your pigs or pullen
Your culvers take, or matchless make
Your Chanticleer or sullen.

When I want provant, with Humphry
I sup, an when benighted
I repose in Paul's with waking souls,
Yet never am affrighted.

That of your five sound senses
You never be forsaken,
Nor wander from your selves with Tom
Abroad to beg your bacon.

I'll bark against the Dog-Star
I'll crow away the morning
I'll chase the Moon till it be noon
And I'll make her leave her horning.

I now repent that ever
Poor Tom was so disdained
My wits are lost since him I crossed
Which makes me thus go chained.

So drink to Tom of Bedlam
Go fill the seas in barrels
I'll drink it all, well brewed with gall
And maudlin drunk I'll quarrel.

Appendix B

The Ogham

I'm including this in the appendix rather than the body of the book because I don't think the Ogham will be a tool that every Fairy Witch will find useful. However, I think that the wisdom of the Ogham – not only the tree alphabet but also the other related Ogham – can be very helpful and worth understanding for those who work in a Celtic framework and who study Irish or Celtic folklore and mythology.

The Ogham that we are most familiar with in a modern context is the Tree Ogham which associates each letter of the Ogham alphabet with a specific tree. However, there are actually many different types of Ogham associations including River Ogham, for example, and Pig Ogham. Each one is layered, both a mnemonic device which associates the letter with a word that begins with that letter and also a mystical system whereby each association has deeper significance related to the ultimate meaning of the symbol. For those seeking to use Ogham, especially magically or for divination, having an understanding of more than just the Tree Ogham is important. There are several good books on the market, including Erynn Rowan Laurie's book *Ogam Weaving Word Wisdom*, Steven Blamires' *Celtic Tree Mysteries*, John-Paul Patton's *The Poet's Ogam* and Skip Ellison's book *Ogham: the secret language of the Druids*. What I would like to offer here is an expanded guide to the symbols and some of the basic associations from several of the Oghams; the symbols themselves can be found in a variety of places including with a quick Google search, so, I am only offering the names and information here. It's important to note that while the words do not seem related when we see them in English in the original Irish they all alliterate, beginning with the same letter as their

The Ogham

corresponding Ogham letter – this is highly significant and needs to be kept in mind. To help the reader with this, I am including the Old Irish names and words as much as possible.

Ogham name: Beithe – pronounced: Beh.

English letter: B.

Literally 'birch tree'.

Tree Ogham – birch.

The Word Ogham describes it as 'faded trunk and fair hair'.

The Alphabet Ogham of Mac Ind Oc says this 'most silvery of the skin'.

The Scholar's Primer tells us that Beithe is the first letter because it was the first ever written, used seven times in a row to warn the God Lugh that his wife was in danger.

Bird Ogham – pheasant (besan).

Colour Ogham – white (ban).

Skill Ogham – livelihood (bethamnas).

Key words for divination use: new beginnings, cleansing, protection.

Ogham name: Luis – pronounced Looh-sh.

English letter: L.

Possibly from 'lus' meaning herb.

In the Tree Ogham itrepresents the Rowan, 'coarthann' or elm

The Word Ogham calls it 'delight of eye, to wit the flame'.

The Alphabet Ogham of Mac Ind Oc says this 'friend of cattle ... for dear to the cattle is the elm for its bloom and for down'.

The Scholar's Primer tells us: 'Delight of eye is mountain-ash, i.e. rowan, owing to the beauty of its berries.'

Bird Ogham – duck (lachu).

Colour Ogham – grey (liath).

Skill Ogham – pilotage (lúamnacht).

Key words for divination use: enchantment, mysticism, protection against magic.

251

Ogham name: Fearn – pronounced Fee-yarn.

English letter: F.

In the Tree Ogham it is the alder tree, Old Irish 'fern', modern 'fearnog'.

The Word Ogham calls it 'shield of warrior-bands'.

The Alphabet Ogham of Mac Ind Oc says this: 'guarding of milk ... for of it [alder] are made the vessels containing the milk.'

The Scholar's Primer tells us: 'The van of the Warrior-bands, that is, alder, for thereof are the shields.'

Bird Ogham – seagull (faelinn).

Colour Ogham – blood red (flann).

Skill Ogham – poetry (filidecht).

Key words for divination: support, protection during attack. Often associated with ravens and divination.

Ogham name: Saille – pronounced Sall-yuh.

English letter: S.

In the Tree Ogham it is the willow tree, Old Irish 'sail'.

The Word Ogham calls it 'hue of the lifeless'.

The Alphabet Ogham of Mac Ind Oc says this 'activity of the bees'.

The Scholar's Primer tells us: 'The colour of a lifeless one, i.e. it has no colour, i.e. owing to the resemblance of its hue to a dead person.'

Bird Ogham – hawk (sebac).

Colour Ogham – 'fine-coloured' (sodath).

Art Ogham – craft of a wright (saírsecht).

Key words for divination: healing, making plans, moving forward.

Ogham name: Nin – pronounced Nin.

English letter: N.

Possibly 'weaver's beam'.

In modern understanding it is associated with the Ash, 'fuinseag' but in the Tree Ogham it is said to be 'maw of spear, or nettles in the woods'.

The Word Ogham calls it 'checking of peace; it is the maw of a weaver's beam as applied to wood, a sign of peace is that'.

The Alphabet Ogham of Mac Ind Oc says this ' fight of women'.

The Scholar's Primer tells us: 'A check on peace is nin, viz., ash, for of it are made the spear-shafts by which the peace is broken.'

Bird Ogham – snipe (naescu).

Colour Ogham – clear (necht).

Skill Ogham – notary work (notairecht).

Key words for divination: peace, creation, stability. A clear path. Bring things together.

Ogham name: Huath – pronounced Oo-uh.

English letter: H.

Literally terror or phantom.

In the Tree Ogham, represented by the Hawthorn, 'sceach', a fairy tree.

The Word Ogham calls it 'a pack of wolves, for a terror to anyone is a pack of wolves'.

The Alphabet Ogham of Mac Ind Oc says this 'blanching of face, fear'.

The Scholar's Primer tells us: 'A meet of hounds is huath, viz. white-thorn; or because it is formidable owing to its thorns.'

Bird Ogham – night raven (hadaig)?

Colour Ogham – 'terrible' (huath)?

Art Ogham – trisyllabic poetry (hairchetal).

Key words for divination: the unknown, fear of the unseen, transition.

Ogham name: Duir – pronounced Doo-ihr.

English letter: D.

The oak 'dair'.

The Word Ogham calls it 'highest of bushes'.

The Alphabet Ogham of Mac Ind Oc says this 'carpenter's work'.

The Scholar's Primer tells us: 'Higher than bushes is an oak.'

Bird Ogham – wren (droen).

Colour Ogham – black (dub).

Skill Ogham – wizardry (draiocht).

Key words for divination: wisdom, strength, protection, growth.

Ogham name: Tinne – pronounced Tihn-nyeh.

English letter: T.

Literally means metal rod.

In the Tree Ogham associated with the Holly 'cuileann' or elderberry.

It is not found in the Word Ogham.

The Alphabet Ogham of Mac Ind Oc says this 'fires of coal'.

The Scholar's Primer tells us: 'holly, a third of a wheel is holly, that is, because holly is one of the three timbers of the chariot-wheel.'

Bird Ogham – starling (truith).

Colour Ogham – dark grey (temen).

Skill Ogham – turning (?).

Key words for divination: fighting, contention, weapons, fire, and smithcraft.

Ogham name : Coll – pronounced Kohl.

English letter: C.

In the Tree Ogham it is hazel.

In the Word Ogham: 'fairest of trees, owing to its beauty in woods.'

The Alphabet Ogham of Mac Ind Oc says this 'friend of cracking'.

The Scholar's Primer tells us: 'Fair wood, that is, hazel, i.e. everyone is eating of its nuts.'

Bird Ogham – not listed.

Colour Ogham – reddish-brown (cron).

Skill Ogham – harp playing (cruittirecht).
Key words for divination: divination, magic, and enchantment, knowledge. Also relates to wealth.

Ogham name Quert, alt. Cert – pronounced Kehrt.
English letter: Q.
Means 'rags'. In modern understanding this is apple 'ull'.
The Tree Ogham gives three options – holly, rowan, or aspen.
The Word Ogham calls it 'shelter of a hind. [and] death sense, it is then his sense comes to him when he goes to his death, that is an apple tree'. By this account it is associated with lunatics, deer, death and apple trees.
The Alphabet Ogham of Mac Ind Oc says this 'force of the man'.
The Scholar's Primer tells us: 'Shelter of a boiscill, that is, a wild hind is queirt, i.e. an apple tree.'
Bird Ogham – hen (cerc).
Colour Ogham – dark (cíar).
Art Ogham – fluting (cuislennach).
Key words for divination: healing, restoration, renewal, nourishment.

Ogham name: Muin – pronounced Mwin.
English letter: M.
Literally means 'neck' or 'back'.
In the Tree Ogham it stands for the vine 'funiuin'.
The Word Ogham calls it 'strongest of effort, back of a man or ox'.
The Alphabet Ogham of Mac Ind Oc says this 'condition of slaughter'.
The Scholar's Primer tells us: 'Highest of beauty is muin, that is, because it grows aloft, that is, a vine-tree.'
Bird Ogham – titmouse (mintan).
Colour Ogham – speckled (mbracht).
Skill Ogham – soldiering (míletacht).

Key words for divination: release, compromises, focus, determination, confrontation, vengeance (basically think the good and bad sides of wine).

Ogham name: Gort – pronounced Guhrt.

English letter G.

Literally 'field'. In the Tree Ogham it is 'cornfield' but is understood as the ivy, 'eidhnean'.

The Word Ogham calls it 'sweeter than grasses. When it is in the blade sweeter than any grass is that grass, to wit, the cornfield'.

The Scholar's Primer tells us: 'Greener than pastures is ivy.'

The Alphabet Ogham of Mac Ind Oc says simply 'ivy'.

Bird Ogham – swan (geis).

Colour Ogham – blue (gorm).

Skill Ogham – smithwork (goibnecht).

Key words for divination: beauty, love, friendship, fidelity.

Ogham name nGetal – pronounced Neh-tahl.

English letter: nG.

Literally 'wounding'.

Associated with the broom plant or reed 'giolcach' in Tree Ogham.

The Word Ogham calls it 'the physician's strength' because of its association with battle and wounding and also calls it 'robe of physicians'.

Not found in the Alphabet of Mac Ind Oc.

The Scholar's Primer tells us: 'A physician's strength is broom, to wit, broom or fern.'

Bird Ogham – goose (ngeigh).

Colour Ogham – green (nglas).

Skill Ogham – arranging (glósnáithe ?).

Key words for divination: separation, warning, courage, direct action.

Ogham name: Straif – pronounced Strahf.

English letter: Str.

Sraib literally 'sulfur'; straif is explained in some later glossaries as meaning 'Blackthorn sloe'.

In the Tree Ogham it is the willowbrake and in modern terms is understood as the blackthorn 'draighean'.

The Word Ogham calls it 'strongest of red' and associates it with Blackthorn sloes.

The Alphabet Ogham of Mac Ind Oc says this 'increasing of secrets'.

The Scholar's Primer tells us: 'The hedge of a stream is sraibh, that is, black-thorn.'

Bird Ogham – thrush (stmolach).

Colour Ogham – bright (sorcha).

Skill Ogham – deer-stalking (sreghuindeacht).

Key words for divination: discernment, cunning, focused protection, the thorn, inner strength, boundaries.

Ogham name: Ruis – pronounced Roosh.

English letter: R.

Literally 'redness'.

In Tree Ogham it represents the elder tree, 'trom'.

The Word Ogham calls it 'intensest of blushes, from the reddening or shame according to fact'.

The Alphabet Ogham of Mac Ind Oc says this 'redness of faces; sap of the rose which causes the redness of faces so that blushing is in them'.

The Scholar's Primer tells us: 'The redness of shame is ruis, i.e. elder.'

Bird Ogham – small rook (rocnat).

Colour Ogham – red (ruadh).

Skill Ogham – feast giving (rannach).

Key words for divination: anger, blushing (i.e. loss of face, embarrassment), endings, completion, be realistic in order to succeed.

Ogham name; Ailm – pronounced Al-ihm.

English letter: A.

The word and its meaning is uncertain.

In Tree Ogham it represents the fir or pine, 'giuis'.

The Word Ogham calls it 'loudest of groaning'.

The Alphabet Ogham of Mac Ind Oc calls it 'beginning of an answer'.

The Scholar's Primer tells us only that ailm is the fir or pine.

Bird Ogham – lapwing (aidhircleog).

Colour Ogham – piebald (alad).

Skill Ogham – sovereignty (airechas).

Key words for divination: hard work, effort. The need for caution. Integrity and good judgement are key.

Ogham name: Onn – pronounced On.

English letter: O.

Old Irish for 'ash tree' or 'stone'.

In Tree Ogham this is given as 'furze or ash' but is understood now as gorse, 'aitenn'.

The Word Ogham calls it 'helper of horses' and 'equally wounding'.

The Alphabet Ogham of Mac Ind Oc says this of it 'smoothest of work'.

The Scholar's Primer tells us only that this is the furze.

Bird Ogham – dun coloured bird (odoroscrach)?

Colour Ogham – dun (odor).

Skill Ogham – literally Ogham writing, euphemistically called 'harvesting' (ogmóracht).

Key words for divination: take action, movement, success, perseverance, relief.

Ogham name: Uir – pronounced Oor.

English letter: U.

Literally 'earth'.

Described in the Tree Ogham as 'thorn' but currently understood as heather, 'fraoch'.

The Word Ogham says of it 'in cold dwellings'.

The Alphabet Ogham of Mac Ind Oc says this 'growing of plants; the soil of the earth'.

The Scholar's Primer tells us only that ur is heath.

Bird Ogham – lark (uiseog).

Colour Ogham – resinous (usgdha).

Skill Ogham – brasswork (umaidecht).

Key words for divination: embrace your talents, plant now to harvest later, effort brings reward with patience.

Ogham name: Edad – pronounced Ehd-ahd.

English letter: E.

The word and meaning are unknown.

In the Tree Ogham it is the yew, now understood as the aspen, 'crithach'.

The Word Ogham calls it 'distinguished wood'.

The Alphabet Ogham of Mac Ind Oc says this 'synonym for a friend'.

The Scholar's Primer tells us: 'that is, ed uath, horrible grief.'

Bird Ogham – swan (ela).

Colour Ogham – dark red (erc).

Skill Ogham – fowling (énairecht).

Key words for divination: endings, death, let go of what you've outgrown. Calm consideration. Trust in your ability to endure.

Ogham name: Idad – pronounced Eed-ahd.

English letter: I.

The word and meaning are unknown. Associated with the yew, 'iur', in the Tree Ogham it is simply called a 'service tree'.

The Word Ogham calls it 'oldest of woods, that is the yew'.

The Alphabet Ogham of Mac Ind Oc says this 'most withered of wood'.

The Scholars Primer tells us only that this is the yew.

Bird Ogham – (?) (illait).

Colour Ogham – very white (irfind).

Skill Ogham – fishing or yew work (íascairecht) or (ibróracht).

Key words for divination: see the big picture. Seek experience, know when to act and when not to act. Bide your time. Don't avoid problems.

Appendix C

Resources

The bibliography of this book contains many excellent books that are great resources for further study on this path. I do want to discuss a few non-fiction books in more depth and beyond these there are other resources that I would recommend looking into including works of fiction as well as movies and some good YouTube videos.

Non-Fiction Books

There are a lot of non-fiction books out there about fairies and many are best avoided, quite frankly. Some though are solid resources and worth reading.

A Dictionary of Fairies by Katherine Briggs – really anything by Katherine Briggs is good as she was an eminent folklorist of her time. This book is my choice to recommend because it's one of my go-to's and is easy to use due to its format.

The Good People: New Fairylore Essays edited by Peter Narvaez – a collection of more recent essays on the subject of fairylore from different Celtic countries, including a lot of anecdotal evidence. A modern version of *The Fairy Faith in Celtic Countries*.

A Practical Guide to Irish Spirituality: Slí Aon Dhraoi by Lora O'Brien – a great overall introduction to modern Irish paganism that includes some good discussion on the Othercrowd. I'd also recommend the author's older book, *Irish Witchcraft from an Irish Witch*.

Fairy and Folktales of the Irish Peasantry by W. B. Yeats – a look at folklore and belief, especially fairylore. I also highly recommend *Celtic Twilight* by Yeats which has some great folklore as well; I like that one so much I carry a copy of it around with me in my bag.

The Gaelic Otherworld by John Campbell – an overview of Scottish folk beliefs and folk lore. There is some really good Scottish fairylore here which can be hard to find elsewhere.

The Fairy Faith in Celtic Countries by W. Y. Evans Wentz – the classic text on the Fairy Faith, it's a bit dated at this point having come out in 1911 but it includes fairy beliefs from a wide array of Celtic cultures.

Scottish Herbs and Fairy Lore – by Ellen Evert Hopman – a great book on traditional Scottish fairy beliefs and related practices.

Elves, Wights and Trolls by Kveldulfr Gundarson – a look at Norse and German fairy beliefs and some comparison with the Celtic beliefs. Very useful for looking at how different closely related cultures viewed their fairies.

The Secret Commonwealth of Elves, Fauns and Fairies by Reverend Robert Kirk[1] – written in the seventeenth century it's a short but fascinating look at traditional Scottish fairy beliefs.

The Secret Commonwealth and the Fairy Belief Complex by Brian Walsh – a review and analysis of Rev. Kirk's book but extremely insightful and should be read in addition to Kirk's book for its commentary on beliefs about fairies.

Meeting the Other Crowd by Eddie Lenihan and Carolyn Green – excellent book on Irish fairy lore.

Faeries by Brian Froud[2] and Alan Lee – excellent artwork and some great tidbits of folklore sprinkled in. I included this in particular for the artwork which encompasses the entire range from attractive to hideous, from grand to humble. Froud also tackles a wide range of beings in his work including those that are often overlooked by other artists.

Fiction

Most fiction which is based around fairies doesn't make a good resource here, for an obvious reason: it's fiction. It was written by someone wanting to tell a good story, not for the purpose of passing on actual belief or folklore. As much as we might like to think that fiction authors are actually inspired by real fairies or trying to tell a true story, much of the fairy fiction on the market is vastly at odds with traditional folklore. There are, however, some that are closer to traditional lore, and so I'm listing those here as resources.

The Faery Sworn Series by Ron Nieto – a trilogy about the granddaughter of a Fairy Doctor in Scotland who teams up with a kelpie to find her grandmother when she goes missing.

The Knowing by Kevin Manwaring – a story that builds off of the life and disappearance of Rev. Robert Kirk. A really interesting story and some great fairylore in it.

Good Fairies of New York by Martin Miller – a bit whimsical but also gritty. A story about Celtic fairies coming to New York and those already there, how their lives collide with several humans.

Lords and Ladies by Terry Pratchett – part of Pratchett's Discworld series, and in fairness his other books are also good, but this one is my particular favourite for fairylore.

Spiritwalk by Charles de Lint – a work of urban fantasy but full of genuine Celtic mythology and folklore, with some touches of the Americas.

Additional Ballads

We only touched on a small selection of ballads in this book but there are many others worth studying. Below is a short list of the main ones I'd recommend; it is of course not exhaustive and most ballads have a variety of versions.

Alice Brand – a ballad about a woman and her lover who flee to live in a forest after the lover kills the woman's brother. The wood is an elfin wood and the King of Fairy sends one of his people to deal with the interlopers. A fascinating look not only at a Fairy King, which is less common, but some protection against fairies and the crossover between fairies and the dead.

Allison Gross – the story of a witch who enchants a man into the shape of a worm. He remains thus until one Halloween when the Seelie Queen is passing by and takes pity on him.

The Wee Wee Man – a ballad set in Cartehaugh like Tam Lin, featuring a person's encounter with a tiny but immensely strong fairy man who performs feats of strength and magic and takes the person into a fairy hall. Useful for insight into fairy powers as well the description of the fairy hall.

Childe Rowland – the story of a young girl who is taken into fairy after going counter-clockwise around a church at noon and her three brothers' separate attempts to rescue her with the advice of a warlock named Merlin. Too long to include in this book but includes a lot of essential fairylore.

YouTube

Ah, YouTube. There's some really interesting stuff on there. Here are a couple of videos I'd recommend:

The Fairy Faith – a documentary that looks at fairy beliefs and anecdotes in America, Ireland and the UK, https://www.youtube.com/watch?v=xYYbrKq3hv0

Irish Fairylore: An Interview with Folklorist Dr. Jenny Butler – a great interview with someone who knows the subject well from an academic perspective, https://www.youtube.com/watch?v=CnDlZLkralU

Folklore Collections by Michael Fortune – Michael Fortune is a treasure; he has spent time and effort recording interviews with people about their beliefs in different parts of Ireland, https://www.youtube.com/playlist?list=PLrw-XMzMCkujsJYziUeyoo__j2RPZUwRT

Eddie Lenihan – there are a few videos of Eddie Lenihan on youTube and I highly recommend them. He is an amazing storyteller and very knowledgeable, https://www.youtube.com/watch?v=Q_ez_g_VqEE

Miscellaneous

Not on youTube but really, really worth watching is the Kin

Fables series, http://www.fiveknightsproductions.com/work.html

One of the best classes I've ever personally attended on fairies was taught by Lora O'Brien. She offers it online, as well as a series of guided meditations and some other classes. Definitely worth looking into, http://loraobrien.net/class/download/

'The poem La Belle Dame sans Merci' by John Keats is an excellent look at fairy beliefs relating to fairies of the Leannan Sí type. Free versions can be found online.

Television and Movies

Secret of Roan Inish – a movie about a family's multi-generational relationship with selkies, called rón in Irish.

The Spiderwick Chronicles – aimed at a very young audience, but seems to capture the idea of some traditional fairies.

Pan's Labyrinth – fairly accurate, although very grim depiction of fairies.

Labyrinth – more lighthearted but truer to older folklore. A story of a girl trying to regain her baby brother from goblins; reminiscent of old changeling stories.

The Last Unicorn – I may be biased but I always really enjoyed this one and think it stays true to the feel of older fairylore.

Krampus – technically a horror movie, of sorts, but it has an interesting take on both Krampus and elves that is not out of line with folklore.

Jonathan Strange & Mr. Norrell – a television series which only lasted for one season but includes a lot of British fairylore.

The television show Torchwood has an episode called 'Small Worlds' that focuses on the Fey in a way that is fairly accurate to some folklore.

Endnotes

1.   Please be certain that you get the book titled *The Secret Commonwealth of Elves, Fauns, and Fairies*. There is another

book that was published in 2005 called *The Secret Lives of Elves & Faeries* by John Matthews. The similarity of the titles can be confusing but only *The Secret Commonwealth* was written by Rev. Robert Kirk and its contents are invaluable in studying fairylore. I do not personally recommend Matthews' book.

2. Brian Froud is also the artist who designed the fairies for the movie Labyrinth and the Dark Crystal. He has quite a few other books of artwork at this point and they are all worth getting, in my opinion, but if you can only get one it should be *Faeries*.

Bibliography

Acland, A., (1997) Tam Lin retrieved from http://tam-lin.org/

Acland, A., (2015) Is Tam Lin a Rape Story? http://tam-lin.org/analysis/Tam_Lin_and_rape.html

Acland, A., (1997) Thomas the Rhymer http://tam-lin.org/stories/Thomas_the_Rhymer.html

Acland, A., (1997) Childe Rowland http://tam-lin.org/stories/Childe_Rowland.html

Aislinge Oenguso http://iso.ucc.ie/Aislinge-oenguso/Aislinge-oenguso-text.html

Allingham, W., (1888) The Lepracaun; or Fairy shoemaker http://www.sacred-texts.com/neu/yeats/fip/fip24.htm

Anderson, G., (2008) *Birds of Ireland: facts, folklore & history*

Ashliman, D., (2005) Night-Mares http://www.pitt.edu/~dash/nightmare.html

Ballard, L., (1991) 'Fairies and the Supernatural on Reachrai' in *The Good People: New Fairylore Essays*

Beachcombing's Bizarre History Blog, (2016) 'In Search of the Earliest Fairy Wings', http://www.strangehistory.net/2016/12/17/search-earliest-fairy-wings/

Becker, M., (2009) An American witch bottle. Retrieved from http://www.archaeology.org/online/features/halloween/witch_bottle.html

Beveridge, J., (2014). *Children into Swans: Fairy Tales and the Pagan Imagination*

Bitel, L., (1991) "In Visu Noctis": Dreams in European Hagiography and Histories

Black, G., (1903) County Folk-Lore, vol. 3: Examples of Printed Folk-Lore Concerning the Orkney & Shetland Islands

Briggs, K., (1967) *The Fairies in Literature and Tradition*

—(1976) *Dictionary of Fairies*

—(1976) *An Encyclopedia of Fairies*

—(1978) *The Vanishing People: Fairy Lore and Legends*

Bruford, A., (1991). 'Trolls, Hillfolk, Finns, and Picts: The identity of the Good Neighbors in Orkney and the Shetlands', in *The Good People: New Fairylore Essays*

Buchan, D., (1991) 'Ballads of Otherworld Beings' in *The Good People: New Fairylore Essays*

Buchan, P., (1828) *Ancient Ballads and Songs of the North of Scotland*

Caffrey, N., (2002) The Elfin Knight Child #2: Impossible Tasks and Impossible Love

Calder, G., (1917) Auraicept na n-Éces: The Scholar's Primer, http://www.maryjones.us/ctexts/scholar_primer.html

Campbell, J., (1902). *The Gaelic Otherworld*

Carmichael, A., (1900) *Carmina Gadelica*

Carson, C., (1956) The Midnight Court

Chambers, R., (1842) *Popular Rhymes, Fireside Stories, and Amusements of Scotland*

Child, F., (1898) *The English and Scottish Popular Ballads*

Cunningham, S., (1985) *Encyclopedia of Magical Herbs*

Cutchin, J., (2015) *A Trojan Feast*

Daimler, M., (2017) Echtra Condla, http://lairbhan.blogspot.com/2017/03/ectra-condla-chaim-meic-cuind.html

—(2017) *Fairies: A Guide to the Celtic Fair Folk*

Danaher, K., (1972) *The Year in Ireland*

Davies, O., (2003) *Popular Magic: Cunning-folk in English History*

D'Este, S., and Rankine, D., (2012) *The Faerie Queens*

DSL (2017) *Dictionary of the Scots Language*

Dobs, M (1929) Zeitschrift fur Celtische Philologie, Vol 18

Douglas, G., (1901) *Scottish Fairy and Folk Tales*

Dúchas.ie (2017) A Story of Lug Dubh retrieved from https://www.duchas.ie/en/cbes/5009087/4985340/5122146

Dunnigan, S., (2016) 'From Fairy Queens to Ogresses: Female Enchanters in Early Scottish Literature', *The Bottle Imp*, Issue 20,

eDIL (2017) Luchorpan http://edil.qub.ac.uk/search?search_

in=headword&q=luchorp

Erickson, W., 1996) *Mapping the Faerie Queene: Quest Structures and the World of the Poem*

Evans, E., (1957) *Irish Folk Ways*

Evans-Wentz (1911) *Fairy Faith in Celtic Countries*

Firth Green, R., (2016) *Elf Queens and Holy Friars*

Gregory (1970) *Visions & Beliefs in the West of Ireland*

Grimm, J., (1888) *Teutonic Mythology,* Vol. 2

Gundarsson, K., (2007) *Elves, Wights, and Trolls*

Gwyndaf, R., (1991) Fairylore: Memorates and Legends from Welsh Oral Tradition, in *The Good People: New Fairylore Essays*

Hall, A., (2005) 'Getting Shot of Elves: Healing, Witchcraft and Fairies in the Scottish Witchcraft Trials', *Folklore,* Volume 116

—(2007) *Elves in Anglo-Saxon England*

—(2007) 'The Evidence for *Maran,* the Anglo-Saxon "Nightmares"' in *Neophilologus,* Vol. 91

Harms, D., Clark, J., and Peterson, J., (2015) *The Book of Oberon: A Sourcebook of Elizabethan Magic*

Harper, D., (2017) Imp, Online Etymology Dictionary

—(2017) Leprechaun, Online Etymology Dictionary

—(2017) Thanks, Online Etymology Dictionary

—(2017) Nightmare, Online Etymology Dictionary

Hartland, E., (1890) *English Fairy and Other Folk Tales*

—(1891) *The Science of Fairy Tales: An Inquiry into Fairy Mythology*

Heddle, D., (2016) 'Selkies, Sex, and the Supernatural', *The Bottle Imp,* Issue 20

Henderson, L., and Cowan, E., (2007) *Scottish Fairy Belief*

Henderson, L., (2016) 'The (Super)natural world of Robert Kirk: Fairies, Beasts, Landscapes and Lychnobious Liminalities', *The Bottle Imp,* Issue 20

Huson, P., (1971) *Mastering Witchcraft*

Hyde, D., (1910) *Beside the Fire: A Collection of Irish Gaelic Folk Stories*

Jackson, N., (1994) *Call of the Horned Piper*

JCHAS (2010) *Journal of the Cork Historical and Archaeological Society*

Jolly, K., (1996) *Popular Religion in Late Saxon England: Elf Charms in Context*

Johnson, M., (2014) *Seeing Fairies*

Kelly, F., (2005) *A Guide to Early Irish Law*

Kirk, R., (1691) *The Secret Commonwealth of Elves, Fauns, and Fairies*

Lecouteux, C., (2003) *Witches, Werewolves, and Fairies: Shapeshifters and Astral Doubles in the Middle Ages*

—(2009) *The Return of the Dead: Ghosts, Ancestors, and the Transparent Veil of the Pagan Mind*

—(2011) *Phantom Armies of the Night: The Wild Hunt and the Ghostly Processions of the Undead*

—(2013) *The Tradition of Household Spirits: Ancestral Lore and Practices*

—(2015) *Demons and Spirits of the Land*

Lenihan, E., and Green, C., (2003) *Meeting the Othercrowd*

Logan, P., (1981). *The Old Gods: The Facts about Irish Fairies*

Lyle, E., (1970) 'The Teind to Hell in Tam Lin', Folklore, Volume 70

Lysaght, P., (1986) *The Banshee: The Irish Death Messenger*

McCain, B., (2009) *The Second Sight*

MacCoitir, N., (2003) *Irish Trees*

—(2006) *Irish Wild Plants*

McCone, K., (1990) *Pagan Past and Christian Present in Early Irish Literature*

MacKillop, J., (1998) *A Dictionary of Celtic Mythology*

MacManus, D., (1959) *The Middle Kingdom: The Faerie World of Ireland*

McNeill, F., (1956) *The Silver Bough*

Miller, J., (2004) *Magic and Witchcraft in Scotland*

Narvaez, P., (1991) *The Good People: New Fairylore Essays*

Newall, V., (1973) *The Witch Figure*

O'Crualaoich, G., (2006) 'Reading the Bean Feasa', *Folklore*, Volume 116

O'hOgáin, D., (1995) *Irish Superstitions*

O'Grady S., (1892), *Silva Gadelica*, Volume 2

O'Súilleabháin, S., (1967) *Nósanna agus Piseoga na nGael*

O'Sullivan, S., (1966) *Folktales of Ireland*

Old Farmers Almanac (2012) http://www.almanac.com/calendar/date/2012-08-17

Olsen, K., and Veenstra, J., (2014) *Airy Nothings: Imagining the Otherworld of Faerie from the Middle Ages to the Age of Reason*

Pocs, E., (1999) *Between the Living and the Dead*

Purkiss, D., (2000) *At the Bottom of the Garden: A Dark History of Fairies, Hobgoblins, and Other Troublesome Things*

Quinn, E., (2009) *Irish American Folklore in New England*

Reppion, J., (2016) *Spirits of Place*

Rieti, B., (1991) *Strange Terrain: The Fairy World in Newfoundland*

Rogers, C., (1869) *Scotland Social and Domestic: Memorial of Life and Manners in North Britain*

Ross, A., (1976) *The Folklore of the Scottish Highlands*

Seo Helrune (2016) *Essays from the Crossroads*

Seo Helrune (2017) 'Maran, Night-Walkers, and Elves, Oh My!', http://www.seohelrune.com/2017/09/maran-night-walkers-and-elves-oh-my.html

Sikes, W., (1880) *British Goblins: Welsh Folklore, Fairy Mythology, Legends and Traditions*

Silver, C., (1999) *Strange and Secret Peoples: Fairies and the Victorian Consciousness*

Sneddon, A., (2015) *Witchcraft and Magic in Ireland*

Walsh, B., (2002). *The Secret Commonwealth and the Fairy Belief Complex*

Westropp, T., (2003) *Folklore of Clare*

Wilby, E., (2005) *Cunningfolk and Familiar Spirits: Shamanistic Visionary Traditions in Early Modern British Witchcraft and*

Magic

—(2010) *The Visions of Isobel Gowdie: Magic, Witchcraft, and Dark Shamanism in Seventeenth Century Scotland*

Wilde, E., (1888) *Irish Cures, Mystic Charms & Superstitions*

Williams, M., (2016) *Ireland's Immortals: A History of the Gods of Irish Myth*

Williams, N., (1991) 'The Semantics of the Word Fairy', *The Good People: New Fairylore Essays*

Vallee, J., (1969) *Passport to Magonia*

Viegas, S., (2009) '17th-Century urine-filled witch bottle found', Retrieved from http://www.msnbc.msn.com/id/31107319/ns/technology_and_science-science/t/th-century-urine-filled-witch-bottle-found/

Yeats, W., (1888) *Fairy and Folktales of the Irish Peasantry*

—(1892) *The Book of Fairy and Folk Tales of Ireland*

—(1902) *Celtic Twilight*

—(1959) *Mythologies*

Moon Books

PAGANISM & SHAMANISM

What is Paganism? A religion, a spirituality, an alternative belief system, nature worship? You can find support for all these definitions (and many more) in dictionaries, encyclopaedias, and text books of religion, but subscribe to any one and the truth will evade you. Above all Paganism is a creative pursuit, an encounter with reality, an exploration of meaning and an expression of the soul. Druids, Heathens, Wiccans and others, all contribute their insights and literary riches to the Pagan tradition. Moon Books invites you to begin or to deepen your own encounter, right here, right now.

If you have enjoyed this book, why not tell other readers by posting a review on your preferred book site.

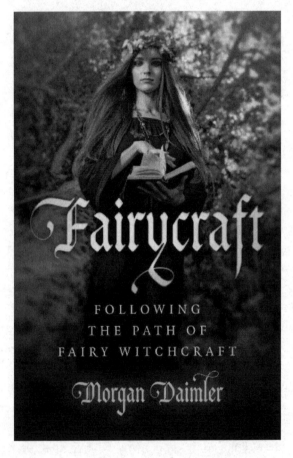

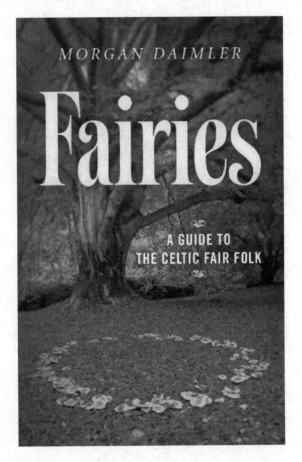

Other books by Morgan Daimler...

Books in the Pagan Portals series

Brigid
Meeting the Celtic Goddess of Poetry, Forge, and Healing Well
978-1-78535-320-8 (Paperback)
978-1-78535-321-5 (ebook)

Fairy Witchcraft
A Neopagan's Guide to the Celtic Fairy Faith
978-1-78279-343-4 (Paperback)
978-1-78279-344-1 (ebook)

Gods and Goddesses of Ireland
A Guide to Irish Deities
978-1-78279-315-1 (Paperback)
978-1-78535-450-2 (ebook)

Irish Paganism
Reconstructing Irish Polytheism
978-1-78535-145-7 (Paperback)
978-1-78535-146-4 (ebook)

Odin
Meeting the Norse Allfather
978-1-78535-480-9 (Paperback)
978-1-78535-481-6 (ebook)

The Morrigan
Meeting the Great Queens
978-1-78279-833-0 (Paperback)
978-1-78279-834-7 (ebook)

Readers of ebooks can buy or view any of these bestsellers by clicking on the live link in the title. Most titles are published in paperback and as an ebook. Paperbacks are available in traditional bookshops. Both print and ebook formats are available online.

Find more titles and sign up to our readers' newsletter at
http://www.johnhuntpublishing.com/paganism
Follow us on Facebook at https://www.facebook.com/MoonBooks
and Twitter at https://twitter.com/MoonBooksJHP